ILEX FOUNDATION SERIES 18

ILLUSION AND DISILLUSIONMENT

Also in the Ilex Foundation Series

ILLUSION AND DISILLUSIONMENT

TRAVEL WRITING IN THE MODERN AGE

Edited by
Roberta Micallef

Ilex Foundation
Boston, Massachusetts

Center for Hellenic Studies
Trustees for Harvard University
Washington, D. C.

Distributed by Harvard University Press
Cambridge, Massachusetts, and London, England

Illusion and Disillusionment: Travel Writing in the Modern Age
Edited by Roberta Micallef

Published by Ilex Foundation, Boston, Massachusetts and The Center for Hellenic Studies, Trustees for Harvard University, Washington, D.C.

Distributed by Harvard University Press, Cambridge, Massachusetts and London, England

Production editor: Christopher Dadian
Cover design: Joni Godlove
Printed in the United States of America

Cover image based upon *Typus Orbis Terrarum* by Abraham Orbelius, 1570. Library of Congress. In the public domain.

Library of Congress Cataloging-in-Publication Data

Names: Micallef, Roberta editor of compilation.
Title: Illusion and disillusionment : travel writing in the modern age / edited by Roberta Micallef.
Description: Boston, Massachusetts : Ilex Foundation ; Washington, D.C. : Center for Hellenic Studies, Trustees for Harvard University ; Cambridge, Massachusetts : Distributed by Harvard University Press, 2018. | Series: Ilex Foundation series ; 18
Identifiers: LCCN 2018020374 | ISBN 9780674984479 (alk. paper)
Subjects: LCSH: Travel writing. | Travelers--Psychology. | Perception.
Classification: LCC G156 .I525 2018 | DDC 910.4--dc23
LC record available at https://lccn.loc.gov/2018020374

Contents

Images

Foreword

I T IS A GREAT PLEASURE to welcome *Illusion and Disillusionment: Travel Writing in the Modern Age* into the Ilex Foundation Series. The volume, edited by Roberta Micallef, provides an excellent companion to *On the Wonders of Land and Sea: Persianate Travel Writing*, edited by Sunil Sharma and Roberta Micallef and published in the Ilex Foundation Series in 2013. Both these collections originated in the lively conversations and wonderfully productive workshops held at Boston University in recent years and dedicated to the topics of travel and travel writing. Together, the articles presented in *On the Wonders of Land and Sea* and its fine new companion, *Illusion and Disillusionment*, address a range of interrelated topics and themes from a variety of disciplinary perspectives; collectively the articles in the pair of volumes greatly illuminate our appreciation of recurrent structures and complexities in the narratives and commentaries that comprise pre-modern and modern travel writing.

The articles in *Illusion and Disillusionment* juxtapose the recorded experiences, observations and inner reflections of a highly varied set of travelers, and repeatedly challenge the generic boundaries of the "travelogue." Like *On the Wonders of Land and Sea*, the present volume incorporates valuable insights arising from the study of Orientalism and post-colonial studies, and at the same time seeks to extend the study of travel writing beyond the frameworks of these approaches. Comprised of the editor's introduction and eight articles, *Illusion and Disillusionment* focuses especially on the recurring emotional patterns represented in the travel accounts of a highly diverse group of individuals, male and female, of various social and professional backgrounds, and of East Asian, South Asian, Middle Eastern, and European backgrounds. These individuals, who undertook their long and often arduous journeys from the eighteenth to the twentieth centuries, traveled in multiple directions, and for a wide variety of purposes. The articles presented in *Illusion and Disillusionment* bring to light a common emotional structure, consisting of four distinct parts: the preconceptions that shape travelers' plans, expectations, and perceptions; the effect of the experience of travel on travelers' perceptions of themselves and of others; travelers' choices of the literary vehicles and stylistic methods by which to express their experiences of travel; and finally – and this element proves especially prominent in the modern context of these travels – their encounters with global inequalities, and the tensions they perceive between travel and tourism. It is fascinating to note the recurrence of even quite specific details, in contrasting contexts, across pairs of articles. It is an unusual and particularly valuable feature of the articles gathered in the present volume that, as a corollary of their emphasis on emotional patterns, they pay substantial attention to the travelers' inner journeys as well as their physical ones. *Illusion and Disillusionment* constitutes an outstanding and extremely stimulating contribution to the study of modern travel literature.

L. Marlow

Executive Editor
Ilex Foundation Series

Introduction

Roberta Micallef

*I*LLUSION AND DISILLUSIONMENT: *Travel Writing in The Modern Age* is the outcome of a faculty discussion group that met over the course of two years (2014–16), at Boston University, culminating in a daylong workshop in 2015. Eight papers were presented at this workshop, followed by a keynote address by Professor James Buzard of MIT, who also participated in the discussion of papers. This project was designed to take the discussion initiated with our previous volume, *On the Wonders of Land and Sea: Persianate Travel Writing*,[1] to a broader level. Through a careful examination of Middle Eastern and South Asian travel narratives, *On the Wonders of Land and Sea* focused attention on modern travelogues in an attempt to understand nineteenth- and early twentieth-century travel writing through a lens other than that of Orientalism or post-colonial studies.[2] The present collection examines a set of travel narratives spanning a longer time period, a wider geography, and, in an interdisciplinary move, several literary and historical genres. The essays included here illuminate a set of interconnected cultural webs and global cultural flows that go far beyond the East-West binary that has dominated the field of travel literature for so long and is only recently starting to be outgrown.[3]

Title and the Organization of the Volume

Across the chronological, geographic, and generic range of the travel accounts considered in this volume, a single emotional structure comes up with surprising frequency. Our title, *Illusion and Disillusionment: Travel Writing in the Modern Age*, is meant to highlight that structure. Our essays probe its contributing elements: the preconceptions that shape how the travelers perceive their voyage and the places they visit; the journey's effect on their self-perception and their notions of other; their stylistic decisions about how to represent their experiences as travelers; and finally, the distinctly modern component: their encounters with global inequalities and the ever-present tensions between travel and tourism.

1. Micallef and Sharma 2013.
2. Micallef and Sharma 2013, 1.
3. Huggan 2009, 1–3.

The works studied in this volume range from the eighteenth to the twentieth centuries and describe male and female East Asian, European, Middle Eastern, and South Asian travelers voyaging around the globe. The travelers included in this volume increasingly benefited from the technological advances and greater freedom of movement afforded by the early modern and modern age to travel long distances, from Europe to India, to North America, to China, or from Japan to North America. Writing in a time period that spanned the consolidation of empires to their collapse, when borders and boundaries were shifting and individuals were reassessing their roles vis-à-vis one another, their families and their "imaginary community," some of the travelers increasingly revealed more about their inner journeys than about what they saw and learned about the lands they were visiting. Some travelers also described what they saw and how it paled in comparison to the descriptions they had read or heard before embarking on their trips. None of the travelers included in this volume were wealthy and none represent class privilege. Every single one, including the women travelers, were professionals and all but one, Yoshiya Nobuko, were traveling for professional reasons. However, even she was a professionally successful woman who funded her trips through her own financially successful writings. As this trip became the subject of one of her books, her voyage also constitutes a "professional" voyage. These travelers had benefitted from the social mobility and opportunities for travel afforded by the modern age and, as importantly, by changes in the workforce and perceptions of professional life, particularly related to gender. In addition, the emergence of our group of travelers as professional men and women allowed us to test with some inspiration from Professor Buzard the question of what is and what is not travel. While these travelers may have been exposed to earlier and more romantic notions of the locations they were visiting, and these notions may have influenced their illusions, their position as "professional" men and women allowed their gaze to be more distanced and ironic.

During the course of our meetings, we intentionally paired readings of texts generated from different parts of the world. Many similar strands run through our analyses of these texts. For example, we discovered that many of our texts challenge the boundaries of travel writing and that the non-European travelers writing autoethnographies in new contact zones enriched the genre. However, whether because of the texts themselves or the interests of their interlocutors, certain geographic-thematic overlaps among the texts arose naturally, and that is how we decided to group them for this volume.

We begin our volume with "Desire, Truth, and Propaganda: Lay and Ecclesiastical Travelers from Europe to China in the Long Eighteenth Century" by Eugenio Menegon. The letters written by his early modern eighteenth-century traveler, the Italian Serafino da San Giovanni Battista (1692–1742) provide a stark contrast to the other travelers and essays in the collection, thus providing a good starting point for our discussion. Penned as utilitarian documents, these letters were not meant for printed public consumption. The correspondence does not offer lengthy reflections on cultural differ-ence, or the meaning of Serafino's voyage. However, the letters do include reports on the logistics of travel, and relate the difficulties of early modern travel, just before the onset of modernity in travel writing. The focus on the material reality in Menegon's essay diverges from the literary representa-tions of voyages included in the rest of the volume, but is also linked to them in its exploration of illusion and disillusionment in missionary travel and activities.

We follow with "Travel, Adventure, and Self-Fashioning: A Frenchman's Journey to New Orleans in 1729" by Elizabeth Goldsmith. Goldsmith explores a travel narrative that was re-discovered in 2005, written by Marc-Antoine Caillot, a seafaring clerk in the French Company of the Indies. Caillot provides us with a much more personal, subjective account, and draws explicitly on literary models as he recounts his travels from Paris to New Orleans. Com-posed in 1730, his memoirs exploit the tropes of an assortment of narrative genres, from literary to legal, while also constituting a highly original and lively tale of the adventures of a young man in the early years of formalized trade routes between France and her colonies in North America. Goldsmith highlights the highly personal voice of the narrator, how he draws on liter-ary models to construct his own traveling persona, and how he tries to keep himself attached to, and promote, a particular idea of French identity in this very early moment in what we might call the history of tourism.

The third essay in this volume is James Uden's contribution, "Gothic Fic-tion, the Grand Tour, and the Seductions of Antiquity: Polidori's *The Vampyre* (1819)." In analyzing the anxieties brought on by the grand tour and the jux-taposition of tourist versus traveler, this essay captures some of the larger questions regarding European travel in the nineteenth century. This trav-eler's gaze is not that of a tourist but rather that of a disillusioned employee, a cynical outsider. He certainly is not Pratt's "seeing-man," or the white male subject "whose imperial eyes passively look out and possess."[4] The next three essays examine South Asian and Middle Eastern travelers: "The Chameleonic Identities of Mohan Lal Kashmiri and His Travels in Persianate Lands," by Sunil Sharma; "Imaginary Travels: Halide Edib's Illusory Encoun-

---

4. Pratt 2008, 9.

ters with India," by Roberta Micallef; and "Fellow Travelers? Two Arab Study Abroad Narratives of Moscow," by Margaret Litvin. The essays in this section share a concern with "autoethnography" and "contact zones." Contact zones as defined by Pratt are social spaces where different cultures, often in asymmetrical power relations, meet and engage one another. Subjects previously separated by geography and history are present in the same space and their stories intersect.[5] Autoethnography refers to the ways in which colonized subjects engage the colonizers' language to represent themselves. These texts are usually addressed to both the narrators' home audience and the metropolitan reader.[6] Sharma's study of Mohan Lal Kashmiri demonstrates the hybridity of this autoethnographic travel text written in English but using Persian travel narrative tropes. Micallef's traveler is writing in English for a metropolitan audience but describing her earlier encounters with India, some of which are distinctly Turkish. For Litvin's travelers the dorm room becomes a contact zone where students from different parts of the globe encounter and confront each other's views of the world.

The final two chapters, "Marie Dugard Goes West: A French Schoolteacher's 1893 Exploration of the American West," by Mary Beth Raycraft and "The Travels of a Japanese 'Girl': Yoshiya Nobuko's 1928 World Tour," by Sarah Frederick, are about two decidedly distinct, single, professional women travelers. In her essay, Raycraft argues that Dugard offers a fresh perspective that challenges national and gendered stereotypes. Having distinguished herself through both teaching and dynamic engagement in Paris education circles, Dugard was selected as the sole female member of the French delegation to the Congress of Education at the World's Columbian Exposition, held in Chicago during the summer of 1893. After giving a lively presentation on the state of girls' education in France at the Congress, Dugard made an abrupt decision to extend her trip and undertook a six-week tour of the western United States. As one of few French women of the time to share impressions about the western United States, Dugard's travel narrative stands out for its balanced, investigative approach and its future-oriented conclusions. Her spirited account challenges national and gendered stereotypes put forth by other travelers and offers readers a fresh perspective on the fascinating yet unsettling customs and conventions of the New World.

The traveler that Frederick is concerned with, Yoshiya Nobuko (1896–1973), was one of Japan's bestselling writers of the twentieth century and a participant in the women's magazine and print culture boom of the 1920s

---

5. Pratt 2008, 7.
6. Pratt 2008, 9.

and 30s. With her proceeds from one of her newspaper novels and movie adaptation deals she and her girlfriend, Monma Chiyo, embarked in 1928 on a world tour, with Paris as the main destination, and published a book-length travelogue in 1929. Beginning her stance as a young woman from the Orient visiting Paris with romantic notions, her travelogue reveals encounters that disrupt those images, including encounters with poverty in Europe, boredom in the face of great culture, and discrimination against immigrants. Yet rather than writing a story of maturation via the journey that might have her growing out of her curiosity or even her desire for the same sex, Yoshiya Nobuko consciously avoids narratives of progress in her travelogue. Instead, she uses repetitions that create insight and ironic criticism via vignettes and self-contained stories, fictional and non-fictional, that highlight the multiplicity of the places she visits even while noting the contradictions in these societies and her own. Frederick's essay pays particular attention to modern forms of mediated representation in Yoshiya Nobuko's travelogue: sections on "movies watched on my trip," photographs, the disconnect between media representations and her direct experience, and the use of modern melodrama plots to tell her own travel stories, sometimes in ways that pointedly reject traditional Japanese travel narrative traditions such as the haiku diaries of Bashō. The chapter ties these moves to Yoshiya Nobuko's own connections to media culture, and the ways these connections allowed for her own mobility and self-awareness as a queer cosmopolitan who could take a "honeymoon" journey without marriage and observe without a sense of hierarchy a quotidian aspect of "the West."

Travel Literature and Genre

In his introduction to *The Cambridge Introduction to Travel Writing*, Tim Youngs, the doyen of travel literature studies, discusses the difficulty of defining travel literature as a "hermetically sealed"[7] genre. Whether focused on the actual trip or not, all the essays in this volume are concerned with works written by authors who physically traveled to a place that they then wrote about but who also imagined that place in myriad ways. Travel writing is seen as overlapping with fiction, autobiography, memoir, ethnography, and letters, to name a few. Uden's contribution examines the intersection of travel and antiquarianism in the early nineteenth century and is partially based on analysis of diaries. Sharma's and Litvin's essays observe how modern writers reshape Persianate and Arabic travel writing traditions in contact with Western languages and/or Western travel writing traditions.

---

7. Youngs 2013, 1–2.

Micallef's contribution looks at the fictionalized nature of first-person travel writing by examining two versions of a text published first in English, a metropolitan language, and four years later in Turkish, the author's natal language. Halide Edib's recollections, while autobiographical and replete with memoir-type details, colorfully demonstrate that reciting past events leads inevitably to the creation of some fiction. Menegon introduces yet another genre in his examination of the communication between Catholic missionaries and their homeland: their letters. Epistolary communication builds a kind of travel narrative while providing historical information. The author who forms the subject of Frederick's chapter explicitly acknowledges the porous divide between travel narratives and fiction. To explore her sexuality, Yoshiya Nobuko chooses a setting that echoes Japanese fictional settings where such an exploration would be possible. Goldsmith's essay examines an experimental travel journal – one voyager's attempt to write an honest, entertaining, and self-consciously French travel narrative at an early moment in the history of transatlantic voyages. Raycraft's analysis shows that Dugard's text, too, is hybrid: part travel narrative and part scientific study, drawing on personal observations, interviews, and official documentation as well as literary sources, but using an appealing diary-like format to seduce European readers.

Motivation for Travel

Tim Youngs has written that a main motivation for travel to Africa, South America and other places in the nineteenth and early twentieth century was to fill the blank spaces on the map.[8] The author of an anthology of primary texts, Geoffrey Nash, adds imperialism and colonialism as the chief stimulus to travel in this period. [9] As we ruminated on the motives and incentives of East Asian travelers to the United States and South Asian or Middle Eastern travelers to parts of the Islamicate world, we had recourse to James Buzard's article on what is *not* travel.[10] Buzard suggests that we study the ways in which travel itself has a history and how what counts as travel changes.[11] We had interesting discussions about the distinction between mobility and travel, tourism and travel which are reflected in our individual essays. We found that the distinction among these categories varies. The motives for travel included in this volume are less varied than the genres, but they go well beyond curiosity and colonization.

Four of the texts are by travelers who embarked on their voyages due to

8. Youngs 2006, 1–18.
9. Nash 2011, xi–xix.
10. Buzard 2005, 43–61.
11. Buzard 2005, 43–44.

the demands of their jobs. According to Susan Bassnett, who studies European gender and travel writing between the Victorian age and the 1920s, the female travelers in the works she has studied often appear to be escaping the constraints imposed by their families or societies, whereas male travelers write of themselves as heroic risk takers.[12] We found that these distinctions were not as clear for our more internationally varied group of travelers, whose national, economic, and professional statuses intersected in various ways to make a gender-based dichotomy impossible. Students on limited scholarships to politically sensitive countries tend to relate ironically to the persona of the heroic risk taker. An unmarried female schoolteacher selected to participate in the International Congress for Education is a pioneer, but the freedom she seeks is professional rather than social or personal. A couple of the travelers representing companies or the Society of Jesus were part of larger economic or cultural colonialism projects, but their self-presentation is not particularly heroic. A traveler discussed by Eugenio Menegon, the Italian Discalced Augustinian Serafino da San Giovanni, complains bitterly about the expense and hardship of the trip to reach China.

Travel and Power

We considered the relationship between power and travel from different vantage points, engaging in a broader conversation that moved beyond the East-West binary in travel and representation. Communities, whether national, ethnic or religious, at some point have to be imagined.[13] We explored how a sense of community and identity based on language, location, gender, class, education, or any combination of these attributes, shifted as our travelers became mobile and changed locations, interacted with other peoples of different classes, or wrote for different audiences in different languages. We questioned whether or not the travelers' imagined communities were as fluid as their identities. Travel writing is also influenced by the narrative and storytelling strategies of different cultures. Many of the travelers included in this book were writing in dominant or prestige languages, such as English or French.[14] A discussion of the contact zone necessarily raises questions about relationality and intersectionalism. As we discussed how contact zones had influenced our travelers' notions of self, identity, and belonging, another concept articulated by Pratt became relevant: the distinction between autoethnography and ethnography. Pratt writes: "Thus if ethnographic texts are those in which European metropolitan subjects represent to themselves their others (usually their conquered others), autoethnographic texts are

12. Bassnett 2002, 225–42.
13. Anderson 1983.
14. Casanova 2013, 379.

representations that the so-defined others construct in response to or in dialogue with those texts."[15] It is not surprising that these would be useful concepts and terms for the travelers from South Asia and the Middle East, in particular those writing in the dominant language. It was interesting and productive to think about dormitories in the study abroad setting as contact zones, or the role of language as a contact space when a Middle Eastern or South Asian writer is writing for a western audience about a community with which he or she has an affinity. Naturally, "the contact zone" is an important space for all parties involved.

The relationship between Byron and his personal doctor Polidori, a young man with literary ambitions, captures the inequities among Europeans. Caillot, the young Frenchman who traveled to New Orleans, finds himself participating in a shipboard ritual enacted by the sailors as their boat crosses the Tropic of Cancer. The fierce-looking crew frightens him. He laughs to relieve himself of his anxieties. Marie Dugard, our other French traveler, has to adjust her preconceived notions about Native Americans when she interacts with them while traveling through the American West. She reflects that the experience has pushed her to acknowledge the complexity of their situation. As a French female traveler, her role vis-à-vis the Native Americans was quite different from that of the American settlers. The Italian missionaries discussed by Eugenio Menegon were sharing the same trade routes as the colonial officials, military personnel, and merchants. This contact zone was not simply one that included the Italians and Chinese. The Japanese traveler Yoshiya Nobuko's reflections about a poverty-stricken French woman, unable to afford shoes but able to give money to a beggar, forces the reader to consider the multiple levels and webs implied in this type of interaction and the relativity of power relations.

While broad, this book does not pretend to be comprehensive. For instance, while we do not all agree with Buzard's move to exclude forced migration literature from the analysis of "travel writing,"[16] the essays in this book do not analyze any accounts of coerced travel caused by war, poverty, trafficking, or environmental degradation. By necessity, the book has left many other geographic, chronological, and thematic gaps as well. Nor do we pretend to offer a unified global theory of travel writing – an effort that would say more about the theorist than the object of study in any case. We hope that our readers will perceive these gaps not as shortcomings but as "blank spaces," invitations and provocations to future scholarly journeys.

15. Pratt 1991, 35.
16. Buzard 2005, 53–56.

Bibliography

Anderson, Benedict. 1983. *Imagined Communities: Reflections on the Origins and Spread of Nationalism.* London: Verso.

Anderson, Jaynie, ed. 2009. *Crossing Cultures: Conflict, Migration and Convergence.* Melbourne: Miegunyah Press.

Bassnett, Susan. 2002. "Travel Writing and Gender." In *The Cambridge Companion to Travel Writing,* edited by Peter Hulme and Tim Youngs. Cambridge, New York: Cambridge University Press, 225–42.

Blanton, Casey. 2002. *Travel Writing: The Self and The World.* New York: Routledge.

Burden, Robert. 2015. *Travel, Modernism and Modernity.* Burlington, VT.: Ashgate Publishing Company.

Buzard, James. 1993. *The Beaten Track: European Tourism, Literature, and the Ways to Culture, 1800-1918.* Oxford: Oxford University Press.

———. 2005. "What Isn't Travel." In *Unravelling Civilisation: European Travel and Travel Writing,* edited by Hagen Schulz-Forberg, 43–61. Peter Lang.

Casanova, Pascale, and Marlon Jones. 2013. "What is a Dominant Language." *New Literary History* 44.3:379–99.

Castillo, Susan, and David Seeds, eds. 2009. *American Travel and Empire.* Liverpool: Liverpool University Press.

Caulfield, Annie. 2007. *Travel Writing: A Practical Guide.* Ramsbury: The Crowood Press.

Clark, Steven. ed. 1999. *Travel Writing and Empire: Postcolonial Theory in Transit.* New York: Zed Books.

Clark, S. H., and Paul Smethurst. 2008. *Asian Crossings: Travel Writing on China, Japan and Southeast Asia.* Hong Kong: Hong Kong University Press.

Cronin, Michael. 2010. *Across the Lines: Travel, Language, Translation.* Cork: Cork University Press.

Euben, Roxanne Leslie. 2006. *Journeys to the Other Shore: Muslim and Western Travelers in Search of Knowledge.* Princeton Studies in Muslim Politics. Princeton: Princeton University Press.

Green, Nile. 2014. *Writing Travel in Central Asian History.* Bloomington: Indiana University Press.

Gupta, Hari Ram. 1943. *Life and Work of Mohan Lal Kashmiri, 1812-177.* Lahore: Minerva Book Shop.

Huggan, Graham. 2009. *Extreme Pursuits: Travel/Writing in the Age of Globalization.* Ann Arbor: University of Michigan Press.

Hulme, Peter, and Tim Youngs, eds. 2002. *The Cambridge Companion to Travel Writing.* New York: Cambridge University Press.

Hooper, Glen, and Tim Youngs 2004. *Perspectives on Travel Writing*. London: Ashgate.

Lambert-Hurley, Siobhan, and Sunil Sharma. 2010. *Atiya's Journeys: A Muslim Woman from Colonial Bombay to Edwardian Britain*. New Delhi: Oxford University Press.

Lisle, Debbie. 2006. *The Global Politics of Contemporary Travel Writing*. New York: Cambridge University Press.

Mee, Catherine. 2014. *Anthem Studies in Travel: Interpersonal Encounters in Contemporary Travel Writing: French and Italian Perspectives*. London: Anthem Press.

Micallef, Roberta, and Sunil Sharma. 2013. *On the Wonder of Land and Sea: Persianate Travel Writing*. Boston: Ilex Foundation.

Nash, George. 2011. "Introduction." In *Travelers to the Middle East from Burchkhardt to Thesiger, An Anthology*, edited by George Nash. London: Anthem, xi–xix.

Pratt, Mary Louise. 1991. "Arts of the Contact Zone." *Professions* January 1, 1991:33–40.

——. 2008. *Imperial Eyes: Travel Writing and Transculturation*. 2nd ed. London: Routledge.

Said, Edward W. 1978. *Orientalism*. Harmondsworth: Penguin.

Sen, Simonti. 2005. *Travels to Europe: Self and Other in Bengali Travel Narratives, 1870-1910*. Hyderabad: Orient Longman.

Siegel, Kristi, ed. 2002. *Issues in Travel Writing: Empire, Spectacle and Displacement*. New York: Peter Lang.

Thompson, Carl. 2011. *Travel Writing*. London: Routledge.

Youngs, Tim. 2013. *The Cambridge Introduction to Travel Writing*. New York: Cambridge University Press.

Youngs, Tim, ed. 2006. *Travel Writing in the Nineteenth Century: Filling the Blank Spaces*. London: Anthem.

Desire, Truth, and Propaganda:
Lay and Ecclesiastical Travelers from Europe to China in the Long Eighteenth Century [*]

Eugenio Menegon

Early Modern Missionary Travel to China

Ah golaccia, golaccia, quante spese fai fare!
(Oh, gluttony, gluttony, how much do you cost us!) [1]

This colorful expression appears in a letter written in March 1738 in Nanchang, Jiangxi province, by the Italian Discalced Augustinian Serafino da San Giovanni Battista (1692–1742) to Procurator Arcangelo Miralta (1682–1751), the ecclesiastical administrator in Macao on behalf of the papal Congregation for the Propagation of the Faith (*Propaganda Fide*).[2] Serafino was then

[*]A preliminary Italian language version of this essay is Menegon 2015. I would like to thank for their comments and encouragement Prof. Gianvittorio Signorotto (University of Modena, Italy) and the members of the Boston University Travel Literature Reading Group.

1. Serafino da San Giovanni Battista to Arcangelo Miralta, Nanchang, 1 March 1738, f. 2v, in Archivio Storico della Congregazione per l'Evangelizzazione dei Popoli or *de Propaganda Fide*, Vatican City (hereafter abbreviated as APF), *Procura Cina*, box 30.

2. The Sacred Congregation for the Propagation of the Faith, in Latin *Sacra Congregatio de Propaganda Fide*, and today officially called "Congregation for the Evangelization of the Peoples," was established in 1622 by order of Pope Gregory XV. *Propaganda* or *Propaganda Fide*, as the Congregation is commonly known and as it will be referred to in this article, was a belated outcome of the institutionalization and bureaucratization of the papacy initiated by the reforms of the Council of Trent (1545–63). Organizationally, Propaganda replicated the structure of older, more established "Sacred Congregations of Cardinals" (*Sacræ Cardinalium Congregationes),* also called "dicasteries" of the papal government (meaning "law-courts" in Greek, and equivalent to ecclesiastical "ministries"), established at the end of the sixteenth century. The Congregations derive their name from the fact that they literally "congregate" cardinals as official collaborators of the sovereign pontiff. Some Congregations were established to assist the pope in the administration of the affairs of the entire Church (e.g. the Congregations of the Holy Office, of Sacraments, of Rites, of the Index of Forbidden Books, etc.), while others assisted him in the administration of the temporal dominions of the Holy See. After a period of experimentation during the first decades of the seventeenth century, the Holy See decided to establish the Congregation of Propaganda to exercise universal jurisdiction on Catholic missions across the world. The delay in the foundation of the Congregation was in part due to the role played by the Spanish Crown, and to a lesser degree by the Portuguese Crown, in defending the rights of royal patronage over missionary work in the colonies, as well as by the resistance of religious orders laboring in mission lands; on the organization of Propaganda, see Pizzorusso 2000.

traveling by boat on Chinese rivers, on the last leg of a long journey from his native Lombardy in Italy to the Qing capital, Beijing, where he would arrive on April 8, 1738, approximately twenty-three months after leaving his convent in Milan, including seven months of residence in Rome, seven months of oceanic sailing (December 18, 1736 to July 20, 1737), and six months in Macao.[3] The expenses he mentioned here were the transportation costs as well as the numerous additional tips and fees that he had been forced to pay since leaving Macao, in order to ship some luxury food items destined to his confreres in the capital. He continued: "my dear wine, my very dear chocolate! Custom fees in Macao, custom fees in Canton, custom fees in Ganzhou, transportation fees [to carry the trunks] across the mountains, loading and unloading to and from the boats."[4]

In fact, in almost all the letters penned during the journey, including the continental crossing of Europe to reach the embarkation port in France, and later during the oceanic sail, Serafino repeatedly remarked on the exorbitant travel costs as the single most pressing and worrisome issue he faced. The letters had no pretense to literary style, and they were not, in fact, "travel literature" in the classic sense of the term. They were instead utilitarian documents, penned to inform his ecclesiastical superiors about his progress across Europe, the oceans and China. These letters were not meant for printed public consumption, like the famous Lettres édifiantes et curieuses on overseas missions published by the Jesuits and their editors in France between 1703 and 1776. They also did not belong to the genre of hagiographic missionary relations circulated as manuscript accounts in convents, and read aloud to novices during meals to inspire their missionary zeal for distant shores. Finally, Serafino's correspondence did not offer any extended reflection on cultural difference, or the meaning of his voyage.[5] What we

3. Serafino left Lombardy for Rome around January 18, 1736; he began his journey from Rome to Beijing, accompanied by Sigismondo Meinardi da San Nicola, probably in August 1736, taking thus nineteen months to reach the Chinese capital, as also confirmed by Sigismondo in his correspondence; see several letters in Archivio di Stato di Roma (hereafter ASR), *Congregazioni religiose, Agostiniani scalzi in Gesù e Maria al Corso*, busta (envelope) 156, registri (fascicles) 117 and 118, unnumbered folios. Unless otherwise noted, the following citations from Serafino's correspondence in this archive will be from the same section, envelope and fascicles; since the folios are not numbered, and the letters are mostly unbound, references for the purpose of documentary identification will only mention the date of the individual letter, the writer and addressee if known, and the acronym "ASR."

4. Here "dear" ("caro" in Italian) is a double entendre, meaning both expensive and desirable: "Caro il mio vino, carissima la mia cioccolata!" Serafino to Miralta, Nanchang, 1 March 1738, f. 2v, in APF, *Procura Cina*, box 30.

5. For a sampling of Jesuit missionary reports about China, including several travel descriptions prepared for the lay public, see Boothroyd et al. 1992, 109-251.

have are, rather, reports on his movements and the logistics of travel, collections of tips for other missionaries who would follow in his steps, requests for financial support to cover the increasing costs of the trip, and reports on his daily life in Beijing. To elicit an appropriate response from the addressees, mostly in the form of financial help, these missives openly relate the discomforts and difficulties of early modern travel. They also offer glimpses of the actual mechanisms of travel in the eighteenth century, and of the patronage networks needed to travel to and reside in China.

Reaching China from Europe remained a difficult task in the eighteenth century, and required the support of multiple networks, both within and without the Church, in Europe, and in Asia. Unlike other European countries, the Italian states did not have a colonial or commercial presence in East Asia in the early modern period. The papacy was the only power in Italy that maintained direct contacts with China, mainly through the religious orders involved in the missions and its own Congregation of Propaganda Fide, a sort of "ministry of missions" of the Holy See. A missionary such as Serafino traveling from Italy to China ought therefore to rely not only on the diplomatic and religious system of the Church, but also on the commercial and secular networks linking Europe and Asia. He had to use means of transportation and financial systems managed by the various Companies of the Indies, the Catholic crowns, private merchants, and Asian states, including, of course, the Qing Empire.

This essay employs Serafino's letters to reconstruct his itinerary, the challenges he faced and the networks he employed to travel, and some of the issues he faced in Beijing. Rather than offering an analysis of literary tropes about travel (which are practically absent in this small corpus), the essay offers a study in contrasts, focusing on the material reality of travel in Serafino's rather prosaic missives, as opposed to the mostly idealized and literary representations of voyages showcased in the rest of this volume. As I will show, from his letters we derive a sense that the difficulties of the journey, the residence in Beijing, and the demanding schedule of work as an artist at the imperial court slowly eroded Serafino's faith in his religious mission. After 1724, when Christianity was officially forbidden in China, the only way for missionaries to legally remain in the imperial capital was to offer technical or artistic skills to the Qing government, thereby also staying close to the center of power, in order to protect better the underground and illegal religious operations of the Church still found in the provinces of the empire. While we do not have a clear sense of what specific motivations might have inspired Serafino to leave Italy, we can suppose that he combined the missionary zeal typical of his religious order with some personal ambition and a sense of adventure. The Order of the Discalced Augustinians (in Latin, *Ordo Augustiniensum Discalceatorum*, acronym OAD) was a reformed branch of the older Augustinian order. Established in 1592, the Discalced Augustinians developed quickly, especially in Italy, attracting many to an austere life of begging and popular missions among the poor and illiterate. Detachment from the world was signaled by the adoption of a religious name, inspired by a saint (in Serafino's case, Saint John the Baptist), and abandonment of the original family surname. The missionary spirit of the order soon led to the creation of missions outside Europe, including northern Vietnam and China.[6] Upon his arrival in Beijing in 1738, in his first report to the vicar general of the order in Rome, Serafino mentioned that he had traveled so far for "the great aim of the conversion of these poor infidels, and to take care of these few Christians [in Beijing]."[7] The "desire for the Indies," often paired with a yearning for martyrdom, was a common urge among early modern missionaries, and received particular attention among the Jesuits.[8] However, the adolescent impulse to reach an imagined far-flung heroic mission confronted its first challenge in the difficult "truth" of actual travel. In fact, superiors often selected for the missions psychologically mature men who could withstand, both physically and mentally, the demands of the voyage, and had enough practical spirit to navigate the political and religious compromises, and the economic strictures, commonly faced in the complex enterprise of maritime travel. In the rest of this essay, therefore, rather than emphasizing ideals and desires, we will focus on the economic and global transportation networks of the early modern era, how our missionary used them to reach distant China, and how the trials of residing on the other side of the world and work in the mission field and at the Qing court eventually might have engendered some disillusionment in Serafino.

Three categories of people traveled to East Asia in the seventeenth and eighteenth centuries: colonial officials and military personnel, merchants, and missionaries. Although the motivations that drove these three groups to the journey were very different, all of them used the same trade routes, with variations depending on the ships' country of origin, and the ports where they were allowed to dock. These trade routes were not, however, open to anyone indiscriminately. The East India Companies and Protestant captains (Dutch, British, Swedish, and Danish), for example, did not look kindly upon

---

6. See Campanelli 2001.

7. See Serafino to Vicar General OAD, Macao, December 18, 1737, in ASR.

8. On the Jesuit "desire for the Indies," see Roscioni 2001, Russell 2011 and 2013, Massimi and Colombo 2014; on the eighteenth-century missionary vocation and travels of priests of the Missions Étrangères de Paris, see Marin 2007.

the Catholic clergy, and for religious and political reasons the missionaries usually tried to avoid a passage on Protestant vessels, opting instead for Portuguese and French ships (and occasionally Spanish). This did not apply to the transport of freight, mail, and money for the missions. In fact, during the eighteenth century, more and more of these items were sent to Asia via the fastest and most efficient trading vessels of northern European powers.

The European trade networks that allowed the missionaries to reach Macao and Canton, however, did not extend inside China. Once they reached the Chinese coast, European merchants had to rely on the sophisticated and dense transport system for the internal exchange of goods within the empire, and by law they could not go beyond a few designated ports open to foreign trade. Canton emerged in the eighteenth century as the only entrepôt within imperial borders open to Westerners.

This was not the case for the missionaries. Until 1724, despite moments of difficulty, the imperial government tolerated Catholic missionary activities in the capital and the provinces. From the strategic outpost of Macao and with the financial support of the Portuguese Crown, the Jesuits succeeded in establishing residences in the Chinese provinces, and insinuating themselves at the Ming court as experts in calendric matters. After the 1644 Manchu takeover of the Ming dynasty and the establishment of the new Qing dynasty, the Jesuits under Portuguese missionary patronage (*padroado*) received the new imperial regime's protection in exchange for their technical-scientific services and their political loyalty. A few of them eventually became official members of the imperial bureaucracy within the Astronomical Directorate, participants in court life, and important diplomatic intermediaries between the Qing Empire and European powers. During the Kangxi reign (1662–1722), the Jesuits, whose contingent increased with the arrival of a French mission sent by Louis XIV, reached the apex of their influence in China. Their personal relationship with the Kangxi Emperor as preceptors and coordinators of editorial, scientific, and artistic projects directly commissioned by the throne, rather than their marginal position inside the imperial bureaucracy (only few of them had official posts), allowed the missionaries to protect and aid the development of the Catholic missions in China. In Beijing, about thirty missionaries worked at court as scientists, technicians, and artists. While most of them were Jesuits of the Portuguese and French missions, a small contingent of the papal Congregation of Propaganda Fide arrived in 1711, and Serafino was intent on reaching them.

The missionaries were in fact the only Europeans the Qing court allowed to enter the empire and reside in the capital. Even after the prohibition of religious proselytizing in the provinces in 1724, during the reign of the third emperor of the dynasty, Yongzheng, the missionaries were allowed to stay on at court, and used their professional identity to protect illegal Christian communities in the provinces, and keep the Beijing churches open. To illustrate the almost absolute monopoly of the Church on direct relations with the interior of the Chinese empire, especially in cultural and religious matters, we leave Serafino on his riverboat for a moment, and consider another Italian, who traveled the same route nearly forty years earlier and whose experience is really the proverbial exception that proves the rule.

Gemelli Careri in China and the Missionary Monopoly on Travel

The only Italian early modern traveler who went to China "for pleasure," so to say, without direct colonial or ecclesiastical patronage, was the native Calabrian and Neapolitan by adoption Giovanni Francesco Gemelli Careri (1648–1724). His story illustrates how the Chinese imperial government allowed only missionaries to enter, travel, and reside long-term in China, and suggests how unusual Gemelli Careri's case was. Unlike missionaries, whose journey was the first act of a life-long dedication to religious proselytizing in China, even if under the guise of arts and sciences, Gemelli Careri was a true "traveler," reaching Asia for the pleasure of learning about different cultures, to satisfy his curiosity, and with the intent of leaving those shores and returning home to narrate his exploits. Such European solo travelers to East Asia were very rare in early modern times.[9]

An official of the viceroyalty of Naples and a volunteer against the Turks in Hungary, Gemelli Careri was an adventurous and ambitious man. Driven by his insatiable curiosity, hope to gain fame, and a wish to escape the intellectually and professionally stifling environment of Naples, he set his mind on reaching the inaccessible imperial capital of China. He embarked on an epic journey in June, 1693, crossing the Ottoman Empire, Persia, and India, from where he reached China. Then he went on to the Philippines, and across the Pacific reached Mexico, to return finally to Naples in December 1698, where he published his famous account of his circumnavigation of the globe in six volumes.[10]

Supporting himself with business transactions from one port to the next (he was a master at calculating commodity prices), and thanks to his skills

9. The Dutchman Samuel van de Putte also traveled out of his own curiosity to Persia, India, Tibet, China, and Indonesia in the early eighteenth century; he was in Beijing in 1734, as recorded by the Jesuit Antoine Gaubil, a member of the French mission at the Qing court. On van de Putte, see e.g. Lequin 1985.

10. On Gemelli-Careri and his journey to China, see de Vargas 1955; Fatica 1998; Doria 2000; Amuso Maccarrone 2000.

as a dissimulator, a good dose of luck, and the sympathy of consuls, colonial officials, merchants, members of religious orders, and scholars, Gemelli Careri arrived in Macao in August, 1695. From there he made it to Canton, in Chinese territory, through the intercession of the Macanese authorities, and once there he went to the residence of the Spanish Franciscans, who ran a mission in the capital of Guangdong. The missionaries were astonished, to say the least, at his unexpected arrival, and did not believe that he had subjected himself to such a dangerous journey just out of a desire to visit Beijing. These were years of struggles between the Portuguese Crown, trying to defend the rights of its royal patronage on the missions, and the Holy See, which had founded the Congregation of Propaganda to break that religious monopoly, and tried to establish a network of vicars apostolic in Asia (the equivalent of bishops in mission territories). The government and the ecclesiastical authorities of Macao looked upon the Spanish Franciscans of Canton with great suspicion, as they swore an oath of obedience to the vicars and sided with the pope, even if they remained subject to the royal patronage of Spain.[11]

Despite statements to the contrary by the Neapolitan traveler, who was fluent in Spanish and French, the friars became convinced that he was a Discalced Carmelite or a priest, secretly sent by the Holy See to visit the missions and establish diplomatic relations with Beijing. They apparently told him that "since a path to China had been open, never had they seen an Italian layman, no less, a Neapolitan, arrive there."[12] In fact, in those years the papacy considered sending a legate to the emperor, an enterprise that would be realized in 1704 with the dispatch of the famous Patriarch and later Cardinal Charles Thomas Maillard de Tournon (1668–1710).[13]

The Franciscans of Canton rightly observed that Gemelli was the first

11. In 1695, the following Spanish Franciscans resided in Canton: Jaime Tarin (1644?–1719), superior of the church *intra muros* of the Porziuncola, and provincial commissar of China for the Spanish Franciscan mission; Agustin de San Pascual (1637? - 1697) and Blas Garcia (1635 - 1699) in the church of St. Francis, outside the city walls; see Wyngaert 1942, 175; Mensaert 1965, 407.

12. "Since I arrived at the time of these disorders, everyone was firmly persuaded that I had been sent by His Holiness, to make a secret inquiry. Some thought I was a Discalced Carmelite, some a priest. And though I made every effort by telling the truth in order to eliminate this suspicion from the minds of the Franciscan Fathers, stating that I was a Neapolitan, that I was traveling only out of my curiosity, that His Holiness had not given me a penny to make such a trip, and that I wanted to know nothing of their Missions, for all that I could not change their strong impression, and they would tell me that since the path of China had been open, never had they seen an Italian layman, no less, a Neapolitan, arrive there"; see Gemelli Careri 1700, IV, 30.

13. On the papal legations to China and their organizational and logistical dimensions, see Menegon 2012.

Italian layman to enter Chinese territory, and he himself admitted in his diary that he had succeeded only thanks to the misunderstandings about his identity. This confirms that the monopoly for long-term residential contacts between China and Europe was firmly in the hands of the missionaries, chiefly the Jesuits at the imperial court. Gemelli Careri was traveling with letters patent of all the major religious orders except the Jesuits, and therefore made use of religious as much as governmental global networks to travel. But to reach Beijing, where the Jesuits were indispensable intermediaries in relations with the West, perhaps it was better to surprise, rather than warn.

As a subject of the Spanish viceroyalty of Naples, Gemelli received in Canton the help of the Spanish Franciscans, but gained as well the protection of Carlo Giovanni Turcotti (1643–1706), superior of the local Jesuit mission, and a native of Varallo Sesia in the state of Milan, then under Spanish Hapsburg rule. Turcotti, being by birth a subject of the Crown of Spain, had traveled to Asia on Spanish vessels, and had initially worked as a missionary in Celebes (now Sulawesi in Indonesia) under Spanish auspices. Once in China, he submitted himself to the Portuguese religious patronage in order to stay more easily in Canton. The *Giro del mondo* thus reports about the meeting between Gemelli and Turcotti:

> Having resolved to go to Peking, I spoke to the Father Superior of the [Spanish Franciscan] Convent [of Canton], where I was staying, to provide me with some reliable fellow [as a guide]. Because of a sense of subordination to the Fathers of the Society [of Jesus], he secretly sent word to Father Turcotti, to hear his opinion. Being a good Lombard, Turcotti told them to let me go, while if it had been a Portuguese, he would have definitely opposed the journey. My determination, nevertheless, still made them suspicious, and they firmly believed that I was a Pontifical Commissar, here to gather secret intelligence on the disorders of China, since they saw I was going to the Court. I believe that this suspicion in fact facilitated my journey, which would have normally been very difficult.[14]

So the journey went on in spite of, or rather, thanks to these suspicions, and once in Nanjing, the metropolis of the south, Gemelli Careri met three Ital-

14. Gemelli Careri 1700, IV, 27. The superior who received Gemelli Careri was the provincial commissioner Jaime Tarin. Gemelli Careri reports that Turcotti had worked in the mission of Ternate (Moluccas). But we know that the Spanish had abandoned the Moluccas in 1663, and that Turcotti arrived in Manila only in 1671. He rather went to the island of Siau (north of Celebes, now known as Sulawesi in Indonesia) in 1674, a mission that the Jesuits abandoned in 1677; see Dehergne 1973, 276.

ian Franciscans sent by Propaganda Fide residing there, including Bishop Bernardino Della Chiesa (1644–1721). They again advised him against travel to Beijing, telling him that "the [Jesuit] Portuguese Fathers do not want any European to have knowledge of the Court, and that if ... [he] went there, no doubt they would have been discourteous to ... [him]." Our indomitable traveler was not discouraged at all, replied with temerity that he would seek hospitality with the Jesuits once in the capital, and continued on his path. Once in Beijing, where he arrived on November 6, 1695, the vice-provincial of the Portuguese mission, the Italian Claudio Filippo Grimaldi (1638–1712), welcomed him at the Jesuit College, but did not grant him a room for fear of imperial sanctions, sending him to an inn in the Chinese part of the city, expressing astonishment at his boldness:

> Father Grimaldi and all the Portuguese Fathers could not but marvel about my arrival at the Court, saying they wondered who had advised me to come to Peking, where no European can enter without a summon from the Emperor. I replied that I had come to Peking with the same freedom that I enjoyed in visiting the courts of the Grand Lord [the Sultan of Turkey], the King of Persia, and the Great Mogul, as those monarchs are no less powerful and protective of their kingdoms than the Emperor of China.[15]

In the following days, according to the version by Gemelli Careri that several scholars have found plausible, Grimaldi, director of the Astronomical Directorate, led him to an imperial audience as if he was a new member of the Jesuit mission, for fear that, if he failed to do so, the Kangxi emperor could learn from his spies of the presence of a visitor lacking government permit.[16]

The *Giro del mondo* was a great publishing success, but for the most prudent among the China missionaries these were times of silence rather than public statements, given the internal disputes over religious jurisdictional issues, and the risk of misinformation about China in general, and their mission in particular. Grimaldi himself revealed to Gemelli that "having read the last time he traveled to Europe so many lies they had published about China, not to reproach many authors of spreading fabrications, he had refrained from issuing anything in print."[17] Gemelli Careri obviously had no such qualms, and, with the stylistic assistance of the erudite Matteo Egizio

15. Gemelli Careri 1700, IV, 97-98.

16. Despite later doubts about Gemelli Careri's account, and even his presence in China, contemporary missionary sources confirm his movements in the Chinese empire; see de Vargas 1955, 430; Margiotti and Rosso 1961, 196–97.

17. Gemelli Careri 1700, IV, 389.

(1674–1745), quickly produced his bestseller, liberally using existing literature on China, much of it, in fact, produced by Jesuit missionaries. Gemelli
Careri did not leave private correspondence: all we know about him comes
from scattered personal remarks within his expansive "encyclopedia" of
world travel. As Giuseppe Tucci, a great explorer himself, observed long ago,
in some parts of his work the reader gets the impression that "the things
surrounding him were mute, and that he was almost blind and inert," while
elsewhere he makes acute and precise observations.[18] Yet, in spite of his limitations, Gemelli Careri aspired to offer an erudite and all-embracing view
of the world, with a certain degree of philosophical ambition. In his preface
he encouraged his readers to believe him, as he offered eyewitness accounts
of what he described. He also dismissed the chatter (*ciance*) of those who
"deem that the world is confined to just the space they can see with their
own eyes, and do not trust that others might have seen those countries
where they themselves are afraid to go, even with their own imagination."[19]
What we find in the personal letters of a missionary like Serafino, however,
is quite different.

The Journey of Serafino: European Networks

Gemelli Careri's aims in his peregrinations were to satisfy his curiosity and
acquire fame through the publication of his travel feats. Serafino's aspirations could not be more dissimilar. Like Grimaldi, the Discalced Augustinian
did not publish any report on his experience in China, and this has spread a
veil of oblivion over him. But it is precisely his ordinary testimony, preserved
in letters never intended for publication, that in fact offers us a complex
and fascinating picture, neither hagiographic nor celebratory, of the social,
economic, and logistical mechanisms of missionary travel to China, and of
the global networks that sustained it. Given the nature of this correspondence, we will take Serafino as a travel companion from Italy to Beijing, to
reconstruct the concrete conditions and obstacles encountered by missionary travelers at the time, show the complexity of the political borders and
economic networks they had to navigate through, and how illusions and
disillusionments followed each other in the process of journeying from Europe to China.

Serafino in Italy

Who was Serafino? We only know his religious name, Serafino da San Giovanni Battista, and we learn some meager biographical information in a

18. Tucci 1949, 110.
19. Gemelli Careri 1728 (Venice edition), IV, 3.

posthumous note that qualifies him as a member of the religious province of the Discalced Augustinians in Milan: "a Milanese noble, relative of the Lords Visconti and of other nobility in Rome."[20] From indirect sources we learn that Serafino was prior of the monastery of S. Ilario in Cremona, Lombardy, between 1728 and 1731, a position from which he seems to have been deposed for conflicts with his superiors. He spent the period 1731–36 in Milan, occupied as confessor in the convent of Saints Cosma and Damiano in Monforte, seat of the provincial prior. Although he apparently succeeded in being reinstated in his priory with the support of the Bishop of Cremona, Alessandro Maria Litta, Serafino decided to leave for Asia in response to an appeal of the Mission Procurator of his order. According to the gossip of the Vincentian missionary of Propaganda Fide Teodorico Pedrini (1671–1746), who was stationed in the Chinese capital, Serafino, once destined for China, nourished the ambition of becoming Bishop of Beijing. In fact, it was not he, but another Discalced Augustinian, Damasceno Salusti della Concezione, who would rise to that dignity a few decades later.[21] Should we believe, with Pedrini, that it was this desire for advancement in the ecclesiastical hierarchy that attracted Serafino to the far-flung mission of Beijing? Or was it rather the adventurous journey and life at the imperial court, as a public artist and an undercover missionary? The sources are silent on explicit motivations, except for the formulaic expression of his desire to convert

20. Quotation from ASR, *Congregazioni religiose: Agostiniani scalzi in Gesù e Maria al Corso*, envelope 277, fascicle 722, "Registro Memorie," f. 96 [bis]; cf. Barbagallo 1978, 15, bibliographic note. Serafino in fact seems to have known members of the Milanese elite, including Count Giuseppe Fedeli, police prefect and secretary of state during the governorship of Eugene of Savoy in Milan; see Serafino's letter dated Paris, October 30, 1736, in ASR. The Count, who received the title in 1717, came from a family of wealthy jewelers, and his father had been general commissioner for transportation in the Duchy of Milan. His brother was the famous Dominican missionary and bishop of Isfahan in Persia, Giovanni Battista Fedeli, better known as Barnaba da Milano; see Sanfilippo 1995. In China Serafino received the name Zhang Chunyi 張純 一–or Zhang Zhongyi 張中 一–, as recorded in materials at the Imperial Palace Archives and at the Zhalan Christian cemetery near Beijing; cf. Standaert 2001, 341.

21. The gossip is in a letter by Teodorico Pedrini to the Secretary of Propaganda, Beijing, October 3, 1744, in APF, *Scritture riferite nei Congressi* (SC), *Indie Orientali e Cina*, vol. 24, 1744-45, f. 81v. The Milanese Alessandro Maria Litta was bishop of Cremona from January 10, 1718 to September 12, 1749, when he stepped down. We find confirmation of the presence of Serafino in Cremona between 1728 and 1731 in the surviving papers of the convent of S. Ilario, preserved in the Archivio di Stato di Milano, Italy (hereafter ASMi), *Fondo di religione*, 4361 and 4364, unnumbered folios, with three references in legal documents signed in 1728 by Serafino. After he left the priory in Cremona, we find Serafino mentioned in the summer of 1731 as confessor in the Milanese convent of SS. Cosma e Damiano in Monforte, seat of the provincial prior (ASMi, *Fondo di religione*, 1100); he is again mentioned as resident in the same Milanese convent in 1735 (ASMi, *Fondo di religione*, 1089, "Acta capituli et definitorii provincialis," April 30, 1735). The "Acta" of June 1737 (ASMi, *Fondo di religione*, 1089), however, record him as already departed for the missions.

infidels and serve local Christians we have mentioned earlier. If Serafino entertained any illusions of success in evangelizing China, however, his fantasies were eventually dispelled by reality. As we shall see, disillusionment started to creep into his correspondence soon after he settled in the Qing capital, when he realized that the life of the court missionaries was far from glamorous or even heroic, and rather that imperial authorities treated the foreigners as "laborers and slaves."[22]

Nonetheless, when leaving his native Italy, he must have been inflamed by a good dose of missionary zeal and sense of adventure, embarking upon what turned into almost two years of travel and training for the mission. Serafino arrived in Rome from Lombardy after a journey by land at the beginning of Lent, in mid-February 1736. In his first surviving letter, he already lamented the excessive cost of the trip, a quite common litany for all the missionaries supported by Propaganda, perpetually short of money. Serafino spent six months in the convent of Gesù e Maria al Corso in Rome, where he and his younger traveling companion, the Turinese Sigismondo Meinardi da San Nicola (1713–67), labored at learning the techniques of painting on enamel, illumination, and clock making. Propaganda had indeed received requests from its missionaries in China for new recruits with these skills, necessary in the imperial art workshops in which the missionaries of the capital were employed. It seems unlikely that an accelerated course of a few months could do miracles. Yet, we read in an inflated recommendation composed by the Discalced Augustinian General Procurator Ildefonso da Santa Maria for Propaganda in the summer of 1736 that Serafino possessed "to perfection the art of making clocks" and was "a master at drawing and miniatures," while Sigismondo was "perfect in the art of making claviers, mappamondi, clocks, and any manual work."[23]

In mid-August 1736, the two were busy preparing for their departure by sea from Civitavecchia, the port of Rome, to Genoa, and, from there, to France. The route Serafino took reflected the geopolitical changes that had occurred in the eighteenth century, when the papacy and members of religious orders outside the missionary patronage systems of Spain and Portugal started using the ships of the East India Companies to reach their Asian missions. The vessels of the Compagnie Française des Indes Orientales, in particular, became the preferred means of transportation for Propaganda missionaries, departing from the port of Lorient in Brittany towards China. The Jesuits of the China Vice-Province, however, still subject to the Portu-

---

22. Serafino to Miralta, July 19, 1739, f. 1v, in APF, *Procura Cina*, box 30.
23. APF, SC, *Indie Orientali e Cina*, vol. 21, 1733–36, f. 680r.

guese *padroado*, continued using Portuguese vessels leaving from Lisbon.[24] Correspondence in the Propaganda Archives reveals that Swedish, Danish, and English ships, often stopping in Cadiz (Spain), were also used to ship silver and trunks to China. For Propaganda missionaries, Paris became one of the stopovers on the way to East Asia, and the papal diplomatic network of nuncios (papal ambassadors), as well as the convents of the missionary religious orders, became the operational structure the travelers could use. Serafino, for example, received letters of recommendation (*lettera commendatizia*) from the Master General of the Dominicans, Tomás Ripoll (d. 1747), and from the General of the Capuchins, Bonaventura Barberini da Ferrara (1674–1743), granting him permission to be housed free of charge in any convent of their orders, especially outside Italy (*precipue extra Italiam*).[25]

Across France

To reach France, the two Augustinians first had to sail from Civitavecchia to Genoa, where they arrived on September 23, 1736. A Discalced Carmelite, Ilarione Negroni, had arranged for them to join him and two Franciscans, all traveling to Asia, on a ship leaving for Marseille. But the sea journey was delayed by practical issues: currency exchange, and buying of clothing for the poor Sigismondo, who lacked "underwear and ... undergarments."[26] In fact, the transportation of their personal baggage and the exchange of currency to pay the journey's expenses were the more onerous and necessary tasks for the travelers. Each time a new border was crossed, money had to be exchanged, and Serafino complained that both in Genoa and in France exchanging his *zecchini* and *scudi romani* into local currencies meant losing value. He immediately notified his procurator in Rome, and wrote to the Prefect and the Secretary of Propaganda as well about this financial difficulty, hoping to receive more funds. The delay cost the travelers the passage for Marseille, and instead of getting on a French *tartane* (*tartana*), Serafino and Sigismondo embarked in early October on a lateen (*latina*) ship headed for Nice in Provence. The ship covered the 150 miles between Genoa and Nice in only twenty-four hours, avoiding a "horrible storm" the following day. The travelers decided to take a buggy (*calesse*) to Aix-en-Provence, and avoid Marseille, and then proceeded to Lyon. In Lyon they faced another difficulty. Taking a stagecoach (*diligenza*) from Lyon to Paris would have meant

24. See Wicki 1967.
25. See copy of the "Lettera commendatizia del Generale de' Cappuccini," September 2, 1736, and a reference to the recommendation letter from the Dominican Master General in letter by Serafino to Vicar General OAD, October 18, 1738, both in ASR.
26. Serafino to Ildefonso da Santa Maria, Genova, September 25, 1736, in ASR.

not only paying an expensive ticket of 100 French *livres* per person, but also considerable transportation fees of six *sols* per *libbra* (i.e. pound) for their heavy baggage (*baulli ... pesantissimi*) of around 300 kilograms, bringing the cost to around 300 *livres*.[27] They then learned that in order to rent a buggy, it would be necessary to obtain a license from the postmaster, with an expense of twenty *écus* per person for the license alone. We can imagine Serafino communicating in his improvised French all along.[28] In a later letter of recommendations for future members of his order taking the same route, he indeed advised as follows: "Since we need to cross all of France, and then embark on French vessels, it is necessary to learn a little bit of French, so as to avoid being subjected to cheating and bullying, so often experienced by Italians in France."[29] He was probably thinking of his own experience.

To save on expenses, Serafino finally decided to rent horses (*cavalcatura*), and have a cart follow them with their trunks to the city of Roanne (he writes "Rouain"), the main point of embarkation on the Loire River, where the two Augustinians took a boat to Orleans. The trip was slowed by adverse winds along the route. Once in Orleans, the two priests boarded a public coach to Paris, reaching their destination, the Discalced Augustinian Convent of Notre Dame des Victoires, in another two days, on October 26. Their baggage continued to follow them more slowly by cart, with a considerable saving, as they only paid half a *sol* per pound.[30] But this further delayed their progress: without appropriate clothes, left in the trunks, Serafino was unable to arrange for an immediate meeting with the papal diplomatic envoy (nuncio) in Paris, Monsignor Raniero D'Elci (1670–1761; posted in France from January 2, 1731 until October 10, 1738).[31]

It is not surprising that the first duty Serafino wanted to discharge in the French capital was to meet the nuncio. This ecclesiastical diplomat had indeed a crucial role in supporting the operations of Propaganda Fide abroad. Nuncios acted as postal nodes for the papacy and the missionary Congregation of Propaganda, receiving and forwarding letters and packages from Rome and from the missions, and using diplomatic channels as much as possible to avoid interceptions and custom fees. They offered intelligence

27. Serafino to Ildefonso da Santa Maria, Paris, September 30, 1736, in ASR. Serafino only mentioned the total expense in *livres* (300) and the cost per pound. One *livre* (Serafino calls it *lira francese*) corresponded to twenty *sols* (*soldi*); Serafino used the weight unit called *libbra*, i.e. Italian pound, corresponding to 330 grams; this means that 300 *livres* would have been enough to pay for 330 kilograms. Here is the math: 300 *livres* x 20 *sols* = 6,000 *sols* / 6 *sols* = 1,000 *libbre* x 330 gr. = 330 kgs.

28. Serafino to Ildefonso da Santa Maria, Paris, October 30 1736, in ASR.

29. Serafino to Vicar General OAD, Macao, December 18, 1737, in ASR.

30. Serafino to Ildefonso da Santa Maria, Paris, November (?) 1736, in ASR.

31. Serafino to Ildefonso da Santa Maria, Paris, October 30, 1736, in ASR.

to Rome, while also implementing central orders on behalf of the Roman congregations. They provided financial services to traveling missionaries, transferring funds coming from Rome to banking agents, even all the way to India and East Asia if necessary. They paid back to the headquarters of East India Companies loans taken by the Procurator of Propaganda in Macao and Canton, upon receipt of letters of exchange, or sent caskets of silver species directly to the Procurator via commercial agents and vessels of the East India Companies. They reimbursed travel expenses of missionaries in transit and connected them to government agencies and royal officials in the country where they resided as nuncios. They obtained needed passports, and often bargained with ship owners or royal agencies for discounted or free passage for missionaries. They purchased gifts on behalf of missionaries, to mollify authorities and the imperial court in China. They also sometimes recommended local priests for missionary service to Propaganda.[32]

While the nuncio certainly informed Rome of the travelers' whereabouts, Serafino also communicated directly with the highest authorities in Rome about the journey, and especially stressed his financial needs. On November 5, 1736, he wrote letters to both the Prefect of Propaganda, Cardinal Vincenzo Petra (1662–1747) and to Cardinal Giuseppe Renato Imperiali (1651–1737), cardinal protector of the Augustinian order and member of the congregation of cardinals supervising Propaganda, to lament the high costs of travel in France, and obviously hoping to obtain more funds.[33]

In Paris, Serafino also tried to communicate with French authorities. For example, he met with Adrian Maurice de Noailles (1678–1766), Maréchal de France, whom he had previously encountered in Crema (Lombardy), where the Maréchal was coordinating military operations in the War of Polish Succession (1733–38). De Noailles extended his patronage to Serafino, who was hoping to be received by the king. However, that meeting did not happen, as the monarch was in Versailles, and the missionaries urgently needed to obtain a sea passage.[34]

During their twelve days in Paris, the two Augustinians obtained

32. On the administrative functions of nuncios in the service of Propaganda, see Pizzorusso 1998. Members of religious orders continued to use their own internal communication networks as well. Sigismondo, for example, suggested to his brother in Turin that he send letters addressed in French to the librarian of the Augustinian convent of Notre Dame des Victoires in Paris, a certain "Father Eustache," who would then forward them to Lorient and China; letter from Lorient, December 18, 1736, in Meinardi 1964, 2.

33. On travel to France and related high expenses, see letter of Serafino to Cardinal Petra, Paris, November 5, 1736, in APF, *Scritture Originali della Congregazione Particolare dell'Indie Orientali e Cina* (SOCP), vol. 42 (1739), ff. 185r–v and 188r; and Serafino to Cardinal Imperiali, same place and date, ff. 186r–187r.

34. Serafino to Ildefonso da Santa Maria, Paris, November (?) 1736, in ASR.

through the nuncio needed documentation and a passage on a French East India Company ship. They then proceeded as fast as they could to Nantes, the capital of Brittany, avoiding this time the capricious winds on the Loire River, even if travel by land cost them double. They then continued to the port of embarkation for the Indies, Lorient, further north along the coast, where they would spend around two weeks waiting for the departure of the China vessels. To find suitable accommodation in the busy town was not easy, and the money was dwindling, as the provisions Serafino was going to buy for the long voyage were sold very dearly there, and eight _livres_ per day were necessary for meals for the two of them alone. Fortunately, his French was sufficient to find assistance from a local merchant, one Monsieur Allègre, who became a sort of agent and helped them to navigate the town.[35]

Since passengers on the ship were simply given a space over the wooden floor of the powder magazine (_santabarbara_), Serafino had to purchase several items to make the trip comfortable. He acquired mattresses and woolen blankets for the first leg of the trip in the cold climate of the northern Atlantic (elsewhere it was in fact rather hot); urinals made of tin (so they would not break with the movements of the sea); cloth napkins and towels; a water pitcher; glasses; and a knife for the dining table. Serafino observed that, curiously, forks and spoons were provided on French ships and in French inns, but never knives. He also purchased some linen cloth, since he learned that in China only cotton was available, and took along all the necessary implements for celebrating the Mass, to avoid borrowing anything from the ship's chaplain.[36]

Each missionary – as Serafino advised in a later letter, obviously based on his own experience – should have a small travel cellar (_cantinella_) with at least fifteen large bottles of Canary wine, both to celebrate mass, and to drink in small quantities "to reinforce the stomach, especially since in China there is only rice wine"; and also some aquavit for the same curative properties. In Lorient he also bought some specialty foods, good to combat seasickness: Seville oranges, apples, and salted sardines with onions. Apparently, preserved fish could prevent vomiting. To mitigate the effects of excessive heat when reaching the Tropics, he took along some containers of "refreshing preserves" (_conserve rinfrescative_). Last but not least, he exchanged all the remaining cash into Spanish _pesos_ (_piastre_), "since that's the only currency that is accepted in China without a loss in value." He observed, however, that even in case one still had French silver _écus_, it would be possible to have

35. Serafino to Ildefonso da Santa Maria, Paris, November (?) 1736, in ASR.
36. Serafino to Ildefonso da Santa Maria, Paris, November (?) 1736, in ASR.

those exchanged in China, "since in China silver is cut into pieces, and the loss of value would be minimal."[37]

To obtain a sea passage, Serafino followed a procedure that he later detailed in his instructions to future missionaries. He first introduced himself to the Director General of the Compagnie des Indes, and was informed that he and Sigismondo would need to embark on the vessel *Prince de Conti*. We do not find details on the price paid for the passage, but we know that the nuncio in Paris had negotiated a discounted fare. The Director was particularly pleased when Sigismondo repaired a clavier he owned, and recommended the traveling party to the vessel's captain. Serafino paid a visit to the captain, and presented him some Genoese candied fruit as a small token of appreciation. He noted that Frenchmen paid much attention to such ceremonies and appreciated good manners, but also that members of religious orders were not particularly esteemed in France, and that it was thus very important to give a clear example of virtue and civility.[38]

Oceanic voyage

The *Condé* and the *Prince de Conti*, two East Indiamen of 600 tons each, left Lorient for China on the same day, December 18, 1736.[39] Serafino and Sigismondo embarked on the *Prince de Conti*, together with two other Italian Discalced Augustinians and two "Minori Osservanti" or "religiosi di S. Tomaso."[40]

Serafino recommended that priests on the ship should scrupulously follow the schedule of recitation of the divine office, and celebrate mass whenever possible. Moreover, a certain distance had to be maintained with the crew and other passengers. In a report for the benefit of future recruits, he suggested that traveling missionaries "should not be on familiar terms with anybody [on the ship]."[41] But the social life of the ship could not be

---

37. Serafino to Ildefonso da Santa Maria, Paris, November (?) 1736, in ASR.

38. Serafino to Ildefonso da Santa Maria, Lorient, December 1, 1736, in ASR.

39. These data are drawn from a variety of Serafino's letters in ASR and Sigismondo's letters in Meinardi 1964; details on the Asia trip of the *Prince de Conti* in 1736–38 are available in the database *Mémoire des hommes* of the French Ministry of Defence http://www.memoiredeshommes.sga.defense.gouv.fr/, with many references to the navigational documents in the Archives nationales, section *Marine*, Paris; and at the Service historique de la défense, Lorient.

40. Meinardi 1964, 2. One of the Discalced Augustinians traveling with them was Adriano da S. Tecla, who would go on to Vietnam (see Meinardi 1964, 6). For a biography of Adriano and a description of the missionary efforts of the Order in Southeast Asia, see Adriano di St. Thecla [*sic*] 2002.

41. Serafino to Vicar General OAD, Macao, December 18, 1737, in ASR.

Image 1. "Ceremony of shaving, on passing the line," from F. B. Spilbury, *Account of a Voyage to the Western Coast of Africa, Performed by His Majesty's Sloop Favourite, in the Year 1805, Being a Journal of the Events Which Happened to That Vessel*, London: R. Phillips, 1807; Wesleyan University Library, used with permission.

totally ignored. The line of the Tropic of Cancer was crossed on January 9, and the Equator on January 25, and the favorable winds helped maintain the course. On that occasion, Serafino reported what he called a "ridiculous ceremony" held by the sailors at the passing of the Equator, an enactment that they called "baptism." This was in fact the well-known line-crossing ceremony also described by Marc-Antoine Caillot in his 1729 transatlantic journey to Louisiana, as detailed in Elizabeth Goldsmith's chapter in the present volume. The ceremony took the form of a raucous hazing affair, where sailors dressed up as members of the court of Neptune or as Africans, and mocked the passengers and officers in a carnival parade, requesting tips. Unlike Caillot, Serafino did not find the situation amusing, and tried to avoid becoming the object of ridicule during the ceremony. In his advice to future missionaries, he recommended giving a contribution of one *peso* per person (less would be *spilorchieria*, stinginess) when a basin was passed around at the end of the function, "to avoid being insulted and be drenched with water from head to toe." Tipping the gunner, the butler (*maestro di casa*), and the waiter serving at the table was also customary, to maintain a good level of service and abide by custom.[42]

The vessel remained at sea until March 14, 1737, when it reached the Dutch colony of the Cape of Good Hope. Sigismondo – Serafino's companion – could send a letter to his brother in Turin from the Cape by way of a returning Dutch ship. He reported that the voyage had been uneventful, favored with constant good weather, and not as difficult as earlier descriptions had led him to imagine: "During these three months we went through winter, and then spring when we sailed close to the Canary Islands, which we did not see. After crossing the equinox line, we encountered summer, and now [on the Cape] we have been enjoying ... a nice autumn [...] In a few days we will again encounter spring in the seas of Asia, without experiencing winter." Here we palpably feel the excitement of the missionaries for what turned out to be a pleasant crossing. Yet, not all ships had the same luck. Sigismondo observed that while at the Cape, he witnessed the arrival from Amsterdam of a Dutch ship, which had taken nine months to reach the colony, and was by the time of its arrival in very bad condition.[43]

The Cape was the ordinary stopover for French ships on the way to Asia to get fresh water, supplies, and some rest, and the missionaries spent around three weeks there. Since the Dutch authorities forbade the open presence of Catholic priests in the colony, the missionaries had to dress in secular garb, with clothes borrowed from the ship's officers. All knew their identity nonetheless, and Serafino commented that as Catholic clergy they had to be particularly careful to be above suspicion, "being in the midst of enemies who observe [us] carefully." They found good accommodation through their ship's captain, spending around one Spanish *peso* per day for their room and board per person. While the climate was very pleasant at the Cape, the warm tropical temperatures experienced in circumnavigating Africa, and those expecting them across the Indian Ocean and beyond, required the shedding of the traditional Augustinian long habit made of thick felt, in favor of shorter and lighter clothes. On April 4 they left the Cape, and the remainder of the journey was rather tranquil, so much so that the captain called it "miraculous" in his logbook, according to Sigismondo. However, on Good Friday the ship encountered a storm that "tossed [the passengers] out of the beds, which look like coffers." The following day, however, recitation of the litanies of the saints brought back a calm sea in time for Easter Sunday.[44] By

42. Serafino to Vicar General OAD, Macao, December 18, 1737, in ASR.
43. Meinardi 1964, 7.
44. Meinardi 1964, 4.

May 3 they sighted the island of Java, but the absence of winds slowed their progress, and they were able to enter the Sunda Straits only on June 9. The ship cast anchor and loaded fresh drinking water there, and once more with favorable winds was able to reach Macao on July 20, 1737.

From Macao to Beijing

The missionaries waited on board for instructions from the Procurator of Propaganda Arcangelo Miralta, and eventually moved to the convent of the Portuguese Dominicans in Macao, where Miralta had his quarters. The following six months were spent awaiting imperial permission to proceed to Beijing, to be issued via the office of the Governor General of Guangdong and Guangxi in Canton. The Augustinians relied in part on the connections of the Jesuits to proceed, and attached themselves to two members of the Portuguese Vice-Province, who since 1737 had been awaiting the required *placet* to reach the capital; these two men were the Italian, Giacomo Antonini (1701–1739), physician, and the Portuguese Felix da Rocha (1713–1781), a new member of the Astronomical Directorate. Serafino presented himself as a painter, and Sigismondo as a clockmaker. Once the imperial decree reached them, the party left Macao by boat for Canton on January 12, 1738. However, when they arrived at the provincial capital two days later, they met with a chilly reception. Apparently, the Jesuits in Beijing had petitioned to pay for the travel of their own men from the south, rather than relying on the imperial government as was customary; this initiative caused consternation among officials, as they could no longer administer the travel funds and profit in the process. Only after three visits to the governor's palace were the missionaries finally received, and still most other officials refused to see them, with the exception of the Manchu general in charge of the Canton garrison.[45] On January 28, the four foreign priests finally left by boat along the riverways. The Augustinians were accompanied by two Christians, who had arrived from Beijing to accompany them, and by a Cantonese cook, also a Christian, called Eustachio.[46]

The first stop was in Shaozhou a few days later, but the trip proceeded very slowly as the river's water level was low. Serafino lamented that the expenses were already becoming excessive, since at each new jurisdiction local soldiers would appear, discharge three salvos of their harquebuses in the air to salute, present themselves with a visiting card from their superior,

45. Serafino to Prefect of Propaganda Fide, Canton, January 28, 1738, in APF, SOCP, vol. 42, ff. 178r–v.

46. Serafino to Miralta, Nanxiong, February 13, 1738, ff. 1r–2r, in APF, *Procura Cina*, box 30.

and ask for tips. Antonini on one occasion offered the soldiers "two horrible sweets as gifts, that were so bad that even Italian dogs would have avoided sniffing them,"[47] and this obliged the travelers to double their tips to move along. Halfway to Nanxiong, moreover, they had to offer a lunch to their boatman and the men pulling the boat upstream on the Bei River. While annoyed at these ceremonies with soldiers and boatmen, Serafino did not seem to find them particularly strange, their opacity only partially increased by linguistic barriers. In fact, tips and rewards were the common lubricant for travel everywhere, no more common in China than in Europe. Sigismondo tried also to train their cook to prepare dishes according to the foreigners' taste, but to no avail. The next city, Nanxiong, was reached only on February 13. They were well received there by the local Manchu military official, but had to remain an extra day due to heavy rain. That day their boatmen got terribly drunk, and recovered from the hangover only the following day. To reach the next stop, the party crossed by land over the Mei Pass using sedan chairs, assisted by sixty local porters (whom they paid one *masso* and six *gondorins* [sic] each, more than usual, since it was Chinese New Year).[48] Once in the town of Nan'an, Jiangxi province, they moved back to water transportation, renting a boat on the Gan River. However, as prices were high due to the approaching festivities of the New Year, they had to bargain hard, finally lowering the fare from 21 to 11.5 *taels* per boat. They arrived in Ganzhou on February 19, the day of the Chinese New Year, and in another six days, after passing the famously dangerous rapids of that region, they reached the provincial capital of Jiangxi province, Nanchang. The river journey was now over, and the rest of the itinerary would be by land, using mule litters (*lettiche*) for the two priests, and mules to transport their baggage.

They spent several days in Nanchang, to have the land travel arranged and the litters built, at a cost of six *taels* each. Since their trunks were too heavy for the litters (which reached capacity with a bed and a person each), they hired some extra mules, and rearranged the contents of some of the trunks, for an average weight of 180 *cates* (around 112 kgs) per mule, and a total cost for all their ten mules of 100 *taels*. Managing the Chinese helpers also required careful accounting. A young servant riding a mule led each of the two mule litters, and needed compensation for the trip all the way to Beijing, as well as for clothing and boots. Serafino thus decided to save

47. Serafino to Miralta, Nanxiong, February 13, 1738, f. 1r, in APF, *Procura Cina*, box 30.

48. Serafino to Miralta, Nan'an, February 19, 1738, f. 1r–v, in APF, *Procura Cina*, box 30. *Maz* (plur. *maces*) and *conderin* or *condorin* were terms used by the Portuguese to indicate sub-units of the Chinese silver *tael* (in Mandarin, *liang*, corresponding to ca. forty grams of silver). One *tael* was equivalent to ten *maces* or 100 *condorins*.

Image 2. A mule litter in northern China in the early twentieth century, in all likelihood quite similar to the *lettiche* used by the missionaries. Photograph by Sanshichiro Yamamoto Studio, Peking, (ca. 1906). [Photo in public domain in Japan and USA: https://commons. wikimedia.org/wiki/File:Sedan_chair_carried_by_mules.jpg]

money by dismissing the Cantonese cook, as he had been too liberal for his tastes with tips and expenses.[49]

The land voyage was blessed by good weather and proceeded rather smoothly, in spite of occasional breakdowns of the mule litters, which necessitated repairs. At a distance of three days' journey from Beijing, where they would arrive on April 9, 1738, two domestics of the Beijing Jesuits reached the traveling party, bringing refreshments. One returned immediately to the capital to announce the arrival of the two new Jesuits and the two Augustinians. He was soon back with more refreshments, chickens, sweets, and wine. On the arrival day, the Jesuit Vice-Provincial André Pereira (1689–1743) traveled outside the city gates to meet them, and invited them to have a banquet at the Jesuit College of S. José. Ignaz Kögler (1680–1746), head of the Astronomical Directorate, visited them as well, in spite of having not yet fully recovered from falling off a horse a week earlier. Finally, the two missionaries got on their litters, and reached the residence of the only Propaganda missionary then in Beijing, Teodorico Pedrini, located at the Xitang

49. Serafino to Miralta, Nanchang, March 1, 1738, f. 1r–4v, in APF, *Procura Cina*, box 30.

(Western Church) in the northwestern part of the city. To their great dismay, they found the rooms reserved for them in disrepair and without any furnishing.[50] But they were finally at their destination. All said and done, the final accounting for the trip from Macao to Beijing cost the Procurator Office a total of 459.3 Portuguese *reais*.[51]

The letters reported in detail place names and distances, travel expenses, small accidents along the route, conflicts among the travelers and with boatmen and porters, and weather changes. We would look in vain for any deeper cultural commentary in these short missives, precariously written on boats or during a stopover at a country inn. They were jotted down to inform superiors of the progress of the journey, not to enlighten a broader public on the nature of China's culture, geography, and customs. These notes offer rare glimpses of specific moments of the journey, capturing for us in micro-historical detail the complexity and difficulties of pre-modern travel. Serafino, however, had a particularly rosy view of his own journey. He had been quite lucky, since the oceanic sail had been remarkably uneventful, and he had met with mostly good weather for the entire trip between Macao and Beijing. After several months in the Qing capital, in October 1738 he wrote a letter to the vicar general of his order in Rome to encourage new recruits, stating that the experience of travel had not been as traumatic as he had been led to imagine before his departure, and that living conditions in China were rather good:

> Please encourage members of our religious order to engage in this holy enterprise, and remove from their minds the fears that people over there placed in our hearts and in the hearts of all those who are about to start this journey. Now that the pilots have learned the right timing to sail, one does not encounter any longer the notorious dangers of the Cape of Good Hope, the passing of the Equator, the Agulhas Bank, the Strait of Java and so on. Rather, those [places] are all crossed in safety by all those who choose the right time to pass them, as the French, English, and Portuguese do. Here [in Beijing], moreover, there is bread and wine and everything else one might need, even if over there [in Italy] they said that there was none. In sum, the situation is not as bad as it is usually painted.[52]

In fact, in order to stimulate new arrivals Serafino was only telling a half-truth, especially on life in the Qing capital. The relief at having reached

50. Serafino to Miralta, Beijing, April 9, 1738, ff. 1r–v, in APF, *Procura Cina*, box 30; cf. also Serafino to Vicar General OAD, October 18, 1738, in ASR.

51. "Stato della Cassa … della Procura 1738," in APF, SOCP vol. 42 (1739), f. 140v.

52. Serafino to Vicar General OAD, October 18, 1738, in ASR.

their final destination without incidents had indeed initially contributed to a sense of elation and optimism despite the modest accommodation they found there, and to build good camaraderie with Propaganda's veteran in Beijing, Pedrini. A few days after their arrival, the new priests, with Pedrini's help, had presented their gifts to the court, including a small painting (*miniatura*) by Serafino. Soon after, in a sign of imperial approval for his work, Serafino had received orders to paint some more miniature scenes on paper, leather, ivory, and on tobacco boxes, receiving clothes, furs, and damask textiles as a reward.

Disillusionment, however, set in pretty quickly, already within the first month: "the emperor makes me work like a mule, and to serve him I have to spend all day at the desk, damaging my eyes to paint the very minute scenes that he likes so much." Moreover, without an assignment of imperial horses, he had to spend his own funds to reach the palace, consuming in the first month more than sixty *taels* of silver for transportation and food.[53] Even accounting for some exaggeration to force his superiors to send more funds, the sense of frustration was already palpable. Disenchantment reached a zenith when Pedrini finally revealed his true personality. On August 1, 1738, barely five months after his arrival in the Qing capital, Serafino wrote two separate letters to Procurator Miralta in Macao, one "official" and more neutral, and another confidential, addressed to him as a "friend" (*amico*) rather than as a superior, asking him to burn it immediately after reading it. Fortunately for us, the procurator not only did not comply, but actually forwarded a copy of the most telling "confidential" excerpts to Rome.[54] In his secretive letter Serafino explained the true reasons why that very day he and Sigismondo had abandoned the residence of the Western Church within the walled city of Beijing, and moved to the small and rather dilapidated house owned by the mission in Haidian, at the gates of the suburban imperial palace complex of the Yuanmingyuan:

> The reasons for our departure listed in the [official] letter [sent to you along with this one], although true and very sincere, could have been overcome if the situation had remained the same as in the first month after our arrival in Beijing. However, later on things changed so much that, besides the distance from the Palace and the considerable expense to go there, we had also to face major inconveniences in

53. Serafino to Miralta, Beijing, May 11, 1738, ff. 1r–4v, in APF, *Procura Cina*, box 30; quotation at f. 4r.

54. Original letter by Serafino to Miralta, Haidian, August 1 (?), 1738, ff. 1r–3v, in APF, *Procura Cina*, box 30; cf. partial forwarded copy in APF, SOCP, vol. 42, f. 56v.

living in that house [with Pedrini], and so, for the former and latter reasons, we decided to leave. [55]

Serafino engaged in a weepy mea culpa for having disregarded the orders of the procurator to go directly to Haidian once in the capital, recognizing that the superior's prudent assessment of the situation was not only accurate, but in fact less shocking than the reality. Pedrini, on the pretext of illness, started refusing his services as interpreter and senior palace missionary to the newly arrived confrères, whose linguistic skills and personal contacts were still insufficient to function properly at court. Yet Pedrini was far from being sick, Serafino observed. Three men – he himself, Sigismondo, and a Chinese priest – had barely succeeded in wresting away from Pedrini's hands a poor Chinese servant whom he was "kicking and punching in the face, while pulling him all bloodied across the grounds [of the residence]." The Vincentian priest, then already in his late 60s, was "a man who for many years now has been using a rod [to beat his servants], and who almost daily punches and kicks [some of them]." He was also violent in his language, and threatened to "strangle" Serafino following an argument over administrative matters. After separating their residences, the two parties reconciled in words, but Pedrini continued to undermine his two confrères, depriving them of the help of a catechist stationed in Haidian, and disparagingly telling his own domestics in Beijing that "now that those two missionaries have left, I can hire two servants in their stead," thus proving that he considered them no better than subordinates at his service. Serafino also added that "his natural satirical wit does not let pass any word, gesture, or action by other missionaries without stabbing them with his tongue and ridiculing them, even in front of domestics."[56]

My examination of around eighty letters that Serafino wrote during the remaining five years of his life – he died on August 9, 1742, at age fifty – confirms his increasing sense of despair at the lack of financial support from Macao and Rome, his frustration at the pettiness and stinginess of the hated Pedrini (who outlived him by four years), and his chafing at the tough working conditions for artisans in the imperial service.[57] The China mission had turned out to be much less heroic and exciting than he probably believed before leaving Italy. Illusion had turned into disillusionment.

55. Serafino to Miralta, Haidian, August 1 (?), 1738, f. 2r, in APF, *Procura Cina*, box 30.
56. Serafino to Miralta, Haidian, August 1 (?), 1738, ff. 2r, 2v, 3v, in APF, *Procura Cina*, box 30.
57. The bulk of Serafino's correspondence can be found in APF, in the following sections: SOCP, vols. 42, 43, 44; SC, *Indie Orientali e Cina*, vol. 23; *Procura Cina*, box 30.

Conclusion

Serafino's unpublished letters are the sole remaining traces of the journey he took from Italy to China, and chronicle for us the difficulties of a man caught between a desire for missionary heroism with its illusory rewards, and the disillusionment he experienced once faced with the truth of Chinese reality. As historians, we could use such sources to probe the mentality of the missionary, the psychological effects of travels, the consequences of cultural dislocation, and the workings of cross-cultural communication. Serafino's short missives, however, are less useful in this regard than many other travel accounts, published and unpublished, that have been extensively studied to understand the European ethnographic gaze and the local dynamics of encounters, including missionary ones.[58] His letters, in fact, are more precious as immediate testimonies of how the structural organization of communication and travel from Europe to Beijing functioned for missionaries in the eighteenth century, outside the older Portuguese patronage system, and how material constraints shaped ideological and religious goals. These sources thus turn out to illuminate the micro-historical study of the materiality of travel, as I have briefly illustrated in this essay. In conjunction with the analysis of more reflexive accounts of cultural difference and of philosophical musings on the meaning of travel, so abundant in published accounts (often post-facto systematizations rather than, like Serafino's letters, instantaneous records of travel), the reconstruction of the actual mechanics of voyages can bridge the gap between the ideal and the material dimensions of travel, and restore for us a fuller understanding of the experience of pre-modern travel.

Serafino's reports reveal the physical infrastructure that sustained cross-cultural contacts. Through the mechanisms and patronage networks offered by Propaganda Fide, the papal nuncios, the King of France, and the French East Indies Company, the journey of our two Augustinians went relatively smoothly all the way to Beijing. In Europe, papal nuncios and religious orders offered a flexible and reliable support network for Propaganda missionaries, in terms of communication, accommodation, transportation, and financial resources. In East Asia, the Procurator of Propaganda in Macao, whose powers were both disciplinary and logistical, acted on behalf of the papacy in a capacity similar to that of the nuncios in Europe. But obviously, within China itself, the support of local Christian guides, both from the Macao-Canton region and from Beijing, and imperial permissions and support

---

58. For a recent survey of European and Chinese sources on travel and ethnography in the early modern period, see Rubiés and Ollé 2016.

for those traveling to the court, made travel by foreign priests with almost no linguistic skills possible.[59] The case of the maverick Gemelli Careri, in its exceptionality, only confirms that travel and extended residence in China outside the missionary system or the occasional tributary embassy was virtually impossible. Yet, both for the vagabond Italian layman, and for generations of Catholic missionaries in the age of sail between the mid-sixteenth century and the nineteenth century, the synergy of European and Chinese social and economic networks offered the needed infrastructure to move people and objects from Europe to Beijing. If this feat of social, economic, and logistical coordination within pre-modern technological confines still astonishes, the limitations of Propaganda's bureaucratic organization could not be overcome, and provoked a certain dose of cynicism and disillusionment among its China missionaries. The Congregation's attempt to control the finances and internal life of the mission from distant Rome and Macao, the uneven quality and training of the missionaries recruited by the Holy See, and the endless jurisdictional conflicts that divided the energies of the China evangelists in competing sub-groups (Portuguese Jesuits, French Jesuits, and Propaganda) often contributed to turning rosy illusions into bitter disappointments.

Table: Chronology of Serafino's Journey from Milan to Beijing, 1736–1738

Date	Travel
Late January 1736	Departs Lombardy for Rome
February 10-15 (?), 1736	Arrives in Rome
August 18, 1736	Prepares to leave Rome for France
After September 2, 1736	Departs from Rome
September 23, 1736	Arrives in Genoa
September 25, 1736	At Genoa, prepares to embark for Marseille or Nice
September 30, 1736	At Genoa, prepares to embark for Marseille with *tartana francese*
October 1, 1736 (?)	Ends up taking a *latina* for Nice, Provence
October 2, 1736 (?)	From Nice, takes buggy to Aix-en-Provence
	Aix-en-Provence to Lyon; Lyon to Roanne [Rouain] on horse and cart; from Roanne by Loire River to Orleans by boat; Orleans to Paris by coach in two days
October 26, 1736	Arrives in Paris (Notre Dame des Victoires)
November 11, 1736	Leaves Paris for Nantes by land
December 1, 1736	Arrives in Lorient

59. On the office of the Propaganda Fide's Procurator in China, see Menegon 2017.

Date	**Travel**
December 17, 1736	Embarks in Lorient
December 18, 1736	Departs Lorient on the ship *Prince de Conti* for China
March 14, 1737	Arrives at Cape of Good Hope
April 4, 1737	Departs from Cape of Good Hope
July 20, 1737	Arrives in Macao
January 12, 1738	Departs from Macao to Canton by boat
January 14, 1738 (or 18?)	Arrives in Canton (Guangzhou 廣州)
January 28, 1738	Departs from Canton by river
Late January–early February, 1738 (?)	Passes through Shaozhou 邵州 by river
February 13, 1738	Arrives in Nanxiong 南雄, by river
February 14, 1738 (?)	Passage of the Mei Pass 梅關 by land
February 15, 1738	Arrives in Nan'an 南安 by river
February 19, 1738 (Chinese New Year's Day)	Arrives in Ganzhou 贛州 by river
February 21, 1738	Rapids on Gan 贛 river
February 26, 1738	Arrives in Nanchang 南昌 by river
	From Nanchang to Beijing by land
April 9, 1738	Arrives in Beijing

Bibliography

Archival Sources

Archivio Storico della Congregazione per l'Evangelizzazione dei Popoli or *de Propaganda Fide*, Vatican City (APF). Series *Scritture riferite nei Congressi* (SC), *Indie Orientali e Cina*, vol. 21 (1733–36) and vol. 24 (1744–45). Series *Scritture Originali della Congregazione Particolare dell'Indie Orientali e Cina* (SOCP), vol. 42 (1739). Series *Procura Cina*, box 30.

Archivio di Stato di Roma, Italy (ASR). *Congregazioni religiose, Agostiniani scalzi in Gesù e Maria al Corso*. Envelope 156, fascicles 117 and 118, unnumbered folios; envelope 277, fascicle 722.

Archivio di Stato di Milano, Italy (ASMi). *Fondo di religione*. Folders 1089, 1100, 4361, 4364, unnumbered folios.

Printed Sources

Adriano di St. Thecla. 2002. *Opusculum de Sectis apud Sinenses et Tunkinenses. A Small Treatise on the Sects among the Chinese and Tonkinese.* Translated by Olga Dror and Mariya Berezovska. Ithaca, NY: Cornell South East Asia Publications.

Amuso Maccarrone, Angela. 2000. *Gianfrancesco Gemelli-Careri. L'Ulisse del XVII secolo. Biografia scientifica di un grande di Calabria.* Reggio Calabria: Gangemi.

Barbagallo, Ignazio. 1978. "Le missioni degli agostiniani scalzi nel Tonchino e nella Cina." *Presenza Agostiniana* 2:28–41.

Boothroyd, Ninette, Muriel Détrie, and Fernand Bunel, eds. 1992. *Le voyage en Chine: anthologie des voyageurs occidentaux du Moyen Age à la chute de l'empire chinois.* Paris: Bouquins.

Campanelli, Marcella. 2001. *Gli agostiniani scalzi.* Napoli: La Città del Sole.

Dehergne, Joseph. 1973. *Répertoire des Jésuites de Chine de 1552 à 1800.* Roma-Paris: Institutum Historicum Societatis Iesu.

Doria, Piero. 2000. "Gemelli Careri, Giovanni Francesco." In *Dizionario Biografico degli Italiani*, vol. 53, 42–45. Roma: Istituto dell'Enciclopedia Italiana.

Fatica, Michele. 1998. "L'itinerario sinico di Giovanni Francesco Gemelli Careri: saggio di decrittazione degli antroponimi europei e dei toponimi cinesi nel *Giro del mondo*." In *Persembahan. Studi in onore di Luigi Santa Maria*, edited by Sitti Faizah, Soenoto Rivai, and Luigi Santa Maria, 45–67. Napoli: Istituto Universitario Orientale.

Gemelli Careri, Giovanni Francesco. 1700. *Giro del mondo del dottor d. Gio. Francesco Gemelli Careri - Parte Quarta - Contenente le cose più ragguardevoli vedute nella Cina.* 4 vols. Napoli: Roselli.

———. 1728. *Giro del mondo del dottor d. Gio. Francesco Gemelli Careri – Tomo Quarto – Contenente le cose più ragguardevoli vedute nella Cina – Nuova edizione accresciuta.* 9 vols. Venezia: Coleti.

Lequin, Frank. 1985. "A 'Mandarin' from Vlissingen in Lhasa and Peking: The Hidden Life of Samuel van de Putte (1690–1745)." *Itinerario* 9.2:73–91.

Maldavsky, Aliocha. 2012. "Pedir las Indias: Las cartas *indipetae* de los jesuitas europeos, siglos XVI-XVIII, ensayo historiográfico." *Relaciones (Zamora)* 33.132:147–81.

Margiotti, Fortunato, and Rosso Sisto, eds. 1961. *Sinica Franciscana. Relationes et Epistolas primorum Fratrum Minorum Italorum in Sinis saeculi XVII et XVIII,* vol. VI. Roma: [Edizioni Sinica Franciscana].

Marin, Catherine. 2007. "Passer sur l'autre rive: de l'Occident à l'Extrême-Orient." In *Les écritures de la mission en Extrême-Orient: le choc de l'arrivée, XVIIIe-XXe siècles, de l'attente à l'arrivée, Chine, Asie du Sud-Est, Japon: anthologie de textes missionnaires,* edited by Catherine Marin, 17–107. Turnhout: Brepols.

Massimi, Marina, and Emanuele Colombo. 2014. *In viaggio. Gesuiti candidati alle missioni tra Antica e Nuova Compagnia.* Milano: Il Sole 24 Ore.

Meinardi, Sigismondo da San Nicola. 1964. *Epistolario. Parte prima. Lettere originali inviate a Torino.* Roma: Edizioni di 'Vinculum' – Rivista interna dello Studentato Teologico di Gesù e Maria dei PP. Agostiniani Scalzi.

Menegon, Eugenio. 2012. "A Clash of Court Cultures: Papal Envoys in Early Eighteenth Century Beijing." In *Europe-China. Intercultural Encounters (16th-18th Centuries),* edited by Luis Filipe Barreto, 139–78. Lisbon: Centro Científico e Cultural de Macau.

———. 2015. "La Cina, l'Italia e Milano: connessioni globali nella prima età moderna." In *Milano, l'Ambrosiana e la conoscenza dei nuovi mondi (secoli XVII-XVIII),* edited by Michela Catto, and Gianvittorio Signorotto, 267–80. Milano: Biblioteca e Accademia Ambrosiana, Classe di Studi Borromaici & Bulzoni Editore.

———. 2017. "Interlopers at the Fringes of Empire: The Procurators of the Propaganda Fide Papal Congregation in Canton and Macao, 1700-1823." *Cross-Currents: East Asian History and Culture Review,* E-Journal 25:26-62.

Mensaert Georges, et al., eds. 1965. *Sinica Franciscana. Relationes et epistolas Fratrum Minorum Hispanorum in Sinis,* vol. VII. Roma: Edizioni Sinica Franciscana.

Pizzorusso, Giovanni. 1998'"Per servitio della Sacra Congregatione de Propaganda Fide': i nunzi apostolici e le missioni tra centralità romana e Chiesa universale (1622–1660)." *Cheiron* 30:201–27.

———. 2000. "Agli antipodi di Babele: Propaganda Fide tra immagine cosmo-polita e orizzonti romani (XVII-XIX secolo)." In *Roma, la città del papa. Vita civile e religiosa dal giubileo di Bonifacio VIII al giubileo di papa Wojtyla*, edited by Luigi Fiorani, and Adriano Prosperi, 478–518. Torino: Einaudi.

Roscioni, Gian Carlo. 2001. *Il desiderio delle Indie. Storie, sogni e fughe di giovani gesuiti italiani*. Torino: Einaudi.

Rubiés, Joan Pau and Manel Ollé. 2016. "The Comparative History of a Genre: The Production and Circulation of Books on Travel and Eth-nographies in Early Modern Europe and China." *Modern Asian Studies* 50.1:259–309.

Russell, Camilla. 2011. "Imagining the 'Indies': Italian Jesuit Petitions for the Overseas Missions at the Turn of the Seventeenth Century." In *L'Europa divisa e i nuovi mondi. Per Adriano Prosperi*, edited by Massimo Donattini, Giuseppe Marcocci, and Stefania Pastore, vol. 2:179–89. Pisa: Edizioni della Normale.

———. 2013. "Vocation to the East: Italian Candidates for the Jesuit China Mission at the Turn of the Seventeenth Century." In *Renaissance Studies in Honor of Joseph Connors*, edited by Machtelt Israëls and Louis Wald-man, vol. 2:313–27 Cambridge, MA: Harvard University Press.

Sanfilippo, Matteo. 1995. "Fedeli, Giovanni Battista." In *Dizionario Biografico degli Italiani*, vol. 45:606–10. Roma: Istituto dell'Enciclopedia Italiana.

Standaert, Nicolas, ed. 2001. *Handbook of Christianity in China, Volume One, 635-1800*. Leiden: Brill.

Tucci, Giuseppe. 1949. *Italia e Oriente*, Milano: Garzanti.

Vargas, Philippe de. 1955. "Le *Giro del mondo* de Gemelli Careri, en parti-culier le récit du séjour en Chine: roman ou vérité?" *Schweizerische Zeitschrift für Geschichte - Revue suisse d'histoire - Rivista storica svizze-ra* V.4:417–51.

Wicki, Josef. 1967. "Liste der Jesuiten-Indienfahrer 1541–1758." In *Portugiesi-sche Forschungen der Gorresgesellschaft. Reihe 1: Aufsätze zur Portugiesischen Kulturgeschichte*, edited by Hans Flasche, vol. VII:252–450. Münster: Aschendorffsche Verlagsbuschshandlung.

Wyngaert, Anastasius van den, ed. 1942. *Sinica Franciscana. Relationes et epis-tolas Fratrum Minorum saeculi XVII et XVIII*, vol. IV. Quaracchi-Firenze: Apud Collegium S. Bonaventurae.

Travel, Adventure, and Self-Fashioning:
A Frenchman's Journey to New Orleans in 1729

Elizabeth C. Goldsmith

O N A COOL DAY in March of 1729, a young man stood on the docks of the French Atlantic port of Lorient, waiting to board a ship that would take him to a new post and a new life in the distant colony of Louisiana. Missionaries and soldiers were paying passengers, and familiar to the crews of transatlantic ships departing for the Americas from France. But Marc-Antoine Caillot was neither. He was a copy clerk, employed by the French Company of the Indies, being sent by his employer to serve on one of the many concessions that the powerful company held around the globe. Louisiana, in fact, was a colony that had been managed more by the Company of the Indies than by the French crown. Caillot's posting to Louisiana would run from July 1729 to May 1731, the year in which the Company handed control of the colony back to the French royal state.

A Company clerk sent to the Louisiana colony in 1729 would have had mixed feelings about the assignment. The sensational collapse of John Law's investment scheme in 1720 meant that Louisiana quickly had become one of the least desirable destinations for anyone interested in making a career in one of the French colonies.[1] By 1729, New Orleans and surrounding outposts had been put under a new administrative team from the Company of the Indies. Attention was turned toward finding a way of reaping profits that would persuade skeptical French businessmen to reinvest in the colony. Against considerable evidence to the contrary, reports were sent home of the suitability of the land around New Orleans for tobacco production. Company administrators, many of them new to the territory, drafted reports that ignored the historical tensions with Indian nations that occupied much of the land being converted to tobacco plantations. When Caillot arrived on the scene in July 1729, these tensions were again coming to a head.

Caillot's story is one that was only rediscovered in 2004, when his manuscript turned up at an auction in Montreal. It was purchased, carefully

---

1. Law created France's first national bank, merged it with the conglomerate Mississippi Company, and encouraged massive reckless investment in company shares. See Murphy 1997.

researched, and edited by Erin Greenwald, and published in English under the title *A Company Man* by the Historic New Orleans Collection Museum and Library.[2] Caillot's narrative is an important addition to a small cluster of extant accounts, each quite distinct in tone and approach, written by French travelers to New Orleans in the early eighteenth century.[3] Caillot, writing in a highly personal voice, is a narrator who composed his work with other writers in mind. He draws explicitly on literary models to construct his own traveling persona, and tries to keep himself attached to, and to promote, a particular idea of French identity in this early moment in the history of transatlantic travel. He narrates his voyage in a lively and playful style, seeming to take great pleasure in his writing, while also facing huge challenges trying to communicate his story to readers in a way that will be both honest and entertaining.

In his youth, Caillot's family was connected with the royal French household. His father was first footman at the Château de Meudon, residence of Louis XIV's oldest son. Marc-Antoine's siblings were eventually given positions in the royal household, while he was offered a clerkship in the Company of the Indies. Trained in the Company's Paris headquarters, he was posted to Louisiana at the age of twenty-one. After returning to France two years later, he was reassigned to the Indian Ocean headquarters of the Company of the East Indies, in Pondicherry. Caillot would stay in the service of the Company of the Indies until his death in 1758 in a shipwreck off the coast of India. By then he had built a successful career for himself, married a niece of a highly placed administrator in the Company, and become quite wealthy.[4]

Over one half of Caillot's account is the story of his voyage from Paris to New Orleans, first across France to the coast of Brittany and the port city of Lorient, from where he set sail for his Atlantic crossing on a ship called the *Durance*. He left Paris on February 19, 1729 and set sail from Lorient a month later, on March 16. His sea voyage to New Orleans took four months, with a stop in Saint Domingue (now Hispaniola, or Haiti), then across the Gulf of Mexico and up the Mississippi on a smaller boat.

The remainder of Caillot's narrative is an account of the Louisiana colony, descriptions of people, animals, plants, fish, food, customs, and above all conflicts between the colonists and the Natchez Indians. Aggravated by

2. Greenwald subsequently has published a detailed study of Caillot's narrative as illustrative of the history of the French Company of the Indies. See Greenwald 2016.

3. The principal works in this cluster are Le Page du Pratz 1758, Hachard 1728, and Dumont de Montigny 1753.

4. See Greenwald 2016, 153–60.

a particularly ruthless French military commander – de Chépart – who had confiscated Natchez lands, these conflicts had been coming to a head in the months prior to the clerk's arrival. The tensions culminated in a war between the Natchez and the French that started in November of 1729, just six months after Caillot's arrival. Company resources were diverted to retaliation, civilian militias were formed, and Company employees, including Caillot, were recruited. Immediately after the French victory in 1731, and also following a fire that destroyed most of his possessions in the house where he had been living, Caillot requested a transfer. He left to return to France on May 4, 1731.

For over 200 years, this manuscript remained unknown to all but the very small audience who first read it. It was probably written, or at least completed in 1731, as Caillot was waiting in France to be re-posted after his return from Louisiana. At some point after that it was stored in either a Company or a private archive in France, and most certainly for some time it was archived in a Breton convent, because our first record of it dates to 1939, when it was brought to Canada by an Augustinian nun from a convent near Lorient. Purchased in 1940 by the Quebec provincial government, it was catalogued in archives of the Quebec Museum of Fine Arts and forgotten until 2004, when it was put up for auction.

It is likely that Caillot was familiar with some of the earlier accounts of French exploration in Louisiana and the Mississippi valley. In his own memoir he engages with the famous expeditions of Robert de La Salle and the many failed attempts to discover the mouth of the Mississippi river.[5] These events were recent enough to inspire in him a certain pride as his own boat headed up the river, though he acknowledged continually how difficult the navigation was. He included, among the many illustrations he produced for his manuscript, a detailed map of the Mississippi at its point of entry into the waters of the Gulf of Mexico, and added labels describing precisely how one had to navigate around the islands in order to proceed upriver. Maps are an important element in his narrative. The manuscript includes maps of the city of New Orleans and several of the islands, forts, and settlements in southern Louisiana.

But for Caillot, the experience of the voyage was at least as important as the destination. While his illustrations and maps are drawn with a care for precise detail and accuracy, they also are placed in the narrative to help capture his own subjective experience of the events that he describes in the text. He is his own illustrator – he produced both the manuscript text and the nu-

---

5. An account of La Salle's 1687 expedition, during which he was murdered by some of his own men, was published in France by a member of the expedition, and widely circulated. See Joutel 1713.

merous watercolors that accompany it. It was extremely rare for the author of a travel account also to be the artist who illustrated it. In fact, in France, travel narratives in Caillot's time did not typically include illustrations at all, and when they did, they were often borrowed from other accounts.[6] His bold full-page watercolors stand out all the more in this respect.

Fig. 1. "Noms des Poissons." The Historic New Orleans Collection, acc. no. 2005.0011 plate 17

In an illustration of new varieties of fish encountered on the sea voyage he includes a tiny image of his ship, looking vulnerable, placed between two waterspouts in the background. In the foreground one of the fish is labeled simply *monstre* (see Figure 1). His map of New Orleans evokes a familiar European space – it shows a city laid out on a grid, with a busy port area in the foreground. Illustrations of the colonial outposts in the wilderness, by contrast, show a few tiny structures and cultivated gardens surrounded by a huge undifferentiated forested area that takes up almost all of the space in the illustration. His most detailed drawings are of the two ships on which

6. On illustration practices in early French travel narratives and comparison with Portuguese and Dutch accounts, see Requemora-Gros 2012, 388–407.

he traveled. The _Durance_, which carried him to Louisiana, looks severe and technical, floating on a flat sea, with sails down. The _Durance_ illustration contrasts dramatically with Caillot's depiction of the ship he finally boarded to take him home. The _Saint Louis_ is drawn merrily bobbing through the waves in full sail. As a decorative touch, he adds an imaginary gun emitting a cloud of smoke in a farewell salute (Figure 2).

Fig. 2. "Le Saint Louis." The Historic New Orleans Collection, acc. no. 2005.0011 plate 21

Unlike the accounts produced by earlier French travelers to the Mississippi Delta, like La Salle and Henri Joutel, Caillot's text does not invoke collaborators to authenticate and fill out his story. He is the mapmaker, the draftsman, the narrator and the principal player in the story he tells. But, also in contrast to many authors of travel accounts in his time, he does not seem to be arguing a particular political or business position. He is not defending his own role in the colonial milieu against calumny or misrepresentation by others. He makes no legalistic gestures toward documentary evidence to support his reports of historical events. Nor does he quote from letters, contracts, or interviews with officials.[7] Caillot's project is avowedly

7. The accuracy of Caillot's account of historical events is possible to verify, however, and has been thoroughly annotated by Erin Greenwald in her edition of the narrative.

personal, written after his return home, from notes he took on the voyage and, he says, for the entertainment of a small circle of friends. As far as we know, he never tried to publish it.

In setting out to write the story of his voyage, Caillot's first gesture is to apologize for his poor style, and to claim that he is telling the simple truth. He sets himself up, as early modern memoir writers often do, as a reluctant writer, responding to the urging of friends who have already heard him tell parts of his story. Here is his prologue:

> It having been proposed to me to share with you, in an abridged form, a brief account of the particulars of my journey to New France, I feel I must warn you about the bad style of the author before carrying this to fruition. I must also advise you about faults that I may have committed here due to my lack of ability. But, on the other hand, those who will read this account will do me honor to give credence to it. To my knowledge I have not said anything untrue. Indeed, I am far from using certain exaggerated digressions, as many historians have done in their works, for the purpose of ornamentation and to attract to themselves the applause of a few people who are infatuated with fable.[8]

So, we are meant to understand that he was a traveler neither "infatuated with fable" nor catering to readers who are, and who did not even initially set out to write his travels. We don't know precisely what kind of written record he may have kept of his voyage as it was happening. But he was a record keeper by training – a copy clerk, after all, and his drawings are those of a skilled draftsman – maps, views of cities and settlements, watercolors of the ships he traveled on, and some of the more unusual fish he observed. But when he remembers his travels and writes them as remembered, he also draws on literary models for his own voice and actions, choosing to refer to himself as a kind of picaresque hero, a "knight errant," like Don Quixote, he says, that most famous of infatuated fabulists.[9]

Caillot's story begins in Paris. He cites the date of his departure (February 19, 1729), and describes his sadness at leaving both the place and his family

8. Caillot 2013, 1. I have deviated from the published translation and rendered Caillot's phrase "infatués par la fable" as "infatuated with fable" and not "infatuated with their fable".

9. Like the missionaries discussed by Eugenio Menegon in this volume, Marc-Antoine Caillot left on his voyage from the port of Lorient, on a ship owned by the French Company of the Indies. Caillot's styling of himself as a gallant adventurer, however, is in marked contrast to the approach to travel taken by the missionaries, who worked diligently in advance to firm up their social networks and prepare themselves for the material conditions of shipboard life, as Menegon outlines.

and friends there. But he immediately reports that his traveling companions were able to convince him of the importance of changing his somber mood if he wanted to survive "even more than a quarter of the way."[10] So he starts by embracing what he calls the "charming strategy of availing myself of some Bacchic liquor." From that moment on, he sustains his forward momentum by relentlessly seeking pleasure and diversion in even the most challenging moments of his travels. Aware that this survival strategy involves a certain amount of self-delusion as well as an artificially produced altered state of mind, he compares himself to Don Quixote:

> the eagerness I had to leave the place where I thought I had left all
> my sorrow made me urge my horse forward with such violence that
> one of its front feet slipped, causing me to fly over his head, harnessed
> pretty much like Don Quixote, except, instead of a lance, I had my
> musket at hand leaning against the saddlebow and my hunting
> horn around me. They both were quite banged up, for as a result my
> musket was broken in half from the fall. This is how I left. [11]

And so chevalier Caillot sets out on his adventures, like Don Quixote with his real weapon broken, but equipped with a musical instrument that he will produce on numerous occasions during his voyage to help him in his effort to cultivate beauty and pleasure in the face of adversity. Like Don Quixote, Caillot seems to believe that "where music is, no evil thing can be."[12] Once arrived in Louisiana, he will continue his practice of introducing music into the wilderness, retreating to the woods to play his hunting horn when he feels particularly lost.

His identification with Don Quixote is specifically mentioned again when during the transatlantic crossing his ship encounters what they fear to be a pirate ship, and the men on board grab all the weapons they can find: "there had never been any knights errant from the time of Don Quixote better armed than we were."[13] Later, when he arrives at the house of a Parisian settler on the Mississippi it seems to him to be an enchanted palace, complete with an elegant feast that makes his heart beat faster, he writes, "like Sancho Panza's did, when by chance Don Quixote found himself at a country wedding and his faithful squire filled his stomach for the time that he had been obliged to fast." [14]

Don Quixote is only used loosely as a model here, but it is clearly a way for

10. Caillot 2013, 2.
11. Caillot 2013, 2.
12. Istel and Baker 1927, 434.
13. Caillot 2013, 26.
14. Caillot 2013, 73.

Caillot to think about and present a literary image of himself to his readers. Drawing on the familiar figures of the knight and his servant, the traveling clerk presents himself as both noble and base, idealizing and earthy, heroic and cowardly. Caillot's approach to his adventures mimics Don Quixote's in several respects. He pays court to women who in reality are not at all ideal. He imagines a house as a palace, a wedding party as a court feast, a hostess as a princess, an Indian boy as a classical Cupid. But as narrator of his own adventure, he presents himself as an actor and takes a playful, ironic distance from his own follies. In this respect, he is closer to another popular figure from legend and literature, and one who figures prominently in Caillot's dramatic imagination, namely his hero, Don Juan, always the actor, who views existence and adventure as an endless masquerade.

Caillot may well have become familiar with both Don Quixote and Don Juan through one of the staged versions of their stories, particularly popular in France. In the case of Don Quixote, Caillot may also have encountered the story through the many printed illustrations that circulated independently of the novel. [15] His narrative is theatrical and visual. He refers to his fondness for theater and masquerade on numerous occasions, including one early on in the text where, still en route to the port city where he was scheduled to depart, he attends productions of two plays by Molière – *The Imaginary Invalid* and *Don Juan.* This latter reference is particularly interesting, since Molière's play focused on the themes of loss of identity and how outward signs on the body, such as costume and demeanor, can be manipulated to destabilize traditional hierarchies and serve personal ambition. Molière's Don Juan is very preoccupied with travel, conquest, and masquerade. Like Caillot, he has wandered far from home in an unfamiliar landscape. His path across this landscape is plotted in a series of seduction scenes. Don Juan is a traveler and a conqueror. He compares himself to Alexander the Great and peppers his speeches with metaphors of colonial conquest and New World discovery to describe his amorous exploits:

> There's nothing sweeter than overcoming the resistance of an attractive woman, and I bring to that enterprise the ambition of a conquering general, who moves on forever from victory to victory, and will set no limit to his longings. Nothing can withstand the impetuousness of my desires: I feel my heart capable of loving all the earth; and like Alexander, I wish that there were still more worlds in which to wage my amorous campaigns. [16]

15. On popular versions of Don Quixote in France, Bardon 1931; Showalter 1972, 1136–44; and Roussillon.

16. *Don Juan,* I, 2.

Don Juan the conqueror of women is a model for Marc-Antoine Caillot. Although he sees himself as a playful imitator of the master as he follows in the footsteps of the European colonizers of New France, Caillot wants to be what the *galant* novels of his day termed a "gentle conqueror," substituting seduction for violence and playful masquerade for deception and treachery.[17]

It is noteworthy, too, that Caillot is traveling in Carnival season, something that he mentions several times at the outset, when he and a traveling companion "go masking to pass the time" in the same town where they attended the production of *The Imaginary Invalid*, and again later when they meet two young women who invite them to a masked ball.[18] The most detailed descriptions of life on board the ship are his explanations of rituals involving disguise and masquerade – the most dramatic being the "baptism of the tropics" initiation ceremony that passengers were forced to undergo when the ship crossed the Tropic of Cancer. This ritual involved all of Caillot's favorite activities – costuming, music, parade, and surprise. He is fascinated and readily joins in the masquerade, lending his hunting horn to the "bizarre symphony," and carefully reporting every detail of the ceremony that culminated with each passenger being dunked in a tub of water on deck.[19] The crew members performing this rite of passage are heavily painted and look fierce. They frighten their victims. But several times Caillot points out that his anxiety about what will happen to him is relieved by his ability to laugh – especially when the ritual was ended.[20]

Caillot's choice of literary models for his narrative is in keeping with his determination to write his travels in a burlesque vain, one that had become quite popular in real and fictional stories of travel and adventure by the early eighteenth century.[21] Laughter, in general, occupies a prominent place in seventeenth-century French travel narratives. It can function to provide a reassuring distance between the narrator and the newness of his experiences. Humorous and often self-deprecating anecdotes of romantic encounters abroad were popular digressions in travel accounts and were thought to be almost a requirement if the author hoped to retain the attention of readers.[22]

---

17. On this "modern" heroic figure in French novels of the period, see Welch 2012 and Welch 2011, especially Ch. 5.

18. Caillot 2013, 8, 13.

19. Caillot 2013, 29–34.

20. See Menegon's essay in this volume, for another reference to this shipboard ritual. Unlike young Caillot, the missionaries en route to China did not enter into the illusion of what they called the "ridiculous masquerade."

21. This point is documented in Bertrand 2007.

22. On this point see Requemora-Gros 2012, 183–88 and 480–86.

Travel writers like Challe, Chapelle and Bachaumont, Regnard, Dassoucy, Courcelles and her friends Hortense and Marie Mancini, use laughter and irony to make light of their difficulties on the road. Readers were meant to be entertained and impressed by the author's capacity to sustain this tone in the most challenging of circumstances.[23]

In the first part of his narrative, while he is still in France and then while he is on the boat taking him to Louisiana, Caillot describes himself in a kind of rehearsal mode. Each place he stops en route to the Breton coast brings unfamiliar experiences and he describes how he responds to these, emphasizing his own resilience in the face of adversity, especially with the help of laughter and pleasure seeking, and always trying to keep company with "pleasant" people. He notes his successes with the ladies he meets, his good luck at receiving invitations from the best society in the towns where he stays, and he is "charmed" when he arrives at the port city of Lorient and meets some young women who are embarking on the same boat on which he is scheduled to leave. He describes his transatlantic crossing as a series of lighthearted adventures, the more unpleasant among them (such as seasickness, storms, threat of pirates and shipwreck, disgusting food) quickly finding happy resolutions, through Caillot's obstinate good nature and consistently playful response to unwelcome events. On board the ship his priority is always to be "gallant" in the face of adversity, attending to the female passengers whenever they are frightened by storms or the threat of pirates, enthusiastically entering into the more playful rituals of shipboard life, and keeping his own fears in check, always ready with an ironic quip when others are fainting, panicked or desperately praying for the ship's salvation.[24] He conducts himself like his hero Don Juan, undertaking an elaborate fake courtship of one of the more gullible young female passengers . This episode he describes as a "farce," a theatrical exercise that gives him the opportunity to practice using the language of love (he includes some of his own flowery speeches), a role that he says he played like an amateur: "I did the best I could, like a man with little experience in that language."[25] When he makes his verbal overtures to the lady, he has a friend hide behind a door as an audience observer, and he describes himself using phrases that evoke Don Quixote:

23. See Goldsmith 2007.

24. In using the term term "gallant" (Fr. *galant*) I am referring to a worldview and aesthetic style cultivated among the French elite in Caillot's time. It is characterized by an outward display of casual sophistication and a "modern" interest in forms of art evoking idyllic worlds where the inhabitants cultivate refinement. For studies of the *style galant* in literature, see Viala 2008 and Denis 2001. For a summary, see Goldsmith 2015.

25. Caillot 2013, 36.

As for myself, I went in with a very sad countenance, and I sat in one of the corners of the cabin. She did not hesitate at all to come over to me and ask me the reason for my sorrow, and why I was so lost in thought, and whether I should not be overcome with joy, since we were destined for one another. At these words I let out a long sigh that almost turned into a huge burst of laughter, but miraculously I kept it in.[26]

Like Don Quixote, Caillot rehearses courtship methods on a lady who in reality is not beautiful. But unlike the "knight of the sad countenance", he knows what he is doing, and has an ironic sense of himself.

By the time the *Durance* made its first landing after crossing the Atlantic, supplies of food and water had run dangerously low. The atmosphere among the crew and passengers was anything but festive or playful. But as soon as land was sighted and the ship headed for the provisioning post of Saint Louis on the island of Saint Domingue, Caillot's gallant good humor – and good fortune – returned. "I took the course of a gentleman and amused myself by fishing through one of the artillery room's portholes, where I caught eight hundred little fish that were good for frying," he writes.[27] With the approach of his destination, though, Caillot shifts the tone of his narrative. His account as a whole is divided in two quite distinct parts. The first is the story of his travel adventures punctuated by romantic escapades and episodes involving trickery and surprise. The second part starts after he has settled in Louisiana and he turns to the description of events, places, and people who would presumably be unfamiliar to his readers in France. In between, as the ship makes temporary landing on the island of Hispaniola, Caillot and his comrades have some escapades that get them into trouble. They manage to return safely to the ship by means of bribes, and favors from sympathetic ladies. To mark their gratitude the group puts on a performance, moving among the anchored ships and then around the fort as though enveloping the traveling community in a protective web of music and beauty:

Then we went from ship to ship the rest of the night, with an orchestra consisting of four violins, bagpipes, a viol, two recorders, a transverse flute, a tromba marina, a tabor, and my hunting horn. All these diverse instruments created quite a pleasant music because of the echoes, which, the further we went away from the harbor, the more they rang out. The sea, being very calm, favored us a great deal.

26. Caillot 2013, 39.
27. Caillot 2013, 48.

We retired about four o'clock in the morning after making a circuit around the fort with all of our instruments.[28]

When, more than a hundred pages into his manuscript, Caillot finally undertakes a description of Louisiana, he seems to become more of an ethnographer. First he describes Indian customs, clothing and other matters, but he still tries to interject the light, ironic tone of a young sophisticate and to present glimpses of Indian life as exotic performance, with himself as sophisticated viewer. He describes Indian dances as comical, like the Breton dances he had observed in France just before leaving. He says that during the calumet or peace pipe ritual the Indians sit like monkeys, also making him laugh. His comparison of Indian boys carrying bows and arrows to "little Cupids in the woods" is suggestive of a landscape painting by Poussin or Claude Lorrain, with small classical figures populating a contemporary countryside.[29]

But he moves back and forth between this slightly disdainful distance and something closer to the urgent style of an early gazette writer, occasionally with startling results. By the time the manuscript was completed the French population back home had learned about the violent confrontation between the French settlers in Louisiana and the Natchez Indians.[30] In Caillot's account, the most striking of his shifts between a playful, *galant* tone and the more serious tone of a journalist comes in the middle of his account of the war with the Natchez. After a shocking description of the torture and mayhem of the first Natchez raid on the colonists, he abruptly changes the subject, as though taking flight into a fantasy of Old World pleasures.

> We were already quite far along in the Carnival season without having had the least bit of fun or entertainment, which made me miss France a great deal.... I went to the office, where I found my associates, who were bored to death. I proposed to them that we form a party of maskers and go to Bayou Saint John, where I knew that a lady friend of my friends was marrying off one of her daughters.... I did not delay in assembling a party,... When we were ready and just about to leave, we saw someone with a violin come in, and I engaged him to come with us ... by another stroke of luck, someone with an oboe, who was looking for the violin, came in to take the violin player away with him, but it happened the other way around, [and] ... they stayed. I

28. Caillot 2013, 60–61.
29. Caillot 2013, 111.
30. At least one internal reference in the text (see p. 90) suggests that the manuscript was completed close to 1731.

had them play while waiting for us to get ready to leave.... we ended
up with eleven in our party. Some were in red clothing, as Amazons,
others in clothes trimmed with braid, others [dressed] as women.
As for myself, I was dressed as a shepherdess in white. I had a corset
of white dimity, a muslin skirt, a large pannier, right down to the
chemise, along with plenty of beauty marks too. I had my husband,
who was the Marquis de Carnaval; he had a suit trimmed with gold
braid on all the seams. Our postilion went in front, accompanied by
eight actual Negro slaves, who each carried a flambeau to light our
way.[31]

The masquerade and festivities that follow become a kind of escape
back to France, or introduction of a French ritual into the violent Louisiana
landscape (this may be the first description we have of New Orleans Mardi
Gras).[32] In terms of the narrative style, it is an abrupt and elaborate return
to his playful tone. There is a description of the wedding party with seduction scenes, drawing on the conventional vocabulary of romance based on
metaphors of captivity, enslavement, assault, and suffering to describe how
he was "wounded" by falling in love with one of the young women at the
ball. It is a scenario evocative of French novels, complete with girls who turn
out to be boarders in a nearby convent pursued by young gentlemen who
vie for their attention, and winding down with the male partygoers comparing notes and concluding "There was not a single one of us who had not
made different conquests."[33] Then, just as suddenly as it began, the interlude
ends: "The hour of our departure finally arrived, and we said good-bye to
the lovely company and to the bride and groom. We left around five-thirty
in the morning, lamenting the end of the Carnival days. This is how I spent
them in the land of Mississippi; now let us return to the narrative of the
Indian war."[34]

What can we make of this unharmonious blend of narrative tones
that Caillot assumes in the story of his adventures that he has left us? Any
reader will be struck by the disruption that occurs once he encounters the
"new world" of Louisiana. Had he originally been hoping or intending to be
able to experience and later report his voyage in the literary mode of Don
Quixote or Don Juan? Was he trying to sustain the mood that he had so en-
ergetically cultivated since his first departure from home, when he invokes

    31. Caillot 2013, 134–35.
    32. For an excellent analysis of French reaction to the Natchez attack and the ways in
which Caillot's description conveys the mindset of the colonists, see White 2013.
    33. Caillot 2013, 139.
    34. Caillot 2013, 141.

a kind of fairy-tale account of his escapades on the last day of Carnival? When Caillot does abruptly abandon the mode of romance and burlesque to turn to descriptions that seem more "realistic," is it safe to assume that his new voice is one in which the novelistic imagination has disappeared altogether? Has Caillot the self-described actor and dreamer suddenly become Caillot the modern ethnographer, gazetteer, and naturalist? In his descriptions of the horrors of war, torture, and massacre, he invokes no literary precursors and includes only one illustration, a tiny drawing inserted in the manuscript, of a captured Indian woman being tortured. His language in these descriptions is short on metaphor and uncharacteristically devoid of personal commentary. Other accounts of the French wars with the Natchez, written by Caillot's contemporaries, have shown just how inventive (and illustrated) these reports could be.[35] At the end of Caillot's description of the bloody conflicts between the French and the Natchez, his narrative returns to a more impressionistic tone. He observes, as though to reassure himself and his readers, that the Tunica Indian chief, who had allied his warriors with the French, had been transformed almost into a Frenchman, wearing French clothes and embracing Christianity. "This chief has been baptized," he writes, "and happily is almost Frenchified."[36]

When Caillot does finally get on a boat to return to France, he also describes that moment as one enabling him to return to the pursuit of pleasure and a state of happiness: "I left New Orleans on April 1 in the year 1731, as happy to the same degree as I had been sad upon arriving there."[37] Before leaving he had made a special appeal to be allowed to return home, citing homesickness – an ailment that was treated in his time as a physical malady, even potentially fatal.[38] The first ship he boards runs aground on a sandbar off the coast, but the passengers escape and return to shore. Finally, he manages to book passage on another ship that would take him home. His illustration of this vessel, the *Saint Louis,* seems to embody his own sense of relief and renewed playful exuberance.

Caillot's story raises some interesting questions about travel and the history of travel narrative in this early period just before the advent of tour-

35. On this point see Sayre 2002. For a thorough overview of reporting on the events see Balvay 2008.

36. Caillot 2013, 144.

37. Caillot 2013, 156.

38. The word 'homesick' entered the English language sometime in the eighteenth century. In French the phrase is 'mal du pays,' and before the nineteenth century, as in Caillot's text, the phrase to indicate homesickness was 'maladie du pays', indicating something closer to physical sickness. Until the twentieth century, the disease of homesickness was thought to be potentially fatal. For a history see Matt 2014.

ism. What are the limits of the French *galant* mode, which a young writer like Caillot seems so determined to carry with him, and keep with him, on his voyage to the borderlands of the French colonial territories? And what literary models – more hidden than Don Quixote and Don Juan in Caillot's account – might persist, or be in the process of being invented, in travelers' descriptions of even the most violent and historically verifiable encounters with Indian nations and their cultures? In an essay on the survival of romance in the age of realism, Nicholas Paige has shown how Don Quixote worked as a model for French romance writers at the end of the seventeenth century. Rather than discouraging readers from seeing themselves in the romance plot, Cervantes had the opposite effect.[39] Caillot's use of Don Quixote and Don Juan as models for his own self-fashioning is similar. In Caillot's design of his own adventures, to borrow Paige's phrase, "the real world does not take the place of romance; it is rather romance that colonizes the real world."[40] In the context of French travel to the colonies, this brings up a more general question: why does Caillot cling to the *galant* tone even in the most incongruous of circumstances? His text seems to demonstrate how the entire colonial project needed its illusions.

The filter of romance and *galanterie* would continue to operate as a reassuring artistic device in representations of indigenous colonized peoples throughout the eighteenth century. In 1735 the composer Jean-Philippe Rameau produced an opera titled *Les Indes galantes*, which included a ballet entrée called *Les Sauvages*. It takes place in a Louisiana forest after the defeat of the Indians by Franco-Spanish troops, and enacts a love story involving an Indian "prince" and a "princess" who is also courted by two soldiers, French and Spanish. The Indian prince wins the lady while the libretto and dancing celebrate a new peace between the Europeans and the Indians. Sixty years later, in his novel eulogizing the Natchez Indians, Chateaubriand would establish the basis for subsequent romantic depictions, in literature and painting, of life in the American wilderness.[41]

In 1730, Caillot is of a young generation of French travelers to America who make the trip not to explore or conquer or flee persecution or even to settle permanently in a foreign land. He makes his way to the new periphery of France to put in some time and advance his career interests within an established business institution – the Company of the Indies. He is also a voyager with an acute sense of carrying with him abroad a cultural identity

---

39. Paige 2011, ch. 2.

40. Paige 2011, 77.

41. See Sayre 2002, 401–7. Chateaubriand wrote *Les Natchez* in the 1790s, after his travels in America, although it was not published until 1827.

that is French. Caught up in his adventure, he tries to sustain and cultivate a playful, ironic, and protective distance from the foreignness of his experiences. He rehearses this strategy from the moment he leaves Paris. He tries to hold on to his ties to French culture and contribute to its introduction and assimilation by the New France that is Louisiana. The fact that he does not quite manage to do so – the inevitability of his disillusionment – is perhaps the most interesting feature of his account.

Bibliography

Balvay, Arnaud. 2008. *La Révolte des Natchez*. Paris: Éditions de Félin.

Bardon, Maurice. 1931. *Don Quixote en France au XVIIe et XVIIIe siècle*. Paris: Honoré Champion.

Bertrand, Dominique, ed. 2007. *Le Rire des voyageurs (XVIe-XVIIe siècles)*. Clermont-Ferrand: Presses Universitaires Blaise Pascal.

Caillot, Marc-Antoine. 2013. *A Company Man: The Remarkable French-Atlantic Voyage of a Clerk for the Company of the Indies*. Edited by Erin Greenwald and translated by Teri F. Chalmers. New Orleans: Historic New Orleans Collection.

Denis, Delphine. 2001. *Le Parnasse galant: Institution d'une catégorie littéraire au XVIIe siècle*. Paris: H. Champion.

Dumont de Montigny, Jean-François Benjamin. 1753. *Mémoires historiques sur la Louisiane*. Paris: C. J. B. Bauche.

Goldsmith, Elizabeth C. 2007. "'Ces enjouées aventurières': stratégies du rire dans les lettres et mémoires de femmes fugitives à l'époque de Louis XIV." In *Le Rire des voyageurs*, edited by Dominique Bertrand, 183–97. Clermont-Ferrand: Presses Universitaires Blaise Pascal.

———. 2015. "*Galant* Culture." In *The Cambridge Companion to French Literature*, edited by John D. Lyons. Cambridge: Cambridge University Press, 85–101.

Greenwald, Erin. 2016. *Marc-Antoine Caillot and the Company of the Indies in Louisiana: Trade in the French Atlantic World*. Baton Rouge: Louisiana State University Press.

Hachard, Marie-Madeleine. 1728. *Relation du voyage des dames religieuses Ursulines de Rouen à la Nouvelle Orléans [...]*, Rouen: A. Le Prévost.

Istel, Edgar and Theodore Baker. 1927. "The Music in Don Quixote." *The Musical Quarterly* 13/3:434–50.

Joutel, Henri. 1713. *Journal historique du voyage que feu M. de La Sale fit dans le golfe du Mexique, pour trouver l'embouchure et la rivière de Missicipi, [...]*. Paris: Étienne Robinot.

Le Page du Pratz, Antoine-Simon. 1758. *Histoire de la Louisiane*. 3 vols. Paris: De Bure l'aîné.

Marine Roussillon. "Quelques hypothèses sur la réception de *Don Quichotte* en France au début du XVIIe siècle." http://donquijotedelamancha.free.fr/Roussillon.pdf, n.d.

Matt, Susan J. 2014. *Homesickness: An American History*. Oxford, U.K.: Oxford University Press.

Molière, Jean-Baptiste Poquelin. 2001. *Don Juan*. Translated by Richard Wilbur. New York: Harcourt.

Murphy, Antoin E. 1997. *John Law: Economic Theorist and Policy-Maker*. Oxford and New York: Oxford University Press.

Paige, Nicholas. 2011. *Before Fiction: The Ancien Régime of the Novel*. Philadelphia: University of Pennsylvania Press.

Requemora-Gros, Sylvie. 2012. *Voguer vers la modernité: Le Voyage à travers les genres au XVIIe*. Paris: Presses de l'Université de Paris-Sorbonne.

Sayre, Gordon M. 2002. "Plotting the Natchez Massacre: Le Page du Pratz, Dumont de Montigny, Chateaubriand." *Early American Literature* 37/3:381–433.

Showalter, English, Jr. 1972. "Robert Challe and Don Quixote." *The French Review* (May 1972): 1136–44.

Viala, Alain. 2008. *La France galante*. Paris: Presses Universitaires de Paris.

Welch, Ellen R. 2011. *A Taste for the Foreign: Worldly Knowledge and Literary Pleasure in Early Modern French Fiction*. Newark: University of Delaware Press.

——. 2012. "From Aesthetic to Ethical Cosmopolitanism in Scudéry's *Le Grand Cyrus*." *Cahiers du Dix-Septième* 14:38-55.

White, Sophie. 2013. "Massacre, Mardi Gras, and Torture in Early New Orleans." *The William and Mary Quarterly* 70/3:497–538.

Gothic Fiction, the Grand Tour, and the Seductions of Antiquity: Polidori's *The Vampyre* (1819)

James Uden

T HE EARLIEST ACCOUNT of the aristocratic vampire in English is also a travel narrative.[1] Published on April Fool's Day, 1819, and in its first printing attributed to Lord Byron, *The Vampyre* was begun three years earlier by a man Byron had employed as his personal doctor, John Polidori (1795–1821).[2] The events of the short story take place not in Transylvania, a vampiric locale made most famous in Bram Stoker's *Dracula* (1897), but while the characters are undertaking a Grand Tour of Europe, with a lengthy stay in Athens. Its central protagonist, a naïve young orphan of great wealth named Aubrey, encounters the mysterious Lord Ruthven at a fashionable aristocratic party, and decides to travel with him. Once in Europe, he discovers that Ruthven lavishes money at disreputable places with disreputable people, and incites those around him to dissipation and ruin. They separate. Aubrey makes his way to Athens, where, with the ancient Greek travel writer Pausanias in hand, he sets out to decipher ancient Greek inscriptions, and also falls in love with a Greek girl, Ianthe. She tells him the local lore concerning the vampire, a creature forced to "prolong his life" by feeding upon the "life of a lovely female."[3] One night, when Aubrey has stayed out too late tracking down a particular ancient monument, he discovers that Ianthe herself has fallen victim to that very fiend. Although Aubrey gradually learns that Lord Ruthven is the vampire who killed Ianthe, they travel together again anyway, only to be set upon by robbers, who shoot Ruthven.

---

1. I would like to thank Roberta Micallef and the other members of the BU Travel Literature seminar for their camaraderie and conversation. Elizabeth C. Goldsmith offered useful comments on an earlier version of this chapter. I am also very grateful to Jerrold E. Hogle, who kept my own travel in this area on a steady path.

2. Polidori 2008. Page references throughout the chapter are to this edition, with one exception: like most critics, I retain the first edition's "Lord Ruthven" for the name of the vampire, an allusion to the Byron figure of the same name in Lady Caroline Lamb's scandalous roman à clef, *Glenarvon* (1816). In later editions, Polidori replaced it with the more broadly parodic "Lord Strongmore," which bears a resemblance to names like "Mr Toobad" and "Mr Listless" in Thomas Love Peacock's Gothic satire *Nightmare Abbey* (1818). On the complicated publication history of *The Vampyre*, see Viets 1969.

3. *The Vampyre*, 46.

As he dies, he forces an oath from his young friend: Aubrey must swear to conceal all he knows about the vampire and the fact of his death. Aubrey gloomily returns to England and sinks into implacable melancholy. Finally, at the end of the story, it is the turn of Aubrey's sister to be presented to the fashionable aristocratic set, and at the event, while "engaged in the recollection that the first time he had seen Lord Ruthven was in this very place," he hears the fateful words whispered in his ear: "remember your oath!"[4] Horrifyingly, Ruthven has returned from the dead, and the cycle appears to begin all over again. As Aubrey regresses further into melancholy, his sister announces her engagement – to Lord Ruthven. Unable to convince anyone of the reality of the vampire, he dies, in frenzy and frustration, of a broken blood vessel. The final line announces that Aubrey's sister too has fallen victim. She "glutted the thirst of a VAMPYRE!"[5]

This story has its origins in one of the most notorious journeys in English literature. Polidori, then only twenty years old, was with Byron in 1816 when he toured from Belgium to Switzerland and visited Waterloo, a tour described in the third canto of *Childe Harold's Pilgrimage* (1816–17). He was there at the Villa Diodati overlooking Lake Geneva when Byron and the Shelleys held the ghost story contest that would inspire Mary Shelley's *Frankenstein,* and *The Vampyre* is clearly adapted from a central idea in Byron's unfinished contribution to that contest.[6] But Polidori's own diary of that journey makes for dispiriting reading. Sometimes he affects an urbane nonchalance. Belgium has "fine avenues, which make us yawn with admiration." A farce in Brussels is fit only "to excite the pleasurable sensation of yawning."[7] Mostly he just seems bored. In Flemish towns, he says, "nothing is striking, all evenness, no genius, much stupidity." At Aachen: "May 8. – Got up late. Went to see the Cathedral: full of people, lower ranks, hearing mass. Miserable painting, architecture, etc."[8] As the tour progressed, Polidori's relationship with Byron – an employer whom he wished to see as a friend, and even as an equal – broke down. By summer's end, he was fired. In a letter written to his sister, he had boasted about Byron that, "I am with him on the footing of an equal, everything alike." Once they had parted, he wrote to his father

4. *The Vampyre,* 54.

5. *The Vampyre,* 59.

6. On the relationship between Byron's fragment and Polidori's story, see the second section of this paper; also Skarda 1989; MacDonald 1991, 88–89, 97–98.

7. Polidori 1911, 44, 60. On the origin of these diaries, see Polidori 1911, 10–11. He had been offered £500 by Byron's publisher for a narrative of the tour, but the work was never finished, and it remained unpublished in his lifetime.

8. Polidori 1911, 45. Cf. MacDonald 1991, 65: Polidori's remarks "suggest a lack of interest in the scenery actually in front of him...."

that the fault was mostly his, a result of the inequality of their relationship. "I am not accustomed to have a master," he wrote.[9] It is clear that Polidori never wanted simply to be Byron's doctor. Already the author of poetry and at least one verse drama, he nursed literary ambitions of his own, but in Byron's train it was difficult not to feel outshone. At a party in Geneva, he laments, "B[yron]'s name alone was mentioned; mine, like a star in the halo of the moon, was invisible."[10]

There has been much scholarly work on *The Vampyre*'s allusions to other Romantic literature, its refracted vision of a tense and competitive (and possibly erotic) relationship between Polidori and Byron, and its formative role in articulating the symbol of the vampire in Gothic fiction.[11] My aim is to complement rather than challenge this work by demonstrating the text's critical engagement with changing discourses of travel and antiquarianism in the early nineteenth century. *The Vampyre* appears at a crucial moment in the prehistory of modern tourism, when the aristocratic institution of the Grand Tour was giving way to more commercialized forms of mass tourism in Europe and, in response, to idealized "Romantic" modes of travel epitomized by Byron himself.[12] It was Polidori who popularized the image of a *traveling* vampire, as opposed to the stationary monster of pre-existing myth,[13] and *The Vampyre* casts a cynical eye over the ideals of the Tour, presenting travel itself as a hollow aristocratic ritual. The behavior of Lord Ruthven is an amalgam of moralists' complaints, an embodiment of the corruptions of the Grand Tour that were already presented in monstrous and exaggerated terms in eighteenth-century satire.[14] At the same time, Polidori unexpectedly gives his protagonist, Aubrey, an interest in ancient ruins, and incorporates allusions to a tradition of British antiquarianism. The narrative in fact spends most of its time among the antiquities of Greece, though

9. Polidori 1911, 211, 216.

10. Polidori 1911, 105.

11. Influential analyses in Rieger 1963; Skarda 1989; MacDonald 1991, 177–203; Gelder 1994, 24–41; important recent work in Budge 2004; Bainbridge 2006; Hogle 2009.

12. Buzard 1993 and 2002; on Byron's position as a symbol for the Romantic traveler, Buzard 1991.

13. Auerbach 1995, 16: "In Slavic folklore ... vampires never ventured beyond their birthplace." The prominence of travel in *The Vampyre* is also a reflection of Byron's unfinished story: MacDonald 1991, 196-197. Ek 2015 proposes a different configuration of vampire and tourist, suggesting a model for the modern citizen's post-political detachment in the vampire's itinerant hedonism.

14. The employment of the vampire as a symbol in satiric texts was not new, as Butler (2010, 52–82) demonstrates. In his Orientalist satire *The Citizen of the World* (1760-61), for example, Oliver Goldsmith wrote that a corrupt magistrate "sucks blood like a vampyre" (1966 [vol. 2], 329), and Voltaire compared "speculators, tax officials, and businessmen" to vampires in his *Questions sur l'Encyclopédie* (1772; cited in Butler 2010, 54).

Aubrey's attempts at deciphering the ancient past are constantly foiled. Polidori lamented the absence or erasure of monuments of history in his travel diary, and Aubrey's failure to connect past and present suggests a much broader cultural disillusionment about the vanishing of classical culture amid the "degeneracy" of modern Italy and Greece. In an immediately post-Napoleonic period, when English tourists were again flocking in large numbers to Europe, *The Vampyre* represents a Gothic translation of satiric tropes, giving sardonic expression to a variety of contemporary cultural anxieties about Continental travel.

Satire, the Gothic, and the Grand Tour

By the early nineteenth century, every stage of the English journey to the Continent had been exhaustively documented and debated. Influential travel guides such as Joseph Addison's *Remarks on Several Parts of Italy* (1705), which plotted points on the Tour through the coordinates of Latin literature, were eclipsed later in the eighteenth century by middle-class accounts of the sensations, emotions, and advice of English travelers to France and Italy.[15] Alongside the proliferation of travel narratives was an equally voluminous – and remarkably consistent – tradition of travel satire and critique. As early as the seventeenth century, Bishop Hall attacked the so-called advantages of travel in *Quo Vadis? A Just Censure of Travel* (1617), describing the "monster" who loses his "love of studies" after traveling to "parts which are most sought to for civility."[16] One correspondent in the periodical the *Spectator* voiced a common complaint by urging that young aristocratic men were being sent over to Europe for finishing too early, before they were really formed, at a time when they should instead be "laying the solid foundations of knowledge."[17] Pope, in the fourth book of the *Dunciad* (1743), describes the young British fop on the Tour who "saunter'd Europe round/ And gather'd ev'ry Vice on Christian ground," while losing whatever classical learning he once had (he "dropt the dull lumber of the Latin store").[18] The debate over the usefulness of the Tour was described in most detail in Richard Hurd's *Dialogues on the Uses of Foreign Travel* (1764), which, in a sign of the longstanding nature of the debate, was cast as a conversation between Lord Shaftesbury and the seventeenth-century philosopher John Locke.[19] Shaftesbury con-

---

15. For accounts of this literature, see Chard 1999; Thomson 2007, 32–39.

16. Hall, 1839 [vol. 12], 109.

17. *The Spectator* (Monday April 28, 1712), by "Philip Homebred" [Philip Yorke?] (Bond 1965, vol. 3, 366–70).

18. *Dunciad* iv. 311–12, 319 (Pope 1943, 374).

19. Hurd, 1811 [vol.4], 87–229. Hurd's treatise is well analyzed in Redford, 1996, 40–43.

tends that only European travel can provide elegance and grace to young British noblemen. Locke counters that education should build *men*, and not trick out dandified gentlemen.[20] When Shaftesbury is led to admit that exposure to fashionable society in Europe could harm impressionable youth, Locke declares that its worth is 'less than the price paid for it, our principles and our morals'.[21]

At the height of its popularity in Britain in the 1790s, the Gothic novel, with its sensationalistic narratives of wicked monks and imprisoned heroines in picturesque French and Italian castles, gave new life to myths of the romantic danger of European travel. Novelists such as Ann Radcliffe drew many of their geographical details from earlier published travel narratives, and obviously traded on the same romance of exotic locales. At the same time, these novels perpetuated the xenophobic assumptions long familiar from moralistic and satiric travel critiques.[22] The Europe imagined by such works is both seductive and sinister, a place of violence and immorality, irrational passions, and "Popish" (Catholic) superstition. Yet it is striking how sinister the corruptions of Europe *already* appear in eighteenth-century satire. Alongside the stereotype of the effeminate fop enamored of French fashion exists a far more threatening figure, the Englishman emptied of his own customs and morals, who turns predatory and malign after his time on the Continent. So, for example, the fourteenth of John Gay's often-reprinted *Fables* (1727) reproaches the "dull lad" who travels prematurely and leads a dissolute life in Europe, only to end up with vice "fitted to his parts" (a punning reference to sexually transmitted disease?). The fable describes a monkey who "resolv'd to visit foreign climes" to learn human ways and becomes the pet of a wealthy lady, before finally returning to his fellow monkeys and dazzling them with the fashionable manners he learned while abroad. But the influence of the worldly monkey transforms the apes into vicious versions of their former selves:

> Now warm with malice, envy, spite,
> Their most obliging friends they bite,
> And fond to copy human ways,
> Practice new mischiefs all their days.[23]

Similarly, Soame Jenyns' verse satire "The Modern Fine Gentleman" (1746)

20. Hurd, 1811 [vol. 4], 136.

21. Hurd, 1811 [vol. 4], 101.

22. On the interdependence of the Gothic and eighteenth-century travel narratives see Chloe Chard in Radcliffe 1986 [1791], xiii–xxii.

23. Gay 1967, 46–49, at 49.

describes the corruption and abasement of a young noble after a spell overseas in France and Italy. Having "glean'd' all the 'follies' of the Tour," he
comes back "a monster of such complicated worth,/ as no one single clime
could e'er bring forth." He turns to politics, then to gambling, and then to
heartless financial exploitation:

> In craft political a bankrupt made,
> He sticks to gaming, as the surer trade;
> Turns downright sharper, lives by sucking blood,
> And grows, in short, the very thing he wou'd:
> Hunts out young heirs, who have their fortunes spent,
> And lends them ready cash at cent per cent....[24]

Travel brings monsters home. Polidori crafts a horror story from a fear that
was already horrifying and sinister in eighteenth-century satire: the xenophobic fear of English transformation by Continental license. Although the
character of the traveling vampire was developed most influentially in Polidori's text, the path was clearly prepared for him by moralists and satirists
who used the language of monstrosity in earlier attacks on the Grand Tour.

Polidori's authorial voice from the beginning of *The Vampyre* is that of a
cynical outsider, intent on puncturing the illusions of both Gothic convention and Byronic hero-cult. "It happened," Polidori begins, "in the midst of
the dissipations attendant upon a London winter, that there appeared at the
various parties of the *ton* a nobleman, more remarkable for his singularities,
than for his rank."[25] The reference to "the *ton*" imitates the foppish Galli-
cizing of the impressionable aristocrats whom Polidori is about to satirize;
Lord Chesterfield complained in a periodical piece that after his visit to the
Continent, his wife and daughter talk "of nothing but *le bon ton*."[26] Polidori
repeatedly suggests in the first part of his story that this stranger, with his
aura of Byronic glamor, is in reality a dull blank canvas, with just enough
charm to satisfy the desires projected on him by the bored "monsters" of the
drawing-room.[27] Gothic villains stereotypically have eyes that "penetrate."[28]

24. Jenyns 1790 [vol. 1], 57–62, at 61.
25. *The Vampyre*, 39.
26. *The World* (Thursday May 3, 1753) (Chalmers 1823, vol. 22, 92–102 at 100).
27. *The Vampyre*, 39. On Ruthven as a reflecting mirror for others' desires, see Bainbridge
2006, 27–28, Hogle 2009, 57.
28. Two influential examples, though the idea is a commonplace: the eyes of Schedoni in
Radcliffe's *The Italian* (1797) are "so piercing that they seemed to penetrate, at a single glance,
into the hearts of men, and to read their most secret thoughts" (2000, 43); in Matthew Lewis'
The Monk (1796), Ambrosio's eyes are "large black and sparkling," and "few could sustain the
glance of his eye at once fiery and penetrating" (1998, 18).

In a deliberate reversal of this trope, Lord Ruthven's dead eyes "seemed not to penetrate, and at one look to pierce through the inward workings of the heart; but to throw upon the cheek a leaden ray...." Ruthven is seductive not to innocent, virginal Gothic heroines, but to those who "felt the weight of *ennui*," and were merely "pleased at having something in their presence capable of engaging their attention." Aubrey, the story's hero, finds Ruthven magnetic, but this is because of his addiction to romance, which, we are told, leads him to substitute fiction for reality ("he soon formed this person into the hero of a romance, and determined to observe the offspring of his fancy, rather than the individual before him"). A milieu beholden to Romantic ideas misrecognizes the tawdry as sublime. "Human feelings and sympathies" were, Polidori writes, "the fashionable names for frailties and sins." Polidori paints his Byron figure not as a genuinely glamorous Gothic villain, but – more cuttingly – as a dull, empty approximation of one.

The decision for Aubrey to travel with Ruthven is presented with the same cynical tone of puncturing aristocratic pretensions. "It was time for him to perform the grand tour," writes Polidori, "a tour which for many generations had been thought necessary to enable the young to take some important steps in the career of vice, put themselves on an equality with the aged, and not allow them to appear as if fallen from the skies, whenever scandalous intrigues are mentioned as the subjects of pleasantry or of praise, according to the degree of skill shewn in their conduct."[29] The travel destinations in the text extend the eighteenth-century Grand Tour itinerary into Greece and Turkey (and omit Paris), but otherwise chart a long-familiar southward arc: from Brussels and "other towns" to Rome, then Athens and Smyrna, then back to southern Italy, Calais, and home again to England. As they progress through the first part of their tour, the fear that haunts the text is less that of blood being sucked by vampires, than of money and reputation being hemorrhaged by callow and impressionable young travellers. With his young companion, Lord Ruthven seeks out "all the centers of fashionable vice." Although his financial affairs are "embarrassed," the vampire spends his money lavishly on the least reputable inhabitants of European cities. In Brussels, Ruthven proves a master at gambling, a seductive pastime against which English moralists constantly inveighed.[30] Europe also offered sex to impressionable English nobles, and, sure enough, once Ruthven and Aubrey reach Rome, the vampire is disinterested in the historical monuments of Rome and spends his time instead "in daily attendance upon the

29. *The Vampyre,* 41. The quotes in this paragraph are drawn from pages 41–44.
30. *The Vampyre,* 43. Moralists' warnings against the seductions of gambling on the Grand Tour: Black 1992, 204–6.

morning circles of an Italian countess," choosing dissipation over education. In a period in which Lord Byron was increasingly seen as an icon for a new, Romantic, anti-touristic form of travel, which was more interested in self-discovery than in the conventional sites and sounds of the Tour, Polidori's satiric Byron figure embodies an over-exaggerated isolation from the world around him. His monomaniacal self-interest makes him insensible to the sublime: "Lord Ruthven in his carriage, and amidst the various wild and rich scenes of nature, was always the same: his eye spoke less than his lip...." In his profligacy and his lack of sensibility, the vampire is in fact the worst kind of tourist. His villainy is a conglomeration of satiric tropes about the misbehavior of Englishmen abroad in Europe.

As critics have long observed, although the last sentence of the story reveals that Aubrey's sister has "glutted the thirst" of the vampire, Polidori's story notably lacks the descriptions of blood-sucking that appear already in Byron's *The Giaour* (1813) and loom so large in later versions of the vampire myth, especially Stoker's *Dracula*. Instead, Polidori's vampire works his evil by spreading a sort of corrupting contagion, a miasma that brings to the surface all sorts of latent vice. Once Lord Ruthven leaves England, we are told that the women with whom he had had contact had now thrown "even the mask" of virtue aside, and had not "scrupled to expose the whole deformity of their vices to public view." Men young and old are inspired to gamble away their fortunes in the vampire's presence, and "formerly affluent youth" sit in debt prisons after he leaves.[31] Lord Ruthven is a monster with "irresistible powers of seduction," whose "licentious habits" are "dangerous to society," and whose evil, by the end of the story, had "influenced" Aubrey's own life.[32] Aubrey himself is infected by Ruthven's dull self-absorption. In the latter part of his travels, he is "benumbed," and he and Ruthven "hastened from place to place, yet they seemed not to heed what they gazed upon," now equally superficial and insensitive tourists.[33] Although the medical notion of "influence" is not developed with any specificity in *The Vampyre*, Simon Bainbridge is surely right to compare these aspects of Polidori's vampire with the Byron figure in Lady Caroline Lamb's *Glenarvon*, whose love is described as a death-dealing infection or disease.[34] Combined with the travel motif, however, the operation of the vampire's evil also evokes the incorpo-

---

31. *The Vampyre* 42, 43.

32. *The Vampyre* 43, 57.

33. *The Vampyre* 50. Samuel Johnson criticizes the English traveler in Europe who "enters a town at night and surveys it in the morning, and then hastens away to another place," making "excursions by which nothing could be learned" (*The Idler*, February 23, 1760, cited in Mead 1914, 396).

34. Bainbridge 2006, 26.

real influence of Continental travel on English youth – the warmer air that
was thought to give license to English restraint, the miasma of Southern
Europe that brought a feverish intensity to travelers' desires. Like Rome or
Florence or Naples, the vampire works his effects by influence, insidiously
drawing travelers from their proper inhibitions and into a moralist's gallery
of vice: gambling, sex, profligacy. Rather than suck blood, Polidori's vampire
spreads bad air.[35]

At the conclusion of *The Vampyre*, the traveling villain miraculously reappears in an aristocratic drawing room, alive again and ready to resume
his seductions. If Ruthven's reappearance is a shocking affirmation of his supernatural power, it is also the climax of Polidori's satiric vision of travel as
a hollow, circular, repetitive aristocratic ritual. Despite Ruthven's financial
affairs being embarrassed, despite his reputation for scandalous amorality,
despite his lavish dissipation on the Continent, despite having *died,* he is
nonetheless granted instant admittance year after year to the fashionable
parties of England's aristocratic elite. The vampire's position as a celebrity
among the "leaders of the *ton*" suggests mockingly that European travel,
as its critics argued, instills no deep moral sense, but merely tricks out a
gentleman with accomplishments to win them a place in dissolute high society. The sheer emptiness of the vampire's personality suggests the vapid
elegance that satirists claim was a result of having traveled. English youth
returned from the Grand Tour, according to William Cowper, "empty, though
refined."[36] If Stoker's Dracula – a driven, purposeful traveler – represents the
threat of "reverse colonization," a fear of the invasion of England by the colonized East, then Polidori's vampire represents the opposite, the dangers of
dissipation and moral death that lurk for the English when they go abroad.[37]
Lord Ruthven epitomizes an entire tradition of attacks on the dangers of
travel. His evil is weighted with the shadow of a century of satire.

Antiquarianism, Travel, and the Desire for the Past

One of the most unexpected aspects of *The Vampyre*, and one seldom remarked upon by scholars of the tale, is the antiquarian interests Polidori
accords to his naïve young protagonist, a story element indebted at least
partly to the classical allusions in Lord Byron's own fragmentary story from
the Villa Diodati. A little over five pages remains (or, more likely, was ever

35. On eighteenth- and nineteenth-century accounts of the air at Rome, and connections
between medical and artistic notions of influence, see Wrigley 2013. Waples 2015 gives a suggestive account of the "miasmatic imagination" in Gothic fiction.
36. "Progress of Error" (1782), line 426 (Cowper 1980 [vol. 1], 274).
37. For "reverse colonization," see Arata 1990.

produced) of Byron's original contribution to the ghost story contest, which also centers on travel.[38] The extant portion of the story does not reveal the true nature of the evil it describes. The word vampire never appears. But Byron seems to have blended the vampire myth, already explored in his 1813 poem *The Giaour,* with scenes from his travel in Turkey with his friend John Cam Hobhouse in 1810. Like *The Vampyre,* Byron's fragmentary vampire narrative gives Gothic life to motifs drawn from travel literature – in this case, travel literature about himself. Byron had already created a poeticized version of his journey with Hobhouse in the second canto of *Childe Harold's Pilgrimage* (1812), but his 1816 vampire story conspicuously reworks elements from Hobhouse's prose narrative of their journey, first published in 1813.

The vampire figure in Byron's text is Augustus Darvell, a man not of embarrassed means but of "considerable fortune and antient family." Fascinated by Darvell's "shadowy restlessness" and impressed by his broad travel experience, an unnamed central protagonist sets out on a journey with him to southern then eastern Europe. The narrative hastens almost immediately to their arrival in Smyrna in Turkey (modern İzmir), where Hobhouse and Byron had spent time in March and April, 1810. One of the centerpieces of Hobhouse's account of Smyrna was his long disquisition on the remains of the majestic Greek Temple of Diana [Artemis] at nearby Ephesus, its ancient rise and ruin, and its appropriation by Christian and then Muslim worshippers. Hobhouse blended antiquarian detail with a mournful sense of the remorselessness of historical change.[39] Following Hobhouse's account, Byron depicts his own characters making their way through "the wild and tenantless track" but "lingering over the broken columns of Diana: – the roofless walls of expelled Christianity – and the still more recent but complete desolation of abandoned Mosques." The characters find themselves in a Turkish necropolis, of a kind that Byron and Hobhouse saw on their travels, and which Hobhouse describes in detail in his narrative of their journey.[40] There the main action of the story fragment takes place. Darvell suddenly grows weak, and declares that he has come to this spot to die. He forces his alarmed companion to take a sacred oath, making him swear that he will "fling this ring into the Salt Springs which run into the bay of Eleusis" on the "ninth day of the Month at noon," then the day after "repair to the

38. In 1819, Lord Byron sent the fragment to his publisher, John Murray, to distinguish his own work from Polidori's *The Vampyre.* Against Byron's wishes, Murray then published the fragment as an appendix to *Mazeppa* (1819). I quote the fragment from Andrew Nicholson's edition of Byron's collected prose (1991, 58–63).

39. Hobhouse 1817 [vol. 2], 106–9.

40. Hobhouse 1817 [vol. 2], 76.

ruins of the temple of Ceres." Byron links the vampiric motif of death and regeneration to details from classical Greek mythology: Eleusis and Ceres [Demeter] evoke the famous ancient Eleusinian mysteries, which celebrated Persephone's symbolic descent into the Underworld and rebirth into the world above. A stork with a snake in its beak then appears – a richly symbolic image, but one that again signals the story's indebtedness to Hobhouse, who included a learned digression on the flight and behavior of storks in the Smyrna portion of his travel narrative.[41] At that point in the story fragment, Darvell dies and is buried, and the narrative stops. Presumably he was to return. Byron lost interest.

This story fragment links the motif of the vampire's oath – the pivotal element adapted by Polidori in *The Vampyre* – to the initiation rituals of ancient Eleusinian cult, which, like the period of Darvell's expected death, were popularly thought to last for nine days.[42] It also explicitly links travel with initiation. The unnamed protagonist says that Darvell had been "deeply initiated into what is called the World – while I was yet in my noviciate." He had "already travelled extensively," and the central character is startled to discover that, when in need of water in the burial ground, Darvell can describe even to his Turkish guides the site of local well with "great minuteness" ("I have also been here before," he explains). This experience ranges well beyond the de rigueur Grand Tour; the story begins in its first sentence with the protagonist's determination to travel "through countries not hitherto much frequented by travellers." Moreover, with its specific references to Turkish landmarks and its details from ancient ritual and cult, the fragment none too subtly casts Byron himself as an insider – an initiate – privileged with the mysterious knowledge that travel can bring. Like his vampire Darvell, Byron has been to these places before. If Lord Byron cannot be reborn in quite the same way as his vampiric character, he can at least return to the previously published accounts of his life and travels and give them new textual life. The re-imagining of his earlier travel experience, and his adaptation of details from his travel partner Hobhouse's text, is a vampiric return (or Eleusinian rebirth), albeit one that Byron ultimately abandoned.

Unlike Byron, Polidori makes a point of presenting his naive protagonist as patently *un*initiated into antiquarian mysteries. Once he installs himself in Athens (separated at this point from Ruthven), he is "soon occupied in tracing the faded records of ancient glory upon monuments...." [43] But he

41. Hobhouse (1817 [vol. 2], 90).

42. See, e.g. Lemprière 1801 s.v. "Eleusinia." For a skeptical modern review of the evidence, see Richardson 1974, 165–66.

43. *The Vampyre*, 44; the quotes in this paragraph from pages 44–47.

struggles to pay attention: "the light step of Ianthe often accompanied Aubrey in his search after antiquities," and as a result he often "forgot, in the contemplation of her sylph-like figure, the letters he had just decyphered upon an almost effaced tablet." Her beauty "might well excuse the forgetfulness of the antiquary," when Aubrey "let escape from his mind the very object he had before thought of vital importance to the proper interpretation of a passage of Pausanias."[44] Later, we hear that he would "tear himself from her, and, forming a plan for antiquarian research, he would depart, determined not to return until his object was attained; but he always found it impossible to fix his attention upon the ruins around him. ..." Indeed, it is his engagement in a solitary antiquarian excursion that lures him into danger of a vampire attack, since he ventures to an area near a wood famous among locals as a "resort of the vampyres in their nocturnal orgies." He was "so occupied in his research, that he did not perceive that day-light would soon end...." In "The Progress of Error" (1782), Cowper satirizes the naïveté of English youth abroad, whose tour guide:

> Points to inscriptions whereso'ever they tread,
> Such as when legible were never read,
> But being canker'd now, and half worn out,
> Craze antiquarian brains with endless doubt....[45]

Yet the situation in *The Vampyre* is different. Cowper's youths are misled by their unscrupulous guide. Aubrey is driven to the ruins, again and again, by the enthusiasms of his own persistent – but disappointed – attempts at antiquarian research.

If this sudden passion for antiquity comes as unexpected after Polidori's description of his protagonist as a dreamy reader of romance, it is nonetheless suggested by his name. Patricia Skarda noticed that Aubrey shares his name with the famous seventeenth-century antiquary John Aubrey (1626–97), though she did not explore the implications of that association.[46] John Aubrey is one of the founding figures of modern archaeology, local history, and cultural anthropology. He also became a byword in the eighteenth and nineteenth centuries for credulousness. Already his encyclopedia entry in the 1747 *Biographica Britannica* describes him as "somewhat credulous, and strongly tinctured with superstition." His nineteenth-century biographer records the stronger judgment of Aubrey's contemporaries that he was

---

44. On the popularity of this Greek author of the second century CE as a travel guide in the early nineteenth century, see Asvesta and Guilmet (2007). Polidori himself, it is worth observing, never traveled to Greece.

45. Lines 391–394 (Cowper 1980 [vol.1], 273).

46. Skarda, 251.

"exceedingly credulous" and "extremely superstitious, or seem'd to be so,"
and the biographer concludes on the basis of Aubrey's published *Miscellanies*
that he was "deeply imbued with superstition."[47] Polidori's Aubrey has arguably inherited his naïve passion for the mysterious from his antiquarian
namesake. But he is also made to inhabit an Aubreyan world: the *Miscellanies,* the only one of John Aubrey's many works of research published in his
lifetime, collects textual and material evidence for apparitions, prophecies,
"transportation by an invisible power," "converse with angels and spirits,"
and other supernatural phenomena.[48] Like Polidori's Aubrey, who grows
fascinated with Ianthe's recounting "the supernatural tales of her nurse," including a local Greek tradition about vampires, John Aubrey collected *aniles
fabulae* (old wives tales) since childhood, beginning with the tales of his own
nurse, and consistently defended the usefulness of oral tradition to his readers.[49] *The Vampyre* incorporates themes associated with the memory of John
Aubrey: the defense of the supernatural, credulity and belief, the passion of
the antiquary, and the importance of folk traditions of knowledge. Vampires
in particular do not appear in Aubrey's antiquarian works, though in a later,
posthumously published work, he described antiquarianism itself as a kind
of reanimation of the dead: "the retrieving of these forgotten things from
oblivion," he wrote, "in some sort resembles the Art of a Conjuror who makes
those walke and appeare that have layen in their graves many hundreds of
yeares."[50] When the story of *The Vampyre* shifts abruptly to its protagonist's
attempts to decipher ancient artifacts, the vampiric motif of reanimation is
temporarily recast as the antiquarian attempt to revive the dead.

Indeed, amid *The Vampyre's* cynical commentary on the empty rituals and
moral corruptions of Continental travel, the character of Aubrey, haplessly
"occupied by his research," speaks surprisingly vividly to the seductions of
antiquity, and the desire – even the erotic desire – for the past. The story
trips lightly over Brussels and even Rome (where Aubrey "went in search
of the memorials of another almost deserted city") but lingers for half its
length in Athens, where Aubrey is attracted both by a beautiful woman and
by undeciphered ancient texts. That these two plot elements occur together,

---

47. Britton 1845. Quotations at pages 6, 8, 43.

48. Text in Aubrey 1972, 1–125.

49. *The Vampyre* 45; on Aubrey and oral tradition, Dragstra 2008. In the preface to his "Re-
maines of Gentilisme and Judaisme," Aubrey wrote that "old wives-fables are grosse things:
but yet ought not to be quite rejected: there may be some truth and usefulnesse be elicited out
of them" (1972, 132).

50. Aubrey 1862, 4, cited in Bauman and Briggs 2003, 74. The great classical scholar Ulrich
von Wilamowitz-Moellendorff similarly compared the work of the historian to an Odyssean offering of blood to the spirits: "we know that ghosts cannot speak until they have drunk blood;
and the spirits which we evoke demand the blood of our hearts" (1908, 25).

and even that they compete for Aubrey's attention, falls very much in line with a trend Chloe Chard has observed in eighteenth- and nineteenth-century travel writing, according to which the seduction of foreign beauties and of classical antiquities are pervasively associated with one another. The desire for the past is eroticized. Both women and ruins present "disguises and obstacles" to the interested foreign viewer, provoking excitement but preventing immediate understanding; hence, mysterious "nymph-like" beauties are frequently to be found among mysterious ancient ruins, and the ruins themselves are often symbolically feminized.[51] Aubrey's desire is ultimately foiled by the vampire, who, we might also assume, following Gothic tropes more broadly, symbolizes a sinister resurgence of the past in the present. Yet Ruthven's endlessly circular existence in *The Vampyre* seems instead to represent the opposite of a historical consciousness or a desire for the past. The narrative shows Ruthven engaging in the same actions again and again, and the cyclical story structure, according to which the monster climactically reappears at a drawing-room party exactly like that of the story's beginning, suggests that he will continue unchanged into the future. Ruthven's own apparent lack of a past is very different from, for example, Stoker's Dracula, who can regale Jonathan Harker in his castle with centuries of Transylvanian history "as if he had been present at them all," as indeed he had been.[52] Lord Ruthven seem to come from nowhere, and the oath in Polidori's story, rather than performing a sacred office in the ritual of rebirth (as in Byron's story fragment), requires Aubrey simply to conceal all that he has learnt in the first part of the story. The narrative ensures that its villain continues to lack a history, a past. Dracula's opponents muster the resources of "mere 'modernity'" against their foe.[53] Aubrey, searching for the past, is foiled by a villain who epitomizes a depthless, superficial present.

Polidori in his extant diary does not exactly betray a passion for the classics, though when he was with Byron and the Shelleys at the Villa Diodati he read the Greek satirist Lucian.[54] In his final published work before

51. Chard 1999, 126–40. Polidori knew Madame de Staël's *Corinne; ou, l'Italie* (1807), perhaps the supreme example of the type, in which the mysterious foreign beauty Corinne becomes the seductive embodiment of classical culture. Polidori cites the novel in his text to Bridgens' sketches (Bridgens 1821, n.p. "Horse Race at Rome in Carnival"), and met de Staël on his travels (Polidori 1911, 146–47). Chard adduces a variety of other English and French versions of the association between antiquities and female beauty, including an episode from William Beckford's *Biographical Memoirs of Extraordinary Painters* (1780).

52. Stoker 2011 [1897], 30.

53. Stoker 2011 [1897], 37.

54. Polidori 1911, 121. He also cites from the Roman satirist Persius in his *Essay upon the Source of Positive Pleasure* (1818, 40; cf. Persius, *Satire* 5.152), and the argument of that work closely resembles the tenth *Satire* of another ancient satirist, Juvenal.

his suicide in 1821, the accompanying text to Richard Bridgens' *Sketches Illustrative of the Manners and Costumes of France, Switzerland and Italy,* Polidori shows some interest in archaeology. The ancient ruins in one sketch, he says, "consist of the Capitol, the three remaining columns to the temple of Jupiter Feretrius, and the colonnade of that commonly supposed to be of Concord. Some excavations having, however, lately been made, doubts have arisen, and the latter ruins are given to the Temple of Fortune."[55] But Polidori more often expresses surprise and resentment about the shallowness of history's imprint in the contemporary world. When he and Byron go to see the tomb of the poet Charles Churchill, he describes children trampling heedlessly over the grave, and complains later of the "shameful" way that current inhabitants of the Roman town of Aventicum in Switzerland have neglected "the antiquities of their fathers."[56] The impressions of Byron on these occasions found elegiac expression in "Churchill's Grave" (1816) and *Childe Harold's Pilgrimage,* but Polidori's thoughts on the slender survival of memorials of the past find more caustic expression in *The Vampyre.* As well as embodying the other evils of the Tour, his villain Lord Ruthven epitomizes this sense of the absence, or even the erasure, of the past. The scenes of Aubrey vainly searching for ancient monuments reflect a familiar desire on the part of travelers to feel the presence of the ancient world in the Mediterranean; the vampire, in his very ability to die then live again unchanged, represents the opposite of this yearning for what is older, what is different, what comes before. Ruthven – "riven," in the Scottish pronunciation – is an agent of forgetfulness and erasure, symbolizing the distance between travelers' classicizing desires and their disenchantment with Europe. The monster's shallow, circular existence, and his victim's disillusionment and disappointments, offer a cynical commentary on travel in the Modern age.

In the words of Chloe Chard, late eighteenth- and early-nineteenth-century travel writings frequently "map out the relation between the ancient past and the present as one in which the past is always posed to resurge disquietingly within the contemporary topography, and use various repositories of memory, such as ruins, antique fragments, and ghosts, as sites and vehicles for such a resurgence."[57] The same is true in Gothic fiction. Mary Shelley's *Frankenstein* (1818) is also a tale of *The Modern Prometheus,* and Polidori's own novel *Ernestus Berchtold* (1819) also carried the subtitle *The Modern Oedipus,* but the relationship between contemporary narrative and ancient myth is not, as in the neoclassical ideal, one of direct modeling of the present

55. Bridgens 1821, n.p., text to image titled "Italian Wine Cart."
56. Polidori 1911, 93–94.
57. Chard 1999, 140.

on the past. The ancient myth remains in the plot as a horrific potentiality, a submerged pattern that lurks below the surface, always threatening to emerge and commandeer the characters towards tragic ruin. It is true that Lord Byron, in his abandoned story fragment about Augustus Darvell, implicitly positions himself as an initiate of esoteric ancient mysteries, in close communion with the past. But Polidori's scenes of frustrated antiquarianism speak eloquently to what was perhaps a more common experience, a disappointing lack of connection with antiquity even on the "classic ground" of Italy and Greece, a sense of failed communion between past and present. In *The Vampyre,* ancient texts even submerge themselves underground, mocking modern attempts to understand them. The Athenian monuments that contained "the faded records of ancient glory," says Polidori, "had hidden themselves beneath the sheltering soil or many coloured lichen," apparently "ashamed of chronicling the deeds of free men only before slaves."[58] The discontinuity between ancient Greece and a "degenerate" modern Greece was a commonplace of Romantic thought. Here the rupture in Greek history is presented as frustrating the English traveler's yearning for history, and this failure is thrown into high relief by the sinister pastlessness of Polidori's villain.

The Illusions of Travel

Readers of *The Vampyre* have long understood the story as a fictionalized account of Polidori's relationship with Lord Byron. The fateful 1816 tour of the Continent brought disappointment to Polidori's career hopes and his desire to establish himself as Byron's peer. His short story expresses that bitterness while presenting itself as fanciful Gothic fiction. But the story's combination of disenchantment and imagination also expresses something broader about the travel experience. Aubrey, our feckless traveler, is an intensely impressionistic youth: he "cultivated more his imagination than his judgment," says Polidori sardonically, and possessed "that high romantic feeling of honour and candour, which daily ruins so many milliners' apprentices."[59] Before he set out on his journey, he fostered his own illusions by reading works of supernatural romance, and was startled at home to find there was "no foundation in real life for any of that congeries of pleasing horrors and descriptions contained in the volumes, which had formed the occupation of his midnight vigils."[60] Like other travelers in this volume – the Arab students in Russia in Margaret Litvin's chapter, for example, or the Don Quixote-

58. *The Vampyre,* 44.
59. *The Vampyre,* 40.
60. *The Vampyre,* 40.

loving Frenchman studied by Elizabeth C. Goldsmith – Aubrey shapes his perception of the world, before he ever sees it, by the texts he has read. As the narrative of *The Vampyre* progresses, Aubrey is disabused of his romantic ideas about Ruthven, who reveals his vices along the journey. But the further Aubrey travels and the longer he is away from home, the more his illusions are confirmed. Ruthven really *is* a vampire. The horrors of his old, nocturnal romance narratives do find a foundation in fact. Read as satire, *The Vampyre* suggests that the corruptions of travel on English youth are all too real. But the narrative also attests to a more dynamic and unstable chemistry between the reality of a foreign place and a person's expectations of it. Dangerously, seductively, preconceptions can become a sort of reality in any attempt to comprehend an unfamiliar place. Fiction becomes lived experience through the eyes of a traveler.

Bibliography

Arata, Stephen, D. 1990. "The Occidental Tourist: *Dracula* and the Anxiety of Reverse Colonization." *Victorian Studies* 33/4:621–45.

Asvesta, Aliki and Céline Guilmet. 2007. "The *Periegesis* and the Topographers (1800–1820)." In *Following Pausanias: The Quest for Greek Antiquity*, edited by Maria Georgopoulou et al, 155–68. New Castle, DE: Oak Knoll Press.

Aubrey, John. 1862. *Wiltshire: The Topographical Collections of John Aubrey.* Edited by John Edward Jackson. Devizes: Wiltshire Archaeological and Historical Society.

———. 1972. *Three Prose Works.* Edited by John Buchanan-Brown. Carbondale, IL: Southern Illinois University Press.

Auerbach, Nina. 1995. *Our Vampires, Ourselves.* Chicago and London: University of Chicago Press.

Bainbridge, Simon. 2006. "Lord Ruthven's Power: Polidori's 'The Vampyre', Doubles and the Byronic Imagination." *Byron Journal* 34/1:21–34.

Bauman, Richard and Charles L. Briggs. 2003. *Voices of Modernity: Language Ideologies and the Politics of Inequality.* Cambridge: Cambridge University Press.

Black, Jeremy. 1992. *The British Abroad: The Grand Tour in the Eighteenth Century.* New York: St. Martin's Press.

Bond, Donald F. (ed.). 1965. *The Spectator.* 5 vols. Oxford: Clarendon Press.

Bridgens, Richard. 1821. *Sketches Illustrative of the Manners and Costumes of France, Switzerland, and Italy.* Text by John W. Polidori. London: Baldwin, Cradock, and Joy.

Britton, John. 1845. *A Memoir of John Aubrey.* London: J. B. Nichols and Son.

Budge, Gavin. 2004. "'The Vampyre': Romantic Metaphysics and the Aristocratic Other." In *The Gothic Others: Racial and Social Constructions in the Literary Imagination*, edited by Ruth B. Anolik and Douglas L. Howards, 212–34. Jefferson, NC: McFarland.

Butler, Erik. 2010. *Metamorphoses of the Vampire in Literature and Film: Cultural Transformations in Europe, 1732-1933.* New York: Camden House.

Buzard, James. 1991. "The Uses of Romanticism: Byron and the Victorian Continental Tour." *Victorian Studies* 35/1:29–49.

———. 1993. *The Beaten Track: European Tourism, Literature, and the Ways to Culture, 1800-1918*, Oxford: Clarendon Press.

———. 2002. "The Grand Tour and After (1660–1840)." In *The Cambridge Companion to Travel Writing* edited by Peter Hulme and Tim Youngs (eds.), 37–52. Cambridge: Cambridge University Press, 37–52.

Byron, Lord G. G. 1991. *Lord Byron: The Complete Miscellaneous Prose.* Edited by Andrew Nicholson, Oxford: Clarendon Press.

Chalmers, A. 1823. *The British Essayists.* 38 vols. London: C & J Rivington, et al.

Chard, Chloe. 1999. *Pleasure and Guilt on the Grand Tour: Travel Writing and Imaginative Geography, 1600–1830.* Manchester: Manchester University Press.

Cowper, William. 1980. *The Poems of William Cowper.* Edited by John D. Baird and Charles Ryskamp. 3 vols. Oxford: Clarendon Press.

Dragstra, Henk. 2008. "Before woomen were Readers": How John Aubrey Wrote Female Oral History." In *Oral Traditions and Gender in Early Modern Literary Texts*, edited by Mary Ellen Lamb & Karen Bamford, 41–53. Aldershot, England: Ashgate.

Ek, Richard. 2015. "The Tourist-Vampire and the Citizen as Ontological Figures: Human and Nonhuman Encounters in the Postpolitical." In *Tourism Encounters and Controversies: Ontological Politics of Tourism Development*, edited by Gunnar Thór Jóhannesson, Carina Ren, and René van der Duim, 139–57. Farnham: Ashgate.

Gay, John. 1967. *John Gay: Fables.* Edited by Vinton A. Dearing. Los Angeles: William Andrews Clark Memorial Library.

Gelder, Ken. 1994. *Reading the Vampire.* London & New York: Routledge.

Goldsmith, Oliver. 1966. *Collected Works of Oliver Goldsmith.* 5 vols. Oxford: Clarendon Press.

Hall, Joseph. 1839. *The Works of Joseph Hall.* 12 vols. Oxford: D. A. Talboys.

Hobhouse, J. C. 1817. *A Journey through Albania, and Other Provinces of Turkey in 1809 & 1810.* 2 vols. Philadelphia: M. Carey and Son.

Hogle, Jerrold E. 2009. "The Rise of the Gothic Vampire: Disfiguration and Cathexis from Coleridge's 'Christabel' to Nodier's *Smarra.*" In *Gothic N.E.W.S. Volume 1: Literature* edited by Max Duperray, 48–70. Paris: Michel Houdiard.

Hurd, Richard. 1811. *The Works of Richard Hurd.* 8 vols. London: T. Cadell and W. Davies.

Jenyns, Soame. 1790. *The Works of Soame Jenyns.* 4 vols. London: T. Cadell.

Lemprière, J. 1801. *Bibliotheca Classica; or A Classical Dictionary.* 4th ed. London: T. Cadell and W. Davies.

Lewis, Matthew. 1998. *The Monk.* Edited by Howard Anderson. Oxford: Oxford University Press.

MacDonald, D. L. 1991. *Poor Polidori: A Critical Biography of the Author of "The Vampyre,"* Toronto: University of Toronto Press.

Mead, William Edward. 1914. *The Grand Tour in the Eighteenth Century.* Boston and New York: Houghton Mifflin Co.

Polidori, John W. 1818. *An Essay upon the Source of Positive Pleasure.* London: Longman, Hurst, Rees, Orme, and Brown.

———. 1911. *The Diary of John William Polidori, 1816, Relating to Byron, Shelley, etc.* Edited by William Michael Rosetti. London: Elkin Matthews.

———. 2008. *The Vampyre and Ernestus Berchtold; or the Modern Oedipus.* Edited by D. L. Macdonald and Kathleen Scherf. Peterborough, Ontario: Broadview Editions.

Pope, Alexander. 1943. *The Dunciad.* Edited by James Sutherland. London: Methuen & Co. Ltd.

Radcliffe, Ann. 1986. *The Romance of the Forest.* Edited by Chloe Chard. Oxford: Oxford University Press.

———. 2000. *The Italian.* Edited by Robert Miles. Harmondsworth, UK: Penguin.

Redford, Bruce. 1996. *Venice and the Grand Tour.* New Haven: Yale University Press.

Richardson, N. J. 1974. *The Homeric Hymn to Demeter.* Oxford: Clarendon Press.

Rieger, James. 1963. "Dr Polidori and the Genesis of *Frankenstein.*" *Studies in English Literature* 3:461–72.

Skarda, Patricia L. 1989. "Vampirism and Plagiarism: Byron's Influence and Polidori's Practice." *Studies in Romanticism* 28/2:249–69.

Stoker, Bram. 2011 [1897]. *Dracula.* Edited by Roger Luckhurst. Oxford: Oxford University Press.

Thompson, Carl. 2007. *The Suffering Traveller and the Romantic Imagination.* Oxford: Clarendon Press.

Viets, Henry, R. 1969. "The London Editions of Polidori's *The Vampyre.*" *Papers of the Bibliographical Society of America* 63/2:83–103.

Waples, Emily. 2015. "'Invisible Agents': The American Gothic and the Miasmatic Imagination." *Gothic Studies* 17/1:13–27.

Wilamowitz-Moellendorff, Ulrich von. 1908. *Greek Historical Writing and Apollo.* Translated by Gilbert Murray. Oxford: Clarendon Press.

Wrigley, Richard. 2013. *Roman Fever: Influence, Infection and the Image of Rome, 1700–1870.* New Haven & London: Yale University Press.

The Chameleonic Identities of Mohan Lal Kashmiri and His Travels in Persianate Lands

Sunil Sharma

TWO DECADES before the Victorian explorer and orientalist Sir Richard Francis Burton (1821–90) visited Mecca disguised as a Muslim hajji, a young native informer in British India, Mohan Lal Kashmiri (1812–77), traveled through Afghanistan, Iran, and Central Asia in the years 1831–34, under a nebulous disguise which was sometimes Muslim (Figure 1). Although Burton's trip was undertaken as a personal adventure while he was on leave from his job with the East India Company, as a young man he had already traveled in disguise through the region of Sindh gathering information for his employers. Similarly, Mohan Lal was nineteen years old when he was handpicked for such a mission because of his fluency in English, the new language of the British colonial administration, and Persian, the lingua franca of a large geographical area in Asia. He was to accompany an exploratory expedition led by Sir Alexander Burnes (1805–41), famously remembered as "Bukhara Burnes," to the lands northwest of British India. The party traveled from Delhi through Panjab, across the Khyber Pass to Afghanistan, Central Asia and eastern Iran, in an attempt to gauge the political situation in the lands that separated the Russian and British empires. Although they were both quite similar in the way that they derived pleasure in playing with disguises, we find that "Burton was far more interested in parading his mastery over a range of identity roles than in actually adopting them,"[1] while Mohan Lal's chameleonic self-representation originated in negotiating several actual and potential identities, i.e. Kashmiri, Hindu, Persianate, Shia Muslim, Christian, Indian, in a cultural climate where these national, religious, and cultural identities were becoming increasingly fixed. And it was as a traveler that he learned that he could actually manipulate his identity as a fluid category, depending on the local geography and history – both of the present and past. The chief source for our information on him are two editions of a travel book that he published in English (Figures 2 and 3), which I argue are autoethnographic accounts of his transformation from a traditional Persian *munshi* (secretary) to a westernized colonial subject.

1. Ghose 2006, 79.

Fig. 1. Portrait of Mohan Lal Kashmiri (Courtesy Wikimedia Commons)

Many travel texts produced by Indians in the first half of the nineteenth century can be categorized as Persianate in style and orientation because of the continued influence of classical Persian literary forms and tropes at this time. In the second half of the century, Persian continued to be used by elites even as travel literature in the vernacular Urdu began to proliferate, while there was a simultaneous confluence of multiple textual and generic traditions, chiefly in the way that English and other Indian languages also came to be increasingly employed in a distinctively Persianate mode.[2] Written in such a literary milieu, Mohan Lal Kashmiri's narrative is a lively account of his travels in the fast disappearing Persophone sphere. His work is located at the nexus of several traditions of writing travel – chiefly Persian and English – reflecting his unique personality, as well as the complex social and cultural realities of late Mughal and pre-1857 British India. It is characterized by an admixture of scientific and lyrical ethnography, with some sections, especially those that describe his encounters with people and visits to places,

2. Daniel Majchrowicz studies this topic in his recent dissertation (Majchrowicz 2015). See especially Chapter 2 on the emergence of Urdu travel writing. I am grateful to Daniel for his insightful comments on this paper, especially with regard to the question of adopting different identities in this period, which apparently was something of a common practice among both the British and Indians.

drawing on various forms of classical Persian poetry. Was this a conscious choice on Mohan Lal's part or was his account a new form of writing in a new language over a palimpsest of a long tradition of Persian learning? An examination of his life and close reading of parts of his travel book will be a help in answering these questions.

Mohan Lal's biography is as complex and fascinating as the cultural history of the nineteenth-century Persianate world east of Iran, a region that would include the modern-day countries of Iran, India, Afghanistan, Pakistan, Tajikistan, and Uzbekistan. There were several facets to his background that would make him particularly suitable for the secret mission led by Burnes. Born into a Kashmiri Pandit family of the Hindu Zutshi community that had long served in the imperial Mughal administration, often as Persian *munshis*, Mohan Lal also took up this lucrative profession. In a similar capacity, his father, Rai Brahmnath "Budh Singh," had accompanied Lord Mountstuart Elphinstone on a diplomatic mission to Peshawar in 1808–9.[3] Budh Singh had two wives, one Kashmiri Hindu and the other a Muslim. Thus, as a child Mohan Lal "moved freely between the domestic worlds of his Brahmin biological mother and his Muslim stepmother, learning the languages and values inherent in each household."[4] This is not so surprising since the Kashmiri Hindu community was highly Persianate in their cultural orientation. Early on Mohan Lal found a life-long patron and friend in Sir Charles E. Trevelyan, a key figure in instituting English-language education at Delhi College in 1828, for the training of a new generation of anglicized Indians. Mohan Lal was among the first six graduates of this pioneering program. Trevelyan was, interestingly, the brother-in-law of Sir Thomas Babington Macaulay, notorious for the Macaulay Minute on Education that in 1835 would render Persian a homeless language in India in favor of English. With his education in English, Mohan Lal "formed the vanguard of new-model Anglicized Indian civil administrators that would expand over the following century"; although there were decided advantages to being chosen for this career path, many men like Mohan Lal "frequently felt the frustration of their consequent dependence on and, often, betrayal by their British employers [... and] suffered deracinization and distancing from their natal communities."[5] Although he did not feel he had full mastery over English, this was the language that he chose to employ for his writings. Mohan Lal

3. *An Account of the Kingdom of Caubul, and its dependencies in Persia, Tartary, and India, comprising a view of the Afghaun nation, and a history of the Dooraunee monarchy* (London: Longman, Hurst, Rees, Orme, and Brown, 1815).

4. Fisher 2006, 240.

5. Fisher 2006, 234.

JOURNAL

OF

A TOUR

THROUGH

THE PANJÁB, AFGHÁNISTÁN, TÚRKISTÁN, KHORÁSÁN, AND PART OF PERSIA,

IN COMPANY WITH

LIEUT. BURNES AND DR. GERARD.

BY

MUNSHÍ MOHAN LÁL,

A NATIVE OF DIHLÍ'.

Calcutta:

PRINTED AT THE BAPTIST MISSION PRESS; AND SOLD
BY THE AUTHOR.

1834.

•

Fig. 2. Title page of the first edition (Courtesy Sunil Sharma)

was a particularly valuable traveler for the British because of his ability to communicate fluently in Persian and English. According to Fisher, "both sides [the British and local people wherever he went] regarded him as a cultural intermediary,"[6] and his experiences in Central and West Asia "clearly affected his self-conceptualization profoundly."[7]

The travel party's leader Alexander Burnes posed as a British army captain who was traveling back home overland, their itinerary taking them from Delhi through Panjab, across the Khyber Pass to Afghanistan, Bukhara and eastern Iran, at a time when the Great Game in which several empires had a stake was already in full play. Burnes knew both Persian and Hindustani, the two languages that would be sufficient for a traveler in these parts. Burnes and Mohan Lal parted ways in Iran, with the former going on to the Caspian region while the latter returned to India. Bukhara Burnes gained instant fame when he published his report in 1834 as the three-volume *Travels into Bokhara, Being an account of a Journey from India to Cabool, Tartary and Persia.*[8] In 1833–34, Mohan Lal published six short pieces that later were part of his travelogue in the *Journal of the Asiatic Society of Bengal* in Calcutta. These were in the style of ethno-archaeological reports contributed by European explorers.[9] Subsequently, while undergoing further training to be a surveyor, he brought out an edited book edition of his travelogue: *Journal of a Tour through the Panjab, Afghanistan, Turkistan, Khorasan, and Part of Persia, in Company with Lieut. Burnes and Dr. Gerard.*[10] During his sojourn in Britain in 1844–1846, where he went after the disastrous so-called First Anglo-Afghan War of 1839–1842 to lobby influential supporters to help him regain his heavy losses in Kabul, he brought out an expanded version of his travel book, with the title, *Travels in the Panjab, Afghanistan & Turkistan to Balk [sic], Bokhara and Herat, and a Visit to Great Britain and Germany.*[11] Although written in English, this work often reads as if it were a translation of a Persian text in the author's use of certain poetic tropes, a highly rhetorical style, and description of the wonders of particular places. At the same time, clearly, there is an attempt to write in a new ethnographic style modeled on European travel narratives. In this regard, it may be useful to employ Mary

6. Fisher 2006, 243.

7. Fisher 2006, 247.

8. Burnes 1834.

9. "A Brief Description of Herat"; "Further Information regarding the Siah Posh tribe or reputed descendants of the Macedonians"; "Account of Kala Bagh"; "A brief account of the origin of the Daudputras"; "A brief account of Masud, known by the name of Farid Shakarganj or Shakarbar"; "Description of Uch Sharif." These all appear in v. 3, 1834.

10. Mohan Lal Kashmiri 1834.

11. Mohan Lal Kashmiri 1846.

TRAVELS

IN THE

PANJAB, AFGHANISTAN, & TURKISTAN,

TO

BALK, BOKHARA, AND HERAT;

AND

A VISIT TO GREAT BRITAIN AND GERMANY.

BY MOHAN LAL, ESQ.,

Knight of the Persian Order of the Lion and Sun; lately attached to the Mission at Kabul.

LONDON:

Wm. H. ALLEN & Co.,

7, LEADENHALL STREET.

1846.

Fig. 3. Title page of the second edition (Courtesy Sunil Sharma)

Louise Pratt's term "autoethnography" to Mohan Lal's travel writings. Pratt has proposed that in contrast with European ethnographic texts, autoethnographic texts are composed by the other "in response to or in dialogue with those metropolitan representations" in a process that involves "collaborating with and appropriating the idioms of the conqueror."[12] It seemed that Mohan Lal could not, or did not want to, give up his connection to the older, more romantic, style of writing.

In the first edition of his book Mohan Lal calls himself a *munshi*, but in the preface to the second edition he is at pains to explain that he was not Burnes's *munshi*: that post was actually filled by Mohamed Ali of Bombay, while he himself was Burnes's Persian secretary. Burnes writes in the preface of his travelogue, "I was also attended by a native Surveyor, Mahommed Ali, a public servant, who had been educated in the Engineer Institution of Bombay."[13] He goes on to declare that

> I also took a Hindoo lad, of Cashmere family, named Mohun Lal, who
> had been educated at the English Institution at Delhi, as he would
> assist me in my Persian correspondence; the forms of which amount
> to a science in the East. His youth and his creed would, I believed, free
> me from all danger of his entering into intrigues with the people;
> and both he and the Surveyor proved themselves to be zealous and
> trustworthy men, devoted to our interests.[14]

It is clear that over time, and when he was preparing his book for a wider English audience, Mohan Lal decided to stretch the truth about his role on the trip and reinvent the role he had played. The English term "secretary" would have been more appealing at this point since it was grander than the traditional *munshi*. In the first edition, Mohan Lal is also apologetic about his limited knowledge of English, as well as his abilities to be a travel writer:

> When I quitted Dihli, I did not know how to keep a diary, or to put
> down the names of places; but by copying a few pages of the journal
> for Mr. Burnes, I immediately possessed myself of the way in which
> the memorandums of a journey are preserved.[15]

This display of modesty is absent in the second edition, presumably because by then he had gained a great deal of confidence in his abilities in English, as well as his position as a traveler. Apart from the different prefaces, the main

12. Pratt 1992, 9.
13. *Travels into Bokhara*, xi–xii.
14. *Travels into Bokhara*, xii.
15. *Journal of a Tour*, iv.

differences between the texts of the first and second editions of Mohan Lal's work include noticeable stylistic changes, deletion of the Persian or Pashto originals of poetry and inscriptions, and the addition of the European part of his travels that he undertook later. Thus, there are two levels of comparisons that can be made here: one between the accounts of Burnes and Mohan Lal, and the other between Mohan Lal's two versions of his narrative. I will do a bit of both in this paper, providing instances where reading the two versions against each other can prove to be a fruitful exercise.

On the eve of his journey, on 20 December 1831, Mohan Lal went to say goodbye to a British friend affiliated with the Delhi College, Mr. B. Fitzgerald, who was ill in bed, and a very affective interaction took place that is more reminiscent of partings in Persian romances; he writes:

> [Mr. Fitzgerald] took me in his arms, sighed, and told me he was very sorry for our separation, but hoped that I should have a successful journey. He gave me a great deal of advice, and told me to be assured of one thing, that this enterprising spirit of mine would secure to me the esteem and admiration of all Europeans, and even my own countryman. We shed a flood of tears at parting, which he seemed to feel very much.[16]

Mr. Fitzgerald died about three weeks later, much to Mohan Lal's sorrow. The display of emotion on Mohan Lal's part when he left his friend and then heard about his death appears to be sincere, but the reader of his narrative is never quite sure when he is performing a certain scripted role, as of two lovers parting in a Persianate narrative or a poem (*ghazal*). There are several other instances of such affective responses to people.

Right from the moment of leaving home, it is clear that Mohan Lal's identity was not fixed, perhaps even to himself, but appropriately malleable for his mission. While traveling in the Mughal and Sikh domains, he was most often taken for a Westerner, as when in Shikarpur, Sindh, he is called a "Farangi" [European] by people in the bazaar.[17] In Peshawar people thought he was an Englishman, not a Kashmiri, "though my clothes were not like an [*sic*] European's."[18] These statements suggest that it had more to do with his physical features, or being in the company of Europeans, that he was often mistaken for one of them. But he did not always correct people's mistakes about who he was. There was a playfulness about his chameleonic identities as we see on the threshold of Central Asia, in the small village of Khail-i-Ak-

16. *Travels*, 1846 edition, 2.
17. *Travels*, 301.
18. *Travels*, 46.

hund [Akhun Khel], on the road between Kandahar and Kabul where Hindus would have been a minority, he writes, "I saw a Hindu making his bread, and said to him, "*Ram, Ram*," which is a compliment. He was quite astonished to hear this, and at the same time to see me in the Afghan dress."[19] In his early travels Mohan Lal retained his own Kashmiri Hindu cook and servants, eating separately from Christians and Muslims, a practice that he gave up later. Over time he seemed to be drawn to Islam, though he also flirted with the idea of being a Christian.

While in Iran, where there would have been fewer Hindus than in Afghanistan, Mohan Lal managed to blend into the local populace, as in the holy city of Mashhad. On September 14, he describes a little adventure:

> I attempted to examine the bath at Mashad, where none but
> Mohammedans are allowed to enter. I nearly risked my character,
> as the merchants, who suspected me to be a Christian, in the late
> journey, were present; but, luckily, for me they could not recognize me
> in the Persian attire, which I had purposely put on.[20]

He could naturally not play these games in official circles. In late February 1833, he described a very cordial meeting in Mashhad with His Royal Highness 'Abbas Mirza, the Qajar crown prince and great proponent of modernization, just before the latter's untimely death. 'Abbas Mirza addressed him as the "Indian Mirza" and "asked me whether I was a Sunni or Shia, and what was my name. 'I am the friend of Panjtan, or five persons,' was my reply. Abbas Mirza was highly glad to hear this."[21] Very often such vague references to his own religious and communal identity not only allowed him to infiltrate various groups, but also be embraced by them. It would seem that the local people figured out what he was *not*, without worrying about what he was, as illustrated by a somewhat touching episode:

> The Mohammedans in Mashad, who became friendly with me,
> though they knew that I was a stranger, having no prejudices,
> were exceedingly delighted by my Persian knowledge, which they
> considered peculiar to their tribe. One Persian, who was respected by
> the party, sighed, and said, if I would be a Shia, or follower of Ali, he
> would willingly marry me to his daughter, who would be the mistress
> of a great fortune after his death. I smiled; and he again said to me,
> "Do not you think that the enlightened creed of the Shias will place
> you in heaven? You will gain nothing in other creeds, but repentance."

19. *Travels*, 324.
20. *Travels*, 166-67.
21. *Travels*, 225.

I said, in reply, that the parents who reared me, with great trouble, expected some service in return from me, when they were old, and I had done nothing for them yet. If I were to stay here, for the sake of beauty and money, without discharging my filial duty, how could I become a happy man? These words made a strong impression upon his heart.[22]

Right from the beginning of his narrative Mohan Lal is highly critical of what he calls the superstitions of all religious groups. Chris Bayly remarks that "Mohan Lal's journeys became a Voltairean tour of the absurdities of pagan religion."[23] Despite his protestations that he had not converted to Christianity, in 1834 he was formally excommunicated from the Kashmiri Brahmin community. Later in life, ironically, he would be drawn to Shiism; he used the alias 'Agha Hasan Jan' and had multiple Muslim wives, but until his death in 1877 he never explicitly identified himself with any religious community nor was he accepted by any group.

While on the road Mohan Lal appears as a hopeless romantic with an eye for beautiful women, never missing an opportunity to record his appreciation of the female form. Traveling in western Panjab, he noted that there was "nothing remarkable in this village except the beauty and cheerfulness of the women"[24] or in the next village about which he wrote, "The women of this village are beautiful, and fond of indulgence. They have power over their husbands, whom they control rather than obey, and do what they like. The climate is temperate and wholesome."[25] In Karnal he couldn't find a room in a hostel because of the number of visitors, until "a beautiful girl came gracefully to me, and said 'Come with me in the next room, where I will prepare a clean bed for you.' I slept very comfortably."[26] Later in his travels he compared Iranian and Afghan women as he crossed the border from Mashhad to Herat; he noted: "They [women of Herat] are not so virtuous as those of Mashad, and like rather to wander in the fields than to stay at home."[27] In Bukhara, he was struck by the beautiful people in the Jewish quarter, "where I scarcely saw a man or a woman devoid of beauty. All of them were handsome, delicate, and attractive. Their eyes were alluring, and their persons enticing, though every one looked half sottish."[28] Remarking on the beauty of a city or region's inhabitants was a common feature of clas-

22. *Travels*, 186.
23. Bayly 1996, 232.
24. *Travels*, 23.
25. *Travels*, 27.
26. *Travels*, 4.
27. *Travels*, 271–72.
28. *Travels*, 127.

sical Persian poetry on cities and in travelogues, thus it is not surprising that Mohan Lal draws on this trope in his narrative. Needless to say, such a lyrical feature is absent in Burnes's travel book.

As Mohan Lal exited the Indian subcontinent and entered the larger Iranian world, his remarks on women became conspicuously absent as he was drawn into an easy homosociality in a society where he had to depend entirely on his Persianate cultural orientation and was less protected by either his own background or his colonial employers. The unspoken rules of comportment and masculinity, conditioned by the rules of the popular Persian love lyric, the *ghazal*, where an expression of same-sex love signified multiple levels of friendship and fealty, allowed him to interact easily with individuals of varied backgrounds and social groups. In Peshawar, the cultural frontier of the two worlds, Mohan Lal performed this ritual with Khwajah Mohammed Khan, the governor's son:

> He came to my place, bearing a watch in his hand. After compliments, he sat upon my bed, and talked a long while with me in the Persian language with the utmost politeness. He was richly dressed, and had a shawl turban on his head, which increased his beauty. He is a very sharp boy of fifteen, and knows poetry. He recited a number of Afghani, or Pashto, and Persian verses: the following is a translation of one of the former [by Rahman Baba], which he prevailed upon me to write, and keep as a remembrance. He took a copy from me of some Hindi verses, which were full of love, and told me, when I returned back to my native city, I must remember to write him a letter.[29]

The recitation of poetry in several languages facilitated a smooth passage for our author, allowing a familiarity with local males who would otherwise have regarded him as an outsider.

A similar incident took place later in the trip, when in Mashhad he was drawn to a boy of sixteen or seventeen years of age named Haidur Ali, in the service of the Qajar Prince 'Abbas Mirza:

> His countenance was graceful, and his elevated eyebrows over his heavy eyelashes looked very singular and charming. His white cheeks and ruby lips shewed the delicacy of all his limbs. His curled locks, behind his ears, hung on a marble neck, and his eyes were azure. I have never seen a boy of such beautiful appearance and elegant manners. When he took leave of me, he said he hoped that we should meet again. We rose up and kissed each other, according to the custom of Persia. I praised his locks, which hung like black snakes on his white face; he laughed and repeated the following verse: "The lock

29. *Travels*, 48–49.

of the Persian and the waist of the Indian are curling."[30]

To anyone familiar with the conventions of classical Persian literature and the world of the literary *mahfil* (gathering), these exchanges would seem to be trite and almost scripted in following the ritual of establishing intimacy and friendship between two people. Mohan Lal seemed to dwell comfortably in the ideal romantic world of the lover and beloved of the *ghazal* world, where the cult of the beardless youth was a staple feature of courtly love.[31] But such Persianate values could sometimes clash with those being inculcated by his newly acquired training in English in the service of the British Empire.

About a month after his encounter with the Iranian youth Haidur Ali in Mashhad, Mohan Lal was in Herat, hosted by a chieftain Sardar Din Mohammad Khan. During his sojourn the host "told me to examine a youth, twenty years of age, who had represented himself as an English scholar. The youth, whose name was Sarkhush, was found to be a liar and deceiver, from the very first question put to him." Although Sarkhush had the right characteristics worthy of a young Persian beloved, he failed in other ways:

> He possessed a fund of Persian knowledge, and was the author of some poetry. He has several very singular habits; for instance, whenever he talks, he puts his little finger sometimes on his lips, and sometimes on his chin. When he speaks, he raises and again lowers the eyelids of his beautiful dark eyes; after that, he closes them suddenly. He asked me to take him to India, and recommend him to some gentleman for a good situation. I answered him, "If you are a good Persian writer, you will get a good situation; otherwise, all these [*sic*] your effeminate actions, instead of gaining the favor of gentlemen, will cause them to dislike you.[32]

It would seem that Mohan Lal's revulsion to the young man's unmanly behavior was brought on by the latter's violation of the norms of courtly conduct (*adab*) and ethics (*akhlaq*) when he lied about his language proficiency in English. In the end, he did not measure up to either Persianate or British standards. These experiences were an important part of Mohan Lal's travel experiences and he did not excise them from the second edition of his travel book, when he sought to reinvent himself as a worldly individual who had received an English education.

In addition to the admiration of beautiful women and young boys, an-

---

30. *Travels*, 195.

31. I discuss the figure of the beardless youth in the context of Persianate travel writing by women in my article, Sharma 2013, 119–31.

32. *Travels*, 213–14.

other prominent feature of classical Persian literary texts that Mohan Lal also favored was the rhapsodic description of places, chiefly the topography and architecture of cities. While in Kabul at the tomb of the Mughal emperor Babur (r. 1526–30) who had taken the kingdom of Delhi, Mohan Lal is transported by the beauty of the garden housing the emperor's tomb, Bagh-e Vafa. He writes that he was "meditating whether I was dreaming of paradise, or had come into an unknown region."[33] Burnes, for his part, was also enthralled by the place: "I have a profound respect for the memory of Baber, which had been increased by a late perusal of his most interesting Commentaries."[34] After quoting from the emperor's memoirs and offering a brief description of the place he declares, "I do not wonder at the hearts of the people being captivated with the landscape, and of Baber's admiration; for, in his own words, 'its verdure and flowers render Cabool, in spring, a heaven.'"[35] Mohan Lal also mentions the memoirs of Babur. "We are highly indebted to the English translation of 'Babar's Memoirs,' which gives us valuable intelligence of the whole country of Kabul."[36] Thus, although Mohan Lal could have read the Chaghatai Turkish text *Tuzuk-e Baburi* in its sixteenth-century Persian translation, like his British companions he knew it as a guidebook through its recent English translation.[37] In his first travelogue he provides the Persian text of two inscriptions: one in a marble mosque built in the time of Shah Jahan located in the same garden complex, and one on Babar's tomb itself.[38] He left these out in his second travelogue, as he did with all such inscriptions and Persian verses, presumably hoping to reach a wider and more general audience for the London edition. Combining his new knowledge with the conventions of traditional romance, he goes on to give a brief account of Kabul's history as the ancient Bactria, along with the mythical connection of Farhad, the legendary Persian character from the love story of Khusrau and Shirin, to the place.

Mohan Lal did not usually provide details about the physical journey it-

33. *Travels*, 74. In the 1834 edition, the language is slightly different: "stood without motion, meditating whether I was dreaming of paradise, or roving into an unknown region," *Journal of a Tour*, 65.

34. *Travels into Bokhara*, 1:141.

35. *Travels into Bokhara*, 1:143.

36. *Travels*, 75. The forms Baber and Babar are both common in South Asia. I use Babur when I am not quoting the two travelers.

37. *Memoirs of Zehir-Ed-Din Muhammed Baber, emperor of Hindustan, written by himself, in the Jaghatai Turki, and tr., partly by the late John Leyden, partly by William Erskine, with notes and geographical and historical introduction; together with a map of the countries between the Oxus and Jaxartes, and a memoir regarding its construction, by Charles Waddington, of the East India company's engineers* (London: Longman, Rees, Orme, Brown, and Green, 1826).

38. *Journal of a Tour*, 65–66.

self or reflect on what travel meant to him. In contrast, Burnes occasionally allowed the reader to share the experience, as when he writes,

> Since leaving Cabool, we had slept in our clothes, and could seldom or ever change them. We had halted among mud, waded through rivers, tumbled among snow, and for the last few days been sunned by heat. These are but the petty inconveniences of a traveler; which sink into insignificance, when compared with the pleasure of seeing new men and countries, strange manners and customs, and being able to temper the prejudices of one's country, by observing those of other nations.[39]

One place where Mohan Lal does provide a realistic description of the experience of travel is when he undertook a sea journey to Europe almost a decade later. Having boarded the *Semiramis* on July 19, 1843 in Bombay, he was elated by his first experience on a ship. But it was the monsoon season and the weather being very rough he wrote, "I thought we were all, myself and my fellow-passengers, going to a watery grave." After a week at sea, the vessel's engine broke and they had to return to shore.[40] The second attempt was more successful but less memorable in terms of such details.

The European section of Mohan Lal's travels was included in the second edition of the travelogue. In this part of the world, he ostensibly did not need to resort to play-acting and disguises. In Europe he was simply the exotic Indian or Kashmiri who had mastered the Persian and English languages. In his early years, he had delineated the hierarchy of civilizations in his travel book: "the Persians are next to the Indians in every thing, and above other nations, except Europeans."[41] The English he found were not only powerful and more advanced than the Persians and Indians in modernization, they were not inferior when it came to all the important qualities he cherished in a civilization: "The manners, customs, life, and modes of society in England are of an elegant and refined style. No country takes such pains in cultivating knowledge, and no parents are so desirous of rendering their children accomplished, by expense and anxious care as those of Britain."[42] In this way, superimposing the structure of one empire over another, he found that they were not all that different. The short European portion of the second edition of his travel book bears comparison to the more detailed early accounts by travelers to the West such as Mirza Itisamuddin and Abu Talib Khan who

---

39. *Travels into Bokhara*, 206.
40. *Travels*, 486.
41. *Travels*, 194.
42. *Travels*, 517.

wrote their accounts in Persian, and Yusuf Khan Kambalposh, who was the
first to write a travel book in Urdu. Mohan Lal's style shares the Persianate
features discussed above with them, but there is something new in his work
as well. A marked shift in the abandonment of this style can be seen a couple
of decades later in an English autobiography by another *munshi* Lutfullah
Khan (b. 1802). Published in 1857, this book also includes a small section on
travel to England at exactly the same time as Mohan Lal.[43] Lutfullah's remarks as a young man on his proficiency in English and physical appearance
are reminiscent of Mohan Lal too:

> I could read and write in the language well enough, and spoke it so
> well that some of my English friends often jestingly interrogated me
> whether both of my parents were natives of India, or one of them
> English, for my complexion and accent, said they, were different from
> the natives. I thanked them with a smile, and said their compliments
> were more than I deserved.[44]

Lutfullah, however, did not seem to have performed his identities in the
same way as Mohan Lal.

Mohan Lal's representation of himself was part of the negotiation of
various identities in the milieu of the peculiar social and historical mosaic
of early nineteenth-century India, where the Mughal dynasty and courtly
culture were witnessing their twilight and the colonial project was already
underway in a large part of the subcontinent. While attention is rightly
focused on his position as one of the earliest among anglicized Indians, a
circumstance that allowed him easily to cross social boundaries and find
a new role for himself in the Great Game of the nineteenth century, his
Persian-language skills and Persianate cultural orientation were equally important factors in his self-redefinition. Persian was still a relevant language
in nineteenth-century India and it was Mohan Lal's knowledge of classical
Persian poetry (*sha'iri*) and courtly conduct (*adab*) that allowed him to cross
the frontier between India and the larger Persian world to its northwest,
rather than just his knowledge of English, as claimed by his mentor, Charles
Trevelyan, who triumphantly declared in the preface to his protégé's book:

> In the person of Mohan Lal we proved to the Mohammedan nations
> beyond the Indus our qualification for the great mission with which
> we have been intrusted, of regenerating India. We convinced them

43. This work has been most recently reprinted as *Seamless Boundaries: Lutfullah's Narrative
beyond East and West*.

44. Lutfullah 2007, 120.

that we are capable of producing a moral change infinitely more
honourable to us than any victory we have achieved.[45]

It is no surprise that Mohan Lal was received cordially by rulers such as Ma-
haraja Ranjit Singh in Lahore, Amir Dost Muhammad in Kabul, the Qajar
crown prince 'Abbas Mirza in Mashhad, Queen Victoria in London, and Kai-
ser Wilhelm Friedrich IV in Berlin, as well as by a host of other people from
disparate backgrounds. All this attention doubtless complicated his sense of
his own importance, but in the end, although he comfortably donned different masks, he was disillusioned as a long-cherished courtly way of life with
Persian as the lingua franca faded into the annals of history before his eyes.

Mohan Lal played a central role in the so-called First Anglo-Afghan War
of 1838–41 after which his more successful work, a voluminous biography of
Amir Dost Muhammad Khan (d. 1863), *Life of the Amir Dost Mohammed Khan
of Kabul* (London: Longman, 1846), was written. In contrast to this work's
newfound importance, his travelogue is hardly looked at now. The details of
his later life have not been properly recorded. Apparently he became disillusioned with the way he was treated by the British and retired at the early
age of thirty-four. According to his biographer, "he was swept away by the
love of wine and women. He could not devote himself to a pursuit, whether
politics or pleasure, half-heartedly; it possessed him entirely."[46] Sir Alexander Burnes met a more gruesome end during the Afghan war. While serving
in Kabul as Resident, in 1841 he was hacked to pieces during the political
turmoil. Mohan Lal was there with him but was able to hide out and save
himself, no doubt due to his ability to adapt to different cultural contexts.
Although Mohan Lal would never achieve the fame and notoriety that a traveler such as the adventurous Sir Richard Burton did, his disguises allowed
him to explore different worlds and also gave him the confidence to publish
his travelogue for a wider audience. Traveling at a very young age had a
profound effect on his self-fashioning and confidence. In the places that he
visited in the Persianate world, especially those that had a link to the Perso-
Islamic or Mughal past, he was an explorer; but he was also a traveler, to
quote James Buzard "roaming free of imposed borders and limitations" who
"veer[ed] into those fertile fields for the imagination which lie to one side or
the other of the tourist's [or explorer's] usual path, there to discover secret
significances and unsuspected spurs to deep feeling – cultural treasures"[47]
such as Mughal gardens and tombs, Timurid mosques and palaces. Unlike

45. *Travels*, xiv.
46. Gupta 1943, 334.
47. Buzard 1993, 35.

Burton for whom "the [British] empire was founded on nothing but naked power,"[48] for Mohan Lal it was the proper successor to the pluralistic and syncretic culture fostered by the Mughals, and did not impose a single identity on its subjects.

Although Persian was fast losing ground to Urdu and English, in Mohan Lal's time it was still an essential component of the repertoire of skills that administrators and their assistants had to offer prospective employers.[49] More than just Persian now, it was the Persianate cultural orientation found in Urdu and Hindustani that allowed people of various classes to interact with each other. Mohan Lal's travel book, as an early example of a genre that is situated between multiple traditions, can be appreciated and understood as a Persianate work in English, and the author's representation of himself is part of the negotiation of various identities in the milieu of the peculiar social and historical mosaic of early nineteenth-century India. He deliberately sought ambiguity in terms of his own identity and social relationships, often approximating the role of the poet-lover in the Persianate *ghazal*, which allowed him to view and record the world around him in a lyrical mode, drawing on the distinctive features of several literary and cultural traditions. But in the end, he was betrayed by all of them and English as a replacement for Persian as the official language did not fulfil the potential it had held earlier. Similar to Halide Edib, the Turkish writer whose life a century later was enmeshed in a sea of political upheavals and who forms the subject of Roberta Micallef's essay in this volume, Mohan Lal drew on his knowledge of the Persianate past to make sense of a changing world. In his encounters with historical places and eventual disillusionment, he is also like the protagonist of Polidori's novel analyzed in James Uden's essay, in that ultimately he is unable to reconcile the past with the present. But while it lasted, Mohan Lal was an imaginative and lively travel writer, who reveled in the attention and fame that travel brought him.

48. Ghose 2006, 80.
49. Fisher 2012, 328–58.

Bibliography

Bayly, Chris. 1996. *Empire and Information: Intelligence Gathering and Social Communication in India, 1780-1870.* Cambridge: Cambridge University Press.

Burnes, Alexander. 1834. *Travels into Bokhara, Being an account of a Journey from India to Cabool, Tartary and Persia.* 3 vols. London: John Murray.

Buzard, James. 1993. *The Beaten Track: European Tourism, Literature, and the Ways to Culture, 1800-1918.* Oxford: Oxford University Press.

Fisher, Michael H. 2006. "Mohan Lal Kashmiri (1812-77): An Initial Student of Delhi English College." In *The Delhi College, Traditional Elites, the Colonial State, and Education before 1857,* edited by Margrit Pernau. New Delhi: Oxford University Press.

———. 2012. "Teaching Persian as an Imperial Language in India and in England during the Late 18th and Early 19th Centuries." In *Literacy in the Persianate World: Writing and the Social Order,* edited by Brian Spooner and William H. Hanaway. Philadelphia: University of Pennsylvania Museum of Archaeology and Anthropology.

Ghose, Indira. 2006. "Imperial Player: Richard Burton in Sindh." In *Travel Writing in the Nineteenth Century: Filling the Blank Spaces,* edited by Tim Youngs, 71–86. London: Anthem.

Gupta, Hari Ram. 1943. *Life and Work of Mohan Lal Kashmiri, 1812-177.* Lahore: Minerva Book Shop.

Lutfullah Khan. 2007. *Seamless Boundaries: Lutfullah's Narrative beyond East and West.* Edited, annotated, and with an introduction by Mushirul Hasan. New Delhi: Oxford University Press.

Majchrowicz, Daniel. 2015. "Travel, Travel Writing and the 'Means to Victory' in Modern South Asia." Unpublished PhD dissertation. Harvard University.

Mohan Lal Kashmiri. 1834. *Journal of a Tour through the Panjab, Afghanistan, Turkistan, Khorasan, and Part of Persia, in Company with Lieut. Burnes and Dr. Gerard.* Calcutta: Baptist Mission Press.

———. 1846. *Travels in the Panjab, Afghanistan & Turkistan to Balk [sic], Bokhara and Herat, and a Visit to Great Britain and Germany.* London: W. H. Allen.

Pratt, Mary Louise. 1992. *Imperial Eyes: Travel Writing and Transculturation.* 2nd ed. London: Routledge.

Sharma, Sunil. 2013. "Delight and Disgust: Gendered Encounters in the Travelogues of the Fyzee Sisters." In *On the Wonders of Land and Sea: Persianate Travel Writing,* edited by Roberta Micallef and Sunil Sharma, 119–31. Boston: Ilex.

Fellow Travelers? Two Arab Study
Abroad Narratives of Moscow

Margaret Litvin

T
HIS ESSAY CONSIDERS "study abroad" as a variety of travel and asks in what ways the literary narrative of study abroad (whether memoir or fiction) can both fit into the academic category of travel literature and help interrogate its usefulness. After analyzing two characteristic vignettes from Sonallah Ibrahim's *Ice*, an Egyptian study abroad novel set in 1970s Moscow, I zoom out to survey the historical circumstances and literary fruits of Arab students' experiences in the USSR and introduce the Arabic *riḥla* genre and a few other relevant intertexts and discursive patterns. I then zoom back in to examine two literary traces of one particular experience: Ibrahim's cohabitation and artistic collaboration with Syrian film director Mohamad Malas while both were filmmaking students.

This essay joins other recent work in both Arabic literature and travel studies, highlighting first the centrality of travel writing genres (collectively, *adab al-riḥla*) in different periods of premodern and modern Arabic literature, and secondly the relevance of Arabic texts to the still largely anglophone field of travel writing studies. One upshot of my exploration is that the "study abroad novel," a type of Arab travel writing but also an attractive form of bildungsroman in other languages, emerges as a distinct literary subgenre and valid object of comparative study, not only on ethnographic but also on formal grounds. (In a purely American context, Merve Emre has defined the study abroad novel as "a popular subgenre of young adult chick lit that features the American girl on a cosmopolitan courtship quest in the Old World."[1] Otherwise, the category of "study abroad novel" as such appears not to have been studied, either as a form of travel writing or a subgenre of bildungsroman.)

A more specific observation concerns the particular figures of Sonallah Ibrahim (b. 1937) and Mohamad Malas (b. 1945) and will be interesting to test on other Arab travelers in Russia: while duly noting the shoddiness of the would-be Communist utopia around them, these two artists seem to spend much of their energy unpacking their own historical baggage. They

---

1. Emre 2013. See also Emre's fascinating "Jamesian Institutions."

share this preoccupation with many if not most travel writers – Peter Hulme rightly notes that "as the earth's wildernesses get paved over, travel writing increasingly emphasizes the inner journey, often merging imperceptibly into memoir"[2] – but in the Soviet political context this takes a particular form. Searching for meaning against the USSR's hollow "friendship of nations" ideology and in the wake of the painfully annulled political union between their two countries, Ibrahim and Malas find each other: an Egyptian novelist and a Syrian film director; two artists as young men. Together they explore a global kaleidoscope of literature and film, mourn their countries' joint past, and struggle to develop a new creative idiom for their respective media. Their friendship is a made-in-the-USSR product, albeit one not determined and perhaps not intended by Soviet policy. Yet they come to Moscow as different personalities whose study abroad narratives take quite different forms, marking different responses to their respective sojourns.

1.

To open up the question about extended study abroad and its possible relationship to the type of "travel" that interests scholars of travel writing, I will start by unpacking two entire short chapters of Sonallah Ibrahim's novel *al-Jalīd* (Ice): the opening chapter, which sets the multicultural dormitory scene, and a chapter describing a spring tourist excursion about midway through the novel.[3]

Ibrahim, one of Egypt's best known living writers, has had a provocative career as the author of a dozen novels including *Tilka al-Rā'iḥa* (1966, trans. as *The Smell of It,* 1971, and *That Smell and Notes from Prison,* 2013); *Najmat Aghusṭus (August Star,* 1974); *al-Lajna (The Committee,* 1981, trans. 2001); and *Dhāt (Self,* 1992, trans. 2001). Unlike most other professional fiction writers in Egypt, he has remained outside the state cultural bureaucracy, never holding a government job or position; in 2003 he spectacularly rejected Egypt's Arab Novel Prize. His best books satirize the vulgarity of Egypt's authoritarian systems and neoliberal consumerist aspirations.

His novel *Ice,* written in 2010 and published in 2011, chronicles a calendar year (1973) in the life of an Egyptian writer/historian pursuing non-degree graduate studies in Moscow. The characters rarely go to class. Instead, the novel gives readers a guided tour of some of the stagnation and sordidness of Brezhnev-era Soviet life: intra-Soviet ethnic tensions; Russian retirees unable to afford a tin of meat; threesomes of drunks splitting bottles of vodka

2. Hulme 2002.
3. Ibrāhīm 2011. My translations. Page references will hereafter be given in the text. The novel's protagonist, Dr. Shukri, recurs in Ibrahim's novels *Amrīkānlī* and *al-Qānūn al-Firansī.*

on the sidewalk; a Kirgiz roommate who brings his Russian girlfriend to live in his four-person dormitory room; pregnant Russian women trying to get abortions; black-marketeering Arab embassy officials; and Arab students' debates about the geographically distant October 1973 War. The Egyptian narrator, Dr. Shukri, records all this in a numbly factual style, punctuating it with the only redeeming sources of beauty available: classical music LPs (Tchaikovsky, Rachmaninoff, Khachaturian), newly acquired Russian vocabulary words, a few achingly beautiful blondes (short skirts, long legs), and strong Georgian tea.

The novel strikes a self-consciously ethnographic tone, presenting a kind of grim tourist guidebook to Soviet life. Russian words occur throughout the novel, transliterated into Arabic and often explained in parentheses or stealth glosses.[4] A particularly frequent word is *obshchezhitie* (dormitory) the setting for most of the novel's events. As we will see, this word – domesticated with the Arabic definite article: الأبشجيتي – closes the novel.[5] Even before the grand anticlimax of that closing, the *obshchezhitie* frames and limits the action, providing the stage for the interaction of the novel's diverse characters, who are often introduced by ethnicity or nationality.

The guidebook effect is strengthened by the book's use of a recent middlebrow typographic convention invented in response to Arabic's lack of capitalization: many transliterated words in *Ice* (and even most of the proper names) are boldfaced for easy reading. Thus when in the opening paragraph the *obshchezhitie's komendantsha* (the supervisor) wants to stick our hero with a fourth roommate and he successfully fends her off, she says,

تفاريش (رفيق) شكري. لادنا (حسناً) ستبقون ثلاثة كما أنتم.

Tovarish (comrade) **Shukri, ladno** (all right), you can remain three.[6]
(7)

When later on the page Shukri's Central Asian roommate speaks up, we are told of both his ethnic appearance and his non-Russian Soviet origin:

4. Some contain small errors, as does the word "Ice," decoratively printed in Russian (in the genitive case) on the novel's cover. Arriving in his 30s and already speaking English, Ibrahim (by his own description) never attained fluency in Russian. Rather than re-transliterate the Russian words in this article through the Arabic, I have followed the Library of Congress system.

5. The word is a compound of *obshche-,* shared or public, and *zhit',* living. Roughly equivalent to the Arabic phrase *bayt al-ṭullāb,* which Ibrahim does not use, this word features the exotically non-Arabic consonants "shch" and "zh." Cairene readers would tend to pronounce his transliteration as "el-obshegiti," with the *g* either soft like *j* (as in literary Arabic) or hard (as in Egyptian colloquial).

6. The Russian words appear in Russian; the parenthetical translations "comrade" and "all right" are given in Arabic.

When she was gone, **Mario** the Brazilian straightened the 1973 wall
calendar near the door. He was slim, about my height, with narrow
nervous eyes, wearing an embroidered wool shirt and jeans. He said,
twisting the earring in his ear: They want to put a Russian student
in with the foreigners so he can report on them. Our roommate
Jalaleddinov, tall with Asian features, from the republic of **Kirgizia**,
one of the republics of the **Soviet Union**, spoke up as though to
deflect suspicion from himself: Well. There's nothing worth reporting.

After this discussion the narrator goes shopping, an attempted sightseeing
experience that quickly hits a dead end. After some minutia about queues,
trivial purchases, and the like, the chapter closes:

My nose began to run; I pulled the flaps of my *shapka* down over
my ears and put on my gloves. I walked carefully on the snow. The
glass front of the *magazin* (shop) was piled, like all the stores, with
pyramids of evaporated milk cans and nothing else. (8)

After buying bread, kefir, and cigarettes, he returns and revives himself
with a cup of "good *grūzīni* (Georgian) tea, the adjective for the **Georgian**
Soviet Republic."[7] (10) And so on. Clearly, Ibrahim does not expect his Egyptian reader to know much about Soviet daily life, geography, or even history.
(And perhaps rightly so: in 2010, the median Egyptian was 24 years old, so
had entered kindergarten after the collapse of the USSR.[8])

A vignette that forms an entire short chapter later in the book, describing
a visit to a bona fide tourist attraction, ironically takes a less guidebook-
like tone. In May of his Moscow year (Chapter 38 of 126), Shukri and his
East German friend Hans take a short walk from their dormitory to one of
Moscow's polemically modernist tourist sites, the "Exhibition of Achievements of the National Economy of the Soviet Union," or VDNKh. Foreigners
residing in Moscow would find this a logical and approved place to go. As
geographers Benjamin Forest and Juliet Johnson have pointed out, VDNKh
was "the most important public showplace for Soviet economic ideology,"
its emphasis shifting after Stalin's death (1951) from celebrating the USSR as
multi-ethnic success story – literally, a union of socialist republics – to showcasing Soviet technological and economic advances, most spectacularly the
space program. As Forest and Johnson put it, ending with a quotation from
Soviet scientist S.B. Il'in:

When the exhibition first became permanent, its pavilions honored
the economic accomplishments of individual Soviet republics, with

7. A Russian speaker would say *gruzinskii*.
8. Roudi 2011, 4.

the golden "Fountain of the Friendship of Peoples" as its centerpiece. Under Khrushchev, the focus shifted from individual republics (which lost their pavilions completely) to economic sectors such as metallurgy, medicine, coal mining, and transportation. In its final form, this vast theme park dedicated to the glorification of the command economy included seventy-two exhibition pavilions, from the Atomic Energy Pavilion to the Pavilion of Large Horned Livestock. Located on 238 hectares on the far northeast side of Moscow, the park attracted thousands of visitors to its economic exhibitions each year. According to one of its Soviet hagiographers, "VDNKh is the Soviet Union in miniature."[9]

But Ibrahim's two protagonists are not there to explore the wonders of Soviet technological achievement. Their tour does not reproduce what Mary Louise Pratt has called the "monarch-of-all-I-survey scene" beloved of male European travel writers.[10] Instead Chapter 38 begins, in the novel's characteristic antiliterary style:

The papers carried the news that the Lebanese Army was wiping out the Palestinian guerrillas in Lebanon. Hans returned from Germany. We went together to the nearby "Exhibition of Achievements of the National Economy of the Soviet Union." Light rain. We walked in past the giant steel statue of a young man holding a hammer and a young woman with a sickle holding hands and striding boldly toward the dawning future. Across from it was the big steel replica of the spaceship Vostok (East) in which Gagarin had flown into space; one of its sides had a painting of several scientists and engineers loading him into the capsule, and the other had Lenin leading the masses into space. We walked through the nuclear energy wing, and the wings devoted to the coal industry, biology, education, physics, trade unions, electrical technology, and agriculture. He said East Germany looked a lot like Russia, but people were more disciplined. (83)

Earlier in the novel, Soviet technology dramatizes the narrator's loss of faith in the Communist utopia: "I shaved with the rough Soviet razor, wondering at the Soviets: They build rockets but can't manage or won't bother to build a decent razor blade." (11) But here such paradoxes are just scenery. The chapter's opening sentence tells us what is really on the narrator's mind: not the successes of Soviet science and industry but the failures of Arab nationalism and, in this case, of its post-1967 bright spot, the armed

9. Forest and Johnson 2002.
10. Pratt 1992, 201–27.

Palestinian liberation movement. Hans, meanwhile, feels homesick for his native East Germany. The various pavilions are enumerated in a desultory orderless list, the narrator's deadpan observation exposing their falsehood but worse, their irrelevance.

Quickly it becomes clear what our two heroes are really doing at VDNKh: meeting women. Through this behavior they are also displacing the evident sexual tension between them and seeking distraction from a love triangle that implicates them both. *Ice* portrays Hans as a successful but very unhappy pickup artist, irresistible to women but apparently more attracted to men. (Implied throughout, this interpretation is graphically confirmed in the novel's closing pages.) Frequently we see Hans escape an awkward social situation by picking up a woman – with whom, however, he is always disappointed. He seems drawn to the narrator Shukri, who for his part is deeply and fruitlessly attracted to their Russian friend Zoya, who in turn (although married to someone else) is in love with Hans. These emotional crossed wires provide the subtext for the Freudian and cosmonautic explorations that follow:

> I asked him about his family; he said his mother was unhappy with the doctor she had married after his father had disappeared in the war, a bad man who had been cruel to him, so he had moved out and left them to themselves. I told him about my mother, who was paralyzed. We were coming up to the mock space capsules that hold two people, taking them up in the air and shaking them. Hans suggested we try one. I said no. He bought two tickets. We noticed a tall girl in a coat and black pants sitting on a bench. She had wide blue eyes and a long face framed by straight black hair, and a full sensuous mouth. He said to her, holding up the tickets: Come with me. She blushed and said she had been up already. He went up to her, sat down next to her, and bummed a cigarette. People passing or sitting nearby were looking at us. I sat on another chair near two girls. I offered them the two tickets to go up, but they said they were scared. Then they laughed shyly. One of them asked me where we were from. All the time they were looking at Hans. He went up in the ride with the girl. They spun in the air, shrieking and laughing. Then they came down. She held his arm. Then she let go of his arm and walked beside him. (83-84)

The amusement park-style ride that "hold[s] two people, taking them up in the air and shaking them," is built to sexualize Gagarin's ride for private consumption, promoting a bodily identification with the Soviet space program. But Hans and the narrator go further: indifferent to Gagarin, they "notice" (apparently simultaneously) only the woman on the bench. Meanwhile the foreign visitors (one Egyptian, the other German and strikingly handsome) themselves become objects of the Soviet exhibition-goers' curiosity, like tourist attractions: "People passing or sitting nearby were looking at us"; "One of them asked me where we were from."

The chapter's closing lines conclude the tourist adventure. In sentences so flat that they become somewhat hard to follow, the narrator experiences another amusement ride (his unpaid admission hardly signaling a well-ordered economy), then leaves VDNKh (another ride, this time by bus) to return to the private apartment where, fleeing the crowded dormitory, he has rented a room from an impoverished retiree. Meanwhile Hans and his new conquest continue to somewhere else, presumably the dormitory. The headache that then assails the backside (*mu'ākhira*) of the narrator's neck suggests, by implication, that Hans will not have a wonderful night either:

> We went to the ride with rectangular capsules that spin fast and gradually rise. We wanted to buy tickets but found the window closed. One of the workers told us that the ride was still open for another hour, but the ticket seller's shift had ended. They took us without tickets. We went up in the box and lay down on our backs looking at the sky. When we came down, she put her hand on Hans' arm. We got on a bus, and she sat next to someone. He asked her about me. She told him I was an Arab. Hans whispered: She knew that from your accent without my telling her, she must have some experience; she works in a store, and she's married. I left them by my house. A terrible headache battered me all night long. I watched it hit my eye, then move upwards, then hit the backside of my neck. I woke up the old woman and she gave me a painkiller. (84)

This brief chapter (in Arabic it is a single long paragraph) manifests many of the thematic and stylistic features that study abroad novels share with other kinds of travel writing: making-strange of local political slogans and cultural formations ("striding boldly toward the dawning future," "leading the masses into space"); an emphasis on identities and interlingual encounters (the attention to foreign accents); and characters who experience a familiar set of emotions associated with travel: intercultural bemusement or bewilderment, sexual loneliness, a sense of time both accounted for and oddly idle, and the peculiar intensity of friendships with fellow internationals that can grow among strangers in a strange land. Ibrahim's flat style eschews the "monarch-of-all-I-survey" pose and the other authorizing strategies of the travel writer. Instead it presents a sequence of events without logical subordination or analysis or even personal reaction, thus reducing the narrator to a pair of eyes, or more accurately, to a camera recording impressions to be developed later. (Before going abroad, he had used the same device "at home" to create the numbly post-traumatic tone of *That Smell.*) Rejecting any claim to understand the people or events described, Ibrahim's narration foregrounds the traveler's sense of estrangement, indifference, and resulting anticlimax: in this chapter the only human connection that really works is the landlady's headache powder.

2.

Sonallah Ibrahim's *Ice* is based on the novelist's own experience studying in Moscow from 1971 to 1973. This experience forms part of a largely overlooked chapter of Cold War history: the thousands of students from several Arab countries (avowedly leftist Iraq, Syria, Egypt, Algeria, Palestine, but also Lebanon, Morocco, Libya, Bahrain, and others) who studied abroad in the USSR and elsewhere in the Eastern bloc.[11] My own research concerns Arab students who went to the Soviet Union, particularly to Russia, and most especially to Moscow, the "Red Mecca" of international Communist fantasy.[12]

The Arab students got to Russia in different ways. Some applied for scholarships offered directly through their governments, or by international groups like the Cairo-based Afro-Asian People's Solidarity Organization; others, like the Iraqis, were recommended through contacts in their local Communist parties. Some flew; others arrived by boat across the Mediterranean.[13] These men and women lived in dormitories or apartments, made friends, took part in official meetings and graduate courses and love affairs. The great majority were in technical fields such as pharmacy or engineering, but they included artists and intellectuals as well.

11. For statistics and analysis, see Katsakioris 2016.

12. For the term "Red Mecca," coined in the interwar period and most commonly used in reference to African diaspora travelers, see, for example, McClellan 2006; Ravandi-Fadai 2015; Pantsov and Levine 2013, 181.

13. For instance, Egyptian retired refrigeration engineer Zakariya Turki, who studied in Kiev and Astrakhan between 1967 and 1972, made the journey from Alexandria via Athens and Istanbul to Odessa "aboard the Russian ship Latvia." His memoir (Turkī 1999) depicts his process of cultural discovery beginning on the boat, where the Arab students are fed "a greasy Russian meal" while the radio plays an exploration-themed song called "Marco Polo," which "the sailors especially liked" (it must have been by Italian-inspired Yugoslav pop star Đorđe Marjanović; see http://sonichits.com/video/Djordje_Marjanovic/Marko_Polo). Turki notices that the ship is sparkling clean and watches the captain and cleaning women take part in the nightly shipboard dance party. In Athens he buys "American apples," his second contact with superpower hygiene (Turkī 1999, 8–9).

The earliest wave of Arab students in the USSR studied at the Communist University of the Toilers of the East (KUTV, operating 1921–38), an institute specially established shortly after the Soviet Union's founding to train revolutionary cadres for "eastern" societies, both domestic (Soviet Central Asia) and foreign (Asia and the Middle East).[14] KUTV was closed in 1938. Later waves of Arab students, arriving during the renewed Bandung-inspired internationalism of Khrushchev's post-Stalin "thaw" or during the Brezhnev-era "time of stagnation," took several paths. Many enrolled at the again specially established People's Friendship University (PFU), founded in 1961 to demonstrate the Soviet commitment to helping advance Third World societies. As Djagalov and Evans have argued, PFU's opening in effect presented Moscow as a replacement for the old imperial metropoles, London and Paris, and tacitly compared the vast new global "periphery" to Russia's own former imperial territories, particularly in Central Asia. That is, as its name suggested, PFU would extend the governing metaphor of the Soviet nationalities policy – "friendship of the peoples" – to the nations of the Third World.[15]

About 5000 Arab students have graduated from PFU since its founding. In total, there are about 200,000 alumni of Soviet and Russian universities and institutes in the Middle East and North Africa, excluding Russian immigrants to Israel.[16] Many attended ordinary Soviet universities (Moscow State University and others), and still others went to technical institutes ranging from schools of industrial engineering to the Gorky Institute of World Literature (founded 1932), the State Institute for Theatre Arts (GITIS, founded in 1878 as the Russian Academy of Theatre Arts and later named after Anatoly Lunacharsky), and the already mentioned film institute, VGIK.

These experiences have left abundant literary traces. The KUTV students wrote autobiographies shortly after arrival for their Communist Party hosts – some are still preserved in Russian archives. Students of every generation published memoirs, whether immediately upon return to their countries or decades later.[17] Arab poets set verses amid the Russian snow. In the 1990s, Arab magazines published lavishly illustrated travel essays about

14. For the fluid distinction between the two, see Kirasirova 2017.

15. For a time PFU was renamed after assassinated Congolese leader Patrice Lumumba; it exists even today. See Djagalov and Evans 1960. I am grateful to Rossen Djagalov for sharing the English draft version of this useful essay, from which I quote here.

16. Savicheva 2010, 16–17.

17. The memoirs of the first Palestinian Arab student at KUTV, Communist and later literary translator Najati Sidqi, were published in Arabic many decades later and have been studied in English only recently. See Tamari 2003 and Tamari 2009.

newly liberated post-Soviet domains.[18] Writers who simply visited the USSR, without studying there, wrote travelogues. And a few novels, including Iraqi exile Gha'ib Tu'ma Farman's *al-Murtajā wa al-Mu'ajjal* and Ibrahim's *Ice*, build on personal Moscow experiences to thematize the travails of a disillusioned Arab nationalist generation against the background of Soviet life. All these works have joined a rich tradition of Arabic study abroad literature, itself an important subgenre of Arabic travel literature, or *adab al-riḥla*.

Travel writing has been an important genre of Arabic prose for over a millennium. It has bequeathed to Arabic and world literature some prominent models both fictional (Sindbad the Sailor) and autobiographical (Ibn Battuta), inspiring a vibrant literary tradition into which writers still inscribe themselves today. Theoretical reasons as well as language barriers explain why this body of work has only recently come to the attention of scholars of travel writing. The great bulk of Arab travel has not followed the contours of European empire; the resulting narratives do not conform to prevalent theoretical models about the projection of European selves into non-European spaces. Yet as Nabil Matar's work over the past 15 years has done much to remind us,

> early modern Arab travelers, merchants, envoys, ambassadors, and clergymen journeyed to London and Rome, Cadiz and Malta, Madrid and Moscow.... From the Mashriq and the Maghreb, Muslim and Christian Arabs read about, translated, and wrote from firsthand experience about the world around them. There was curiosity in their travel.... Arab writers [in contrast to their early modern European counterparts] described what they saw, carefully and without projecting unfounded fantasies.... The Arabic travel accounts cannot therefore be approached through the theoretical models with which European accounts have been studied by writers as different as Stephen Greenblatt, Edward Said, and Gayatri Spivak.... Despite being in what Mary Louise Pratt defines as "contact zones," the writers viewed travel as a means of experiencing rather than denouncing that which was culturally and socially different.[19]

As it happens, "the earliest surviving instance of sustained first-person travel narrative in Arabic" chronicles a trip from Baghdad to what is now central Russia: Aḥmad Ibn Faḍlān's colorful tenth-century travelogue of visiting the Volga Bulghars for Abbasid caliph al-Muqtadir, recently re-edited

---

18. For instance, Mohamed Mansi Qandil wrote travelogues of Uzbekistan and Kazakhstan for the Kuwait-based glossy magazine, later incorporating them into his novel *Qamar 'alā Samarqand*. See Qandīl 1996; Qandīl 2009; and Litvin 2011.

19. Matar 2003, xxxii.

and retranslated by James Montgomery as *Mission to the Volga*.[20] While the people Ibn Fadlan met were Viking Rus, not Russians in any recognizable linguistic or ethnic sense and certainly not objects of imperial envy – Ibn Fadlan calls them "the filthiest of all God's creatures," as uncivilized as the "roaming asses" of Quran 74:50[21] – it is interesting to see this geographic region capturing the Arab political and literary imagination so early on.

At its core, Arabic travel writing shares the fundamental rhetorical priority displayed by its Anglophone and Francophone counterparts: to establish the narrator's credibility through observation of foreign peoples and climes. However, this aim is pursued by different strategies; in Arabic (Ibn Fadlan's imperial arrogance notwithstanding), it has most often been achieved *not* by denigrating the locals or showcasing the psychological depth of one's reactions to the new place, but by emphasizing the knowledge gained during the trip. As Roxanne Euben and others have noted, the Arabic travel narrative is intimately connected with what Euben calls a Muslim "ethos" of *riḥla fī ṭalab al-ʿilm*, or "travel in search of knowledge."[22] Starting in twelfth-century North Africa and Muslim Spain, scholars would write a *riḥla* narrative as a kind of curriculum vitae, enumerating the centers of learning they had visited, the scholars at whose feet they had learned, and the religious authority they had thus acquired.[23] In their case this entailed a voyage eastward to the traditional centers of Islamic learning: Baghdad, Damascus, and Jerusalem.

This *riḥla* genre was a natural model for nineteenth-century Arab intellectuals sent abroad in search of secular kinds of knowledge during the *nahḍa* or Arab Enlightenment. Their voyages revived and explicitly alluded to the early modern tradition of "traveling in search of knowledge" – but now headed mostly to points north and west: Paris or London, though also St. Petersburg (an 1840s example survives) and eventually such centers as New York, Moscow, and Berlin.

Optimistically curious at first and later disillusioned, their study abroad travelogues – one could fruitfully compare examples as diverse as Rifaʿa Rafi' al-Tahtawi's 1820s exploration of Paris, Louis 'Awad's 1937–40 mission to Cambridge, Sayyid Qutb's angry exposé of 1950s Greeley, Colorado, and Mohamed Makhzangi's dark impressions of post-Chernobyl Ukraine – have been published and received within the horizon of expectations of the *riḥla*

20. The quotation is from NYU's promotional material. See http://nyupress.org/books/9781479803507.

21. Sīrāfī and Faḍlān 2014, 76. For a film fictionalization of Ibn Fadlan's adventures, see McTiernan and Crichton 1999.

22. Euben 2006, esp. 34–38.

23. On Abū Bakr ibn al-ʿArabī and the medieval *riḥla* tradition see Garden 2015 and Touati 2010.

genre. This genre has imposed its own standard plot and tropes: the collision of languages, the shock of meeting foreign women, confusion over ethical norms, and so on.

Modern Arab study "missions" were secular but never fully desacralized, as Rasheed El-Enany's exploration of the term (in the context of ʿAwad's study abroad memoir) reveals:

> *Ṭālib Baʿtha* translates literally as "mission student," but the roots *ṭalaba* and *baʿatha* are fraught with transcendental connotations in Arabic. A *ṭālib* is not only a student in the commonplace sense of the word, but also a "seeker" of knowledge or truth and the Prophetic tradition which enjoins the faithful "to seek knowledge if even in China" is one of the most quoted in Arabic in educational contexts. On the other hand, the noun *Baʿtha* … means "mission" and the root *baʿatha*, apart from its basic meaning of "sending out," is also the repository for such semantic variety as "resurrection; renaissance; rebirth; revival." Indeed the word *mabʿūth*, a derivative of this root, is used in Arabic to refer to the prophet of Islam as the one sent by God, much in the same way as the more common *rasūl* [Messenger] which is derived from a root with a similar meaning.[24]

The intercultural encounter is gendered and often troped as sexual. Benjamin Smith summarizes:

> A motif employed by many texts is to dispatch an Arab male protagonist to Europe where he meets a female European counterpart. This relationship becomes the prism through which that Arab male learns about the West and its cultural and social mores. The relationship also frequently develops into a sexual relationship where the Arab protagonist experiences liberation from the traditionalism of his society. Variations on this repetitive motif are presented in Tawfīq al-Ḥakīm's *ʿUṣfūr min al-Sharq* (*Bird of the East*, 1938), Yaḥyā Ḥaqqi's *Qindīl Umm Hāshim* (*The Saint's Lamp*, 1944), Suheil Idris's *al-Ḥayy al-Lātīnī* (*The Latin Quarter*, 1953) and al-Ṭayyib Ṣāliḥ's *Mawsim al-Hijra īlā al-Shimāl* (*The Season of Migration to the North*, 1966). Casting the encounter through this particular gender dynamic inverts traditional patriarchal power dynamics, as the female characters become embodiments of the powerful West.[25]

Later Arab variations on the genre self-consciously refer to these ex-

---

24. El-Enany 2006, 77.
25. Smith 2014, 18–19.

pectations even as they frustrate them. Perhaps the most successful and provocative variation is Salih's *Season of Migration*, a study-abroad-gone-wrong novel that systematically exposes the hypocrisies and delusions underlying the genre, from Arab subservience and self-Orientalization to European liberal racism. Other notable variations include study abroad narratives by female authors such as Radwa Ashour, Fadia Faqir, and Somaya Ramadan. Working against a richer genre background than their European or American sisters, such writers use study abroad trips to Europe or America to create "heterogeneous spaces that allow a multiplicity of perspectives to co-exist," thus claiming their voices as politically engaged and often feminist Arab writers.[26]

Arab study abroad narratives set in Moscow should be read in light of this literary tradition. I cannot document this yet, but it seems likely that the *riḥla* genre not only influenced how Arab intellectuals wrote about their study abroad in the USSR but actually shaped the way they experienced it, similar to the way it shaped how Arab writers (here, Louis 'Awad in Paris) encountered Europe:

> Just being in the Latin Quarter is enough to unhinge one. I look
> around me and I see nothing extraordinary – people in hats, streets,
> buildings. But the idea! The idea that I was in the Latin Quarter, where
> all Egypt's men of letters had tramped about made me tremble. O God!
> When would I tramp about in this quarter like Zakī Mubārak, al-Ṣāwī –
> and Tawfīq al-Ḥakīm ... and write as they have?[27]

However, the Soviet study abroad experience was mediated through other intertexts too, notably Arab intellectuals' prior readings in Russian literature. As we will see, they read before they traveled – a readymade source of disillusion. Soviet-subsidized translations of the Russian classics were more affordable in Cairo or Damascus than novels by Arab or European authors, so they were widely read. As I have shown elsewhere, nearly every Arab intellectual who writes or talks about Russia includes somewhere in his or her narrative a personal canon of important Russian writers, usually presented in non-chronological order to signal the depth of the writer's emotional bond with their works.[28]

Another key source of influences was the disorienting diversity of dormitory life. Rooms were shared, with students of different nationalities often living together: a true "contact zone" in Pratt's sense ("the space in which peoples geographically and historically separated come into contact with

---

26. Logan 2012, 2. On Ashour in New York see also Smith 2014, Chapter 3.
27. Quoted in El-Enany 2006, 77.
28. Litvin 2011.

each other and establish ongoing relations, usually involving conditions of coercion, radical inequality, and intractable conflict"), though here with a many-sided rather than binary shape.[29] On the cultural level, the Arab students in the dorms encountered a global kaleidoscope of artistic sources and models. They imbibed not only Russian and Soviet culture (in all its forms, from official to semi-forbidden to bootleg and *samizdat*) but a heady mix of cultures: Eastern European books and films, local and international music, and Western cultural products from Shakespeare to John Ford movies, all seen simultaneously through Arab and Soviet eyes. On the more basic social and political level of everyday life, Arab students faced intense and challenging social contacts, not only with "the locals" but more intimately with other Arab expatriates – in some cases, fellow Arabs with whom they might not have crossed paths otherwise.

3.

On January 25, 1973, a young Sonallah Ibrahim moved into Room 403 of the student dormitory of the All-Soviet (later all-Russian) State Institute of Cinematography, or VGIK, in Moscow. Already living there were Mohamad Malas and his roommates, fellow Syrian filmmaking students Haitham Haqqi and Samir Zikra.

Malas has gone on to become internationally known as one of the founders of Syria's auteur cinema. Born in 1945 in the Golan Heights town of Quneitra, he was vividly marked by Israel's unimpeded conquest of his hometown in 1967. His works include the films *Quneitra 74* (1974), *Aḥlām al-Madīna* (*Dreams of the City*, 1983), the documentary *Al-Manām* (*The Dream*, 1987), his masterpiece *Al-Layl* (*Night*, 1992), and more recently *Bāb al-Maqām* (*Passion*, 2005), the Civil War-time *Sullam ilā Dimashq* (*Ladder to Damascus*, 2013), as well as published film scenarios and fiction. At the time, however, he was just a twenty-eight-year-old aspiring director approaching the end of film school – a career in which he had ended up almost by chance, as he has told interviewer Tahar Chikhaoui:

> During my childhood I believed, I felt, I wanted to become a writer or a man of letters. I had a deep desire to travel and see the world, but I didn't have the means to do so. I was told that the only way to leave was to apply for studies abroad and that I should apply to programs. That year, 1968, the only scholarships abroad that were offered were for film directing. I applied, I was accepted, and I was sent to study cinema. At the end of the program, I returned home as a film director.[30]

29. Pratt 1992, 6.
30. Chikhaoui 2006, 139.

Sonallah Ibrahim, like Malas, was technically a student of the young Russian art film director Igor Talankin (1927–2010). But in fact he already strongly identified as a novelist and had come to Moscow to write. He had already served five and a half years as a political prisoner in Egypt and two years as an editor for the East German wire service Allgemeine Deutsche Nachrichtendienst in East Berlin. When Malas first met Ibrahim in person – having already heard him tapping on his typewriter from down the hall – he was impressed by his "sweet sparkle" and unmistakably "monkish" air.[31]

The two roommates became inseparable, their many conversations blossoming into a collaboration on Malas' 1974 graduation film, a short called *al-Kull fī Makānihi wa Kull Shay 'alā Mā Yurām, ȳa Sīdī al-Ḍābiṭ (Everything is in Place, and All is Well, Officer Sir)*. The film, which has survived, incorporates Ibrahim's prison experience, addressing the 1967 defeat as experienced by information-deprived political prisoners reading three-day-old newspapers inside an Egyptian prison. They co-wrote it, and Ibrahim and some three dozen other Arab students in Moscow acted. At the same time Ibrahim was finishing his novel, *August Star*, about Egypt's Soviet-funded Aswan High Dam, clipping newspapers for another projected novel examining Egyptian history from 1967 to 1973, and taking notes for the book that nearly 40 years later became *Ice*.

Malas was taking notes too. He has recently published his "film diary," with variant screenplays and journals of the film, and his related volume of memoirs published in 2011 includes a brief "Portrait of Sonallah Ibrahim."[32] Comparing the two 2011 texts, Malas' edited diary in "Portrait" and Ibrahim's fictionalization of the same experiences in *Ice,* yields some nearly verbatim resonances that make the differences of shape and attitude all the more striking.[33] Malas' "Portrait" vibrates with admiration for Sonallah Ibrahim and even enacts a kind of incorporation of Ibrahim's experiences and perspective; *Ice,* by contrast, gives the character based on Malas a much smaller role and instead makes the German Hans the narrator Shukri's roommate. This is part of a larger difference: the arc of Malas' Moscow memoir moves toward discovery and artistic self-realization in the context of a formative friendship, whereas everything about *Ice*, from its January-to-January setup to its frigid tone, is emplotted as a dehumanizing circle, a winter with no escape.

31. Malas 2016, 206.
32. For screenplay versions and stills from the set, see Malas' film diary, Malaṣ 2003. Portions of this diary were distilled into the essay "Portrait of Sonallah Ibrahim" included in Malaṣ, *Madhāq al-balaḥ*. I quote from my translation: Malas, "Portrait of a Friend: Sonallah Ibrahim."
33. There may be other echoes in Russian state archives as well, which I hope to explore in the future.

Both narratives' literary allusions raise a question that could pertain to many travelers: to what extent were these two young students intellectually or emotionally present in their host country at all? Their pre-Moscow readings had certainly included Russian literature; in fact, Ibrahim has written that Gorky's novel *The Mother* had prompted him to join the Egyptian communist organization Haditu in the first place; in prison he had studied news accounts of Yevtushenko and Voznesensky, writing out excerpts on scraps of cigarette packages.[34]

In Moscow, however, we rarely see Shukri reading Russian literature (except Solzhenitsyn), though he does report hearing a poem by Mayakovsky and one by Yevtushenko, and he quotes Vladimir Vysotski's protest ballad "A Song for Serezhka Fomin." Most of the books cited are Arab (for example, a political tract by Palestinian Yusuf al-Khatib) or Western, including Thornton Wilder's *Ides of March* (1948), Arthur Koestler's anti-Communist *Darkness at Noon* (1940), Graham Greene's *The Comedians* (1966), "an article on Cervantes," and Miles Copeland's *Game of Nations* (1970). The characters watch films by Iosseliani, Pier Paolo Pasolini, Damiano Damiani, Egyptian director Hasan al-Imam, and several Bulgarian directors, as well as "an old American film directed by John Ford" (43); they discuss a *Hamlet* production by "the Polish director Wajda," comparing it to other versions.

Local cultural developments are reported laconically, highlighting the hypocrisy and stagnation of the Soviet literary scene:

> *Izvestia* published an open letter from 31 prominent writers attacking Solzhenitsyn and Sakharov. Among the signatories were Sholokhov, author of *And Quiet Flows the Don*, Konstantin Simonov, and Aitmatov. (115)

Malas, too, shows us dorm discussions centered not on an all-Russian syllabus but on Arab political concerns and mainly Western books:

> We always sat in the middle of the room, looking like a theatre set on a stage. Our fourth wall was the forest, apparently our only spectator for these daily performances. A few subjects always pervaded our dialogues: Dos Passos, Graham Greene, Freud, Dostoevsky, prison, Quneitra, love, womankind, and we always ended with the previous night's dreams.[35]

This list includes only one Russian writer, and no Soviets. Some of these works are by actively anti-Communist writers receiving support from the CIA: perhaps Graham Greene and John Dos Passos, like Koestler, were being

---

34. Creswell 2013, "Translator's Introduction".
35. Malas 2003, 223.

passed around and discussed in the dorm as a kind of badge of resistance to the Soviet regime.[36] Other foreign media were available as well. On New Year's Eve 1973–74, while their Russian dormmates were getting dangerously drunk, the Arab friends sat in their room, reading aloud from "the letters to the editor section of Playboy Magazine."[37]

As the last example shows, however, this global literary kaleidoscope was received and appreciated within a Soviet context: the life of the dormitory. Unavoidable and ugly, this life showcased in microcosm the bankruptcy of the very internationalism that had underwritten the Arab students' scholarships to the USSR. Here was great international diversity – but one that brought no "friendship of nations" but racism, homophobia, hypocrisy, and pervasive violence.

Malas' memoir opens with a horrific example: a brutal sexual assault on an East German friend named Kurt (a prototype for *Ice's* Hans) on January 6, 1973. (I will summarize this scene in describing how it occurs in Ibrahim's novel, discussed below.) As I have shown elsewhere, for Malas this scene is redeemed by friendship. His text highlights the racialized non-Russian Soviet attackers' violence as well as the hypocritical internationalism and "cowardice without borders" of the ethnic Russian student council leader. By having Kurt barge in on Sonallah's telling of his prison tale, the narrative symbolically links this cowardly violence to the Nasser regime's attack on its patriotic Communist intelligentsia, both the mass imprisonment of leftists in Egypt and the related 1959 murder of Syro-Lebanese Communist Farajallah al-Helou in Damascus. Yet the rape of Kurt unexpectedly becomes an occasion for heightened intimacy with his friend Sonallah Ibrahim, as Malas witnesses the horrific event almost through Ibrahim's prison-traumatized eyes and verbalizes, on the spot, his own ambition to become a novelist too.[38]

Following the arc of this relationship, Malas' memoir ends with a deeply affecting image of spring, rebirth, loving artistry, and clarified vision:

> Today Sonallah woke up earlier than usual. He didn't take his usual period of matinal contemplation in bed. He didn't bury his head in his hands. He didn't put on his glasses to stare at the little squares of wood flooring. He didn't start doing his funny calisthenic leaps. He didn't pick up his razor or the water bottle for the toilet. Instead he got up in a hurry, smiled to the sun, and pulled out a knife, which he poked into the paper taped over the wood frame between the two

36. On both, Saunders 2000.
37. Malas 2003, 223.
38. Malas 2003, 210.

panes of the window. Then he moved the knife, cutting the paper entirely, and pulled on the latch. The window opened and fresh air came into the room. He took a piece of rag, wet it with water, and began wiping away the sticky traces of tape on the window. The air became clearer and the sun brighter.

He sat down at his desk, picked up a newspaper from 1970, and stared at it for a while. Then he picked up his scissors and cut out a little piece. Perhaps it was a political news item or an advertisement or a notice of a wedding or a suicide or a case of madness. He pasted the item to a sheet of white paper, wrote two or three words under it, then repeated the same process with another newspaper from another day or another year.

He did these things again and again, over and over, as though the newspapers were endless. His papers piled up in front of him like the days.[39]

Ibrahim's January-to-January novel, by contrast, buries the window-clearing scene in a less significant point. Instead *Ice* closes where Malas' memoir begins: with the sudden and extreme violence of the rape. The latter closely parallels the event narrated by Malas (much of the dialogue recurs verbatim), but it is deployed differently. The fictionalized attackers still come from racialized non-Russian minorities within the USSR and use the same homophobic slurs. But Kurt becomes Hans, and Orthodox Christmas moves forward fifty-one weeks to become New Year's Eve 1974. Ibrahim removes the references to his narrator's own past: Nasser, Arab politics, and the story of prison. Instead Hans interrupts the friends' Arabic conversation about a trivial topic, the traditions of celebrating the New Year in Egypt.

Most significantly, the attack on Hans comes at the end of a dysfunctional New Year's room party. New Year's Eve is a fraught time both for Russian culture, where it represented the biggest holiday of the forcibly secularized Soviet year, and for Ibrahim's personal history, since the Egyptian security services had arrested him on that night in 1959. At the party, lonely students are shown wandering in looking for other students, perhaps dancing or talking or eating a bit, and going out again. A student named Anastasia comes in with a transistor radio to listen to Brezhnev's New Year's address at midnight. The narrator Shukri goes upstairs in search of the long-legged Czech student Svetlana but is disappointed to learn she is away in Prague. Later he encourages his attractive friend Anar, a shy Muslim girl from Azerbaijan, to pursue Hans, although the latter is already in the clutches of Anastasia. The narrator's tone is wooden (after reading Malas, we can describe it as post-

39. Malas 2016, 225.

traumatic). The party scene, like the novel as a whole, works to show how the heartlessness of Soviet society leads denizens of the same building to ignore or dehumanize each other. Then this happens:

> We ran back to the room. The door was open and some things
> were strewn beside it. Three big stocky Soviet guys were standing
> there screaming angrily. One of them was the head of the student
> committee. Another had Central Asian features. The third looked like
> a Cossack. I saw **Hans** crouching naked in a corner. The Asian student
> yelled: You Arabs! Homos like him! Or else why would you take him in
> and protect him? The student club leader jumped in, saying sternly:
> Shut up, you can't say that. He turned to us and added: They caught
> **Mikha** fucking him. Together they dragged **Hans** out to the hall,
> kicked him toward the stairs with their feet, then pushed him so he
> fell all the way down. They ran down after him. Just before dawn they
> brought him back, wrapped in a gray blanket. He was completely
> naked. They put him down on the bed and went out. One of them
> turned to us and said: Maybe this stuff is normal in your country, but
> under the Soviet constitution it's punishable by five years. (218–19)

Shukri and his friend Hamid (the Malas-based character) suggest seeking medical help for Hans, who refuses. Then, unable to sleep, the narrator puts on his many layers of winter clothing and goes outside in disgust. But his last excursion of the book is even more a failure than his first: his freezing extremities soon drive him back to the dormitory:

> **Hamid** left the room to go sleep somewhere else. I took off my clothes
> and got into bed, but sleep did not come. The gray dawn light pierced
> the window. I stood up and got dressed: clothes, overcoat, shapka,
> scarf, gloves. Then I left the *obshchezhitie*. The snow was falling thick
> and fast. It covered everything with white, even the trees. It started
> to accumulate on my overcoat, my hat, and my eyebrows. My fingers
> and toes began to freeze. I turned around, heading back toward the
> *obshchezhitie*. (219)

There is nowhere else to go, no exploring to do. Inside is hell (the existentialist hell of other people), but outside is only frozen snow. Like the Moscow year itself, the narrator's path forms a depressing circle.

Conclusion

Ibrahim's *Ice* and Malas' "Portrait" take contrasting approaches to the same set of Moscow dormitory experiences. The novel is anti-literary in style and ugly in content, while the memoir, perhaps more honestly, piles on the literary effects, depicting two bright young men who want only to write, to understand the histories that have (de)formed them, to turn a violent "scene" into literary art, and to converse in the center of the room "as though on a theatre stage."

Both these texts – Malas' earnestly, Ibrahim's ironically – contribute to Arabic study abroad literature, fleshing out its eastern wing. They show how travel for study abroad can erode the very internationalist ideals – both among the students and their Soviet hosts – that brought it about in the first place. They thus provide material for fruitful comparison not only with Arab study abroad literature about other countries (such as France, Britain, or the United States) but with the global genre of Red Mecca disillusion writing (by students of African, African-American, Eastern European, and other backgrounds) and works such as Ismail Kadare's recently retranslated *Twilight of the Eastern Gods*, set at the Gorky Institute in 1958.[40]

Generically, these works blur the categories over which scholars have sometimes puzzled. In so doing they help us address James Buzard's question of "what counts as travel." It is not only that "what counts as travel changes" from one historical moment to another,[41] but also, that doing a "travel literature reading" of a work of literature can open up unexpected and fruitful angles even on works that might not traditionally fit the category or might sit awkwardly on its borders. Malas was a bona fide student on a government scholarship, a "*ṭālib baʿtha*" in Louis ʿAwad's sense, but Ibrahim was an expatriate, a temporary exile, and his narrative is the one that better repays a "travel reading." It turns out that even a stay of several years, "indeed the duration traditionally required of anthropological fieldwork," can continue to elicit "the original frisson of interrogation of and by the other."[42] For over a year *Ice*'s narrator and his friends skitter like tourists on the surface of Russian society, dipping in only for brief encounters that in most cases shock or disappoint. Yet this is the bemused and alienated perspective from which Ibrahim writes about Egyptian society, too. Whether abroad or at home, the narrator never forgets that he is a stranger in his out-of-joint surroundings – and neither can Ibrahim's readers.

40. Kadare 2014.
41. Buzard 2005, 43.
42. Clark 1999, 17.

Works Cited

Buzard, James. 2005. "What Isn't Travel." In *Unravelling Civilisation: European Travel and Travel Writing*, edited by Hagen Schulz-Forberg, 43–61. Brussels: Peter Lang.

Chikhaoui, Tahar. 2006. "Interview with Mohamad Malas." In *Insights into Syrian Cinema*, edited by Rasha Salti. New York: ArteEast.

Clark, Steven H. 1999. "Introduction." In *Travel Writing and Empire: Postcolonial Theory in Transit*, edited by Steven H. Clark. London: Zed Books.

Creswell, Robyn. 2013. "Translator's Introduction." In *That Smell and Notes from Prison*. New York: New Directions Publishing.

Djagalov, Rossen, and Christine Evans. 2009. "Moskau, 1960: Wie man sich eine sowjetische Freundschaft mit der Dritten Welt vorstellte." In *Die Sowjetunion und die Dritte Welt: UdSSR, Staatssozialismus und Antikolonialismus im Kalten Krieg 1945-1991*, edited by Andreas Hilger. Munich: Oldenbourg.

El-Enany, Rasheed. 2006. *Arab Representations of the Occident: East-West Encounters in Arabic Fiction*. London: Routledge.

Emre, Merve. 2013. "Bloody Abroad." *Boston Review*, June 5. http://bostonreview.net/books-ideas/bloody-abroad.

———. 2015. "Jamesian Institutions." *American Literary History* 27, no. 2 (March 16): 226–55.

Euben, Roxanne Leslie. 2016. *Journeys to the Other Shore : Muslim and Western Travelers in Search of Knowledge*. Princeton: Princeton University Press.

Forest, Benjamin, and Juliet Johnson. 2002. "Unraveling the Threads of History: Soviet–Era Monuments and Post–Soviet National Identity in Moscow." *Annals of the Association of American Geographers* 92, no. 3 (September 1): 524–47.

Garden, Kenneth. 2015. "The Riḥla and Self-Reinvention of Abū Bakr Ibn Al-ʿArabī." *Journal of the American Oriental Society* 135, no. 1: 1-17.

Hulme, Peter. 2002. "Travelling to Write (1940–2000)." In *The Cambridge Companion to Travel Writing*, edited by Peter Hulme and Tim Youngs, 87–102. Cambridge, UK: Cambridge University Press.

Ibrāhīm, Ṣunʿ Allāh. 2011. *al-Jalīd: riwāya*. Cairo: Dār al-Thaqāfa al-Jadīda.

Kadare, Ismail. 2014. *Twilight of the Eastern Gods*. New York: Grove/Atlantic.

Katsakioris, Constantin. 2016. "Les étudiants de pays arabes formés en Union soviétique pendant la guerre froide (1956-1991)." *Revue Européenne des Migrations Internationales* 32, no. 2: 13-38.

Kirasirova, Masha. 2017. "The 'East' as a Category of Bolshevik Ideology and Comintern Administration: The Arab Section of the Communist

University of the Toilers of the East." *Kritika: Explorations in Russian and Eurasian History*, vol. 18, no. 1: 7–34.

Litvin, Margaret. 2011. "Egypt's Uzbek Mirror: Muḥammad Al-Mansī Qandīl's Post-Soviet Islamic Humanism." *Journal of Arabic Literature* 42, no. 2–3 (January 1): 101–19.

Logan, Katie Marie. 2012. "Reading, Writing, Roaming: The Student Abroad in Arab Women's Literature." M.A., University of Texas. https://repositories.lib.utexas.edu/handle/2152/ETD-UT-2012-05-5390.

Malas, Mohamad. 2016. "Portrait of a Friend: Sonallah Ibrahim." Translated by Margaret Litvin. *Alif: Journal of Comparative Poetics*, no. 36: 201–25.

Malaṣ, Muḥammad. 2003. *al-Kull fī makānih! wa-kull shay' 'alá mā yurām sayyidī al-ḍābiṭ: mufakkirat film*. Damascus: Dār al-Madá lil-Thaqāfa wa-al-Nashr.

Matar, Nabil I. 2003. "Introduction." In *In the Lands of the Christians: Arabic Travel Writing in the Seventeenth Century*. London: Routledge.

McClellan, Woodford. 2006. "Black Hajj to 'Red Mecca': Africans and Afro-Americans at KUTV, 1925–1938." In *Africa in Russia, Russia in Africa: Three Centuries of Encounters*, edited by Maxim Matusevich, 61–84. Trenton, NJ: Africa World Press.

McTiernan, John, and Michael Crichton. 1999. *The 13th Warrior*, Touchstone Pictures.

Pantsov, Alexander V., and Steven I. Levine. 2013. *Mao: The Real Story*. New York: Simon and Schuster.

Pratt, Mary Louise. 1992. *Imperial Eyes: Travel Writing and Transculturation*. London: Routledge.

Qandīl, Muḥammad al-Mansī. 2009. *Moon Over Samarqand*. Translated by Jennifer Peterson. Cairo: American University in Cairo Press.

——. 1996. "'Alá Ṭarīq al-Ḥarīr. (2): Uzbikstān ... Bilād Niṣf al-Ibtisāma." *Al-'Arabī*, November.

——. 1996. "'Alá Ṭarīq al-Ḥarīr. (1): Kāzakhstān Bilād al-Suḥūb wa-al-Wu'ūd." *Al-'Arabī*, October.

Ravandi-Fadai, Lana. 2015. "'Red Mecca' – The Communist University for Laborers of the East (KUTV): Iranian Scholars and Students in Moscow in the 1920s and 1930s." *Iranian Studies* 48, no. 5 (September 3): 713–27.

Roudi, Farzaneh. 2011. "Youth Population and Employment in the Middle East and North Africa: Opportunity or Challenge?" United Nations Expert Group Meeting on Adolescents, Youth and Development: Population Division, July 22. http://www.un.org/esa/population/meetings/egm-adolescents/p06_roudi.pdf.

Saunders, Frances Stonor. 2000. *Who Paid the Piper?: The CIA and the Cultural Cold War*. London: Granta Books.

Savicheva, Elena. 2010. *RUDN i Arabskiy Vostok*. Moscow: Peoples' Friendship University of Russia.

Ṣidqī, Najātī. 2001. *Mudhakkirāt Najātī Ṣidqī*. Beirut: Mu'assasat al-Dirāsāt al-Filasṭīnīya.

Sīrāfī, Abū Zayd Ḥasan ibn Yazīd, and Aḥmad Ibn Faḍlān. 2014. *Two Arabic Travel Books: Accounts of China and India and Mission to the Volga*. Edited by Tim Mackintosh-Smith, James E Montgomery, Shawkat Toorawa, and Philip Kennedy. Library of Arabic Literature. New York: NYU Press.

Smith, Benjamin Lenox. 2014. "Writing *Amrika*: Literary Encounters with America in Arabic Literature." PhD, Harvard. https://dash.harvard.edu/handle/1/13095487.

Tamari, Salim. 2009. "The Enigmatic Bolshevik from the Holy City." In *Mountain against the Sea: Essays on Palestinian Society and Culture*, 167–75. Berkeley and Los Angeles: University of California Press.

———. 2003. "Najati Sadqi (1905–79): The Enigmatic Jerusalem Bolshevik." *Journal of Palestine Studies* 32, no. 2: 79–94.

Touati, Houari. 2010. *Islam and Travel in the Middle Ages*. Chicago: University of Chicago Press.

Turkī, Zakarīyā.1999. *Ṣaʿīdī fī bilād al-Rūs*. Cairo: Dār al-Thaqāfa al-Jadīda.

Imaginary Travels: Halide Edib's Illusory Encounters with India

Roberta Micallef

Introduction

URKISH AUTHOR, intellectual and prominent political figure Halide Edib Adıvar (1884–1964) published *Inside India* in 1937 in English while in voluntary exile[1] in France. A shorter version in Turkish was serialized as "Today's India" in the newspaper *Tan* between March 16, 1938, and August 2, 1938. Two years later, between 28 December 1940 and 8 February 1941 it was reprinted with some additions in another Turkish newspaper, *Yeni Sabah*.[2] In 2014, the complete Turkish volume entitled *Hindistan'a Dair*, was made available to readers. *Inside India* combines biography, memoir, social and political commentary about Halide Edib's trip, as well as details of her illusory encounters with India before she actually traveled to that country. Decades later Edward Said, in his seminal text, *Orientalism*, showed us that travel writers were influenced by previous cultural representations that they had encountered. In both versions of her narrative, Halide Edib shares the cultural information about India that she encountered before meeting any Indians or traveling to India herself.

Adıvar's accounts of her trip to India provide her readers with examples of a type of twentieth-century self-reflexive ethnography and of social commentary travel narrative, which transcends gender boundaries and easy classification.[3] Her texts are rich in information about the pre-partition[4] Muslim-majority Indian cities and the landscape of important figures of the Indian social and political scene. Thus, they represent excellent examples of New Travel Writing, which Dea and Birkett define as a fusion of biog-

---

1. Halide Edib Adıvar and her husband Dr. Adnan Adıvar went into voluntary exile in 1925, when opposition to the Republican People's Party was suppressed. In what follows, I shall refer to the author variously as Halide Edib, Edib, or Adıvar.

2. Eray Ak, "Halide Edib Adıvar Hindistan'a Dair," *Cumhuriyet Kitap Eki*, August 11, 2014.

3. Bassnett 2002, 225.

4. The Partition of India refers to the partition of the British Indian Empire that led to the creation of the Dominion of Pakistan and the Union of India (later Republic of India) on 15 August 1947.

Adıvar Halide Edib, "Hindistan'a Dair," *Yeni Sabah*, February 5, 1941, p. 2.

raphy, memoir and fiction.[5] One of the tenets of New Travel Writing is the importance of "how we see" rather than "what we see."[6] Clearly, how we see is influenced by prior information about what we are looking at. Adıvar's inclusion of her illusory encounters with India allows her readers to observe the prism through which she is gazing at India. At the same time, the manner in which she chooses to narrate these texts serves to present Halide Edib to her readers as an authority figure on this topic and believable to both the English-speaking and Turkish-speaking audience.

Inside India begins with a "Preface" and an "Introductory";[7] The Turkish version, *Hindistan'a Dair,* has parallel sections entitled "Ilk Sözler" (*First Words*) and "Hindistan'ın Kapı Eşiğinde" (*On the Threshold of India*).[8] Since the two texts differ I will analyze these parallel sections in their different linguistic contexts to understand how they function to represent this complex author to her audience and how they frame what is "seen," by whom and when. While the differences between the two texts and the related details

5. Youngs 2014, 8.
6. Youngs 2014, 8.
7. Adıvar 2002, 3–5 and 6–12, respectively.
8. Adıvar 2014, 15–18 and 18–39. These pages are the first part of this section of the book.

are of great interest to students of the interwar time period, pre-partition India, and travel literature, what is most exciting is the complex interaction between webs of presentation and representation of self and others that participate in forming identities.

The Preface/The First Words

Structurally both sections of *Inside India* and *Hindistan'a Dair* are similar. Edib explains that this particular text is an anomaly in her larger oeuvre and presents three reasons why she is bold enough to write such a book. However, the Turkish text has an additional section explaining its relation to the earlier English book.

The "Preface" to *Inside India* and its counterpart in *Hindistan'a Dair* both begin with a well-worn trope – Halide Edib declares that she is engaging in this task of describing another culture unwillingly, but she also establishes what a qualified interlocutor she is for such a task:

> It has been a rule of life not to write anything about a country not my own beyond personal impressions, and that very rarely. I have not made an exception to this rule even in the case of England, a people I have known since early life, a culture which has formed me side by side with my own, a country where I have lived for more than four years, not counting the numerous visits made at different periods. I break the rule in writing *Inside India*.[9]

In the Turkish edition, Halide Edib distances herself somewhat from English culture, which is reduced to a conduit to Western culture:

> It has happened that I have written my impressions shortly about foreign countries and nations. But it was as if I had made it a rule not to write a long and serious work about them. I got to know the Western world via English culture.[10]

She seems to be arguing that her familiarity with Western culture allows her to see India in a different light, but her Turkishness allows her yet another vantage point, which creates a more complete picture. Her familiarity with English culture, which is emphasized in the earlier text, qualifies her as being able to speak about this region since she brings both the Eastern – Turkish and Muslim – vantage point and an understanding of the culture of those who had ruled India since 1858.

The author provides the same three reasons as to why she can write

9. Adıvar 2002, 3.
10. Adıvar, 2002, 15.

about India, and yet in all three cases the details are different. In *Inside India* she writes:

> First, I felt India to be nearer to my Soul-Climate than any other country not my own.... Even among Hindu friends who have kindly opened their homes to me, a people whose social structure is so different from my own, I felt entirely at home. And it is this senses of belonging in a spiritual sense which has made me take the liberty of writing about Indians so freely.[11]

Whereas in *Hindistan'a Dair*, Edib writes:

> I did not find India foreign to my own Soul-Climate. I did not find these people who opened up their homes to me, who lived in a completely different manner strange at all. I haven't analyzed the reason for this properly myself either. Only this spiritual oneness that I felt during the India trip gave me the courage to write about them in an open and free manner.[12]

With these sentences, Halide Edib is maintaining her distance from India and at the same time establishing herself as part of the same collective as her Turkish readers. Here the Indians and India are firmly "they." While in the English text the author writes that she felt at home, in the Turkish text she writes that she didn't feel strange at all. Between the English and the Indians, she is closer to the Indians. Between the Turks and the Indians, she is closer to the Turks. The author uses the term Soul-Climate (or *ruh iklimi* in Turkish) to indicate that spiritually she feels close to the people of India, whether Muslim or Hindu, but she acknowledges that there are vast differences between her society and India, thereby affirming the fact that she is, despite everything, a visitor.

Halide Edib presents her second reason for writing this text as a promise made to a good friend. She cannot break her promise to Dr. Ansari, she writes, a friend and one of the founders of the new Jamia Millia University and its chancellor from 1928 to 1936. He had invited her to India and had since died. Edib's second reason for writing this book underlines her visitor status, as well as fulfilling multiple other functions. Edib informs the reader that she has a prominent friend who is a doctor and an Indian and close enough to her that he can make such demands. In other words, she is seen as worthy of such tasks by a prominent Indian.

The Turkish version captures a similar sentiment, a promise given to a dear friend, who has since departed. However, the conclusion of the para-

11. Adıvar 2002, 3.
12. Adıvar 2002, 15.

graph is shorter and significantly different. Here she writes, "There is no salvation from a promise given to the dead. Because of that I took it as a sacred debt good or bad to write the work to the end."[13] The author omits any mention of the fact that the conclusions she has reached may not be correct or that what she perceives as the "truth" may be different from what the Indians themselves see as the "truth." She also omits the part of the English text where she writes that she is impressed with how the Indians in India have "frank" discussions about their problems. Omitting the first statement removes any doubt about her objectivity or the nature of truth. The second part may have continued to be problematic in Turkey, which remained a one-party state for twelve years after its founder Mustafa Kemal Atatürk's death in 1938.[14]

This second reason for writing *Inside India* shows her readers that Halide Edib has a unique vantage point. Her gaze is unlike that of the English male or female traveler. In an essay about English-language travelogues and gender between the Victorian age and the 1920s, Bassnett writes that women travelers differ from more socially conformist women and from male travelers who use the journey as a means of discovering more about their own masculinity. According to Bassnett, the women travelers in the volumes she has studied appear to be escaping the constraints placed upon them by their families or societies, whereas male travelers wrote of themselves as heroic, risk takers.[15] Halide Edib was traveling to India on the invitation of Muslim intellectuals to give a series of lectures. During January and February 1935, Halide Edib gave eight lectures at the Jamia Millia Islamia (National Muslim University) in New Delhi.[16] The fact that she was an invited and honored guest, a woman who was to deliver lectures at a university to an audience of prominent men, tells the reader that this author is no ordinary traveler, male or female. We know from Halide Edib's earlier autobiographical works that she was neither a socially nor a politically conformist woman. In *The Turkish Ordeal* (1928),[17] she writes about her fears and trepidation before giving a rousing, nationalist speech to a large crowd on June 6, 1919. In exposing the damage her father's polygamous marriage did to family harmony in *House with Wisteria* (1926), Halide Edib broke social mores. Halide Edib had already shattered any constraints placed upon her by family or society.

13. Adıvar 2002, 16.
14. Mustafa Kemal Atatürk, the founder and first President of the Republic of Turkey died in 1938. The Adıvars went into self-imposed exile because Adnan Adıvar was accused of being part of a conspiracy to assassinate Atatürk. Open discussions of the issues facing the Republic of Turkey at this time would have been frowned upon.
15. Bassnett 2002, 226.
16. Hasan 2002, viii.
17. Adıvar 1928, 31.

Halide Edib first provides the readers with information about herself. If we agree with Hulme and Youngs, "travel writing consists of predominantly factual, first-person prose accounts of travels that have been undertaken by the author-narrator."[18] It becomes clear that the author is concerned with her ability to narrate India "truthfully." There are many versions and many visions of India depending on the observer's vantage point. She reiterates the fact that what she produces in this volume will not be the "objective truth." She writes, "The conclusions I have reached may not be right. What I say about India need not be the truth as the Indians themselves see it, but it is the truth I see and believe."[19] Halide Edib's gaze is not one that reflects a singular, dominant culture. Perhaps she recognizes the relationship between power, travel, empire, and capitalism that became articulated in postcolonial studies decades later. Halide Edib has a more varied gaze. On the one hand, her use of pronouns serves to distinguish her from "Indians themselves"; on the other hand, she is not suggesting that her perspective or their perspective is the one and only "true" perspective, but rather that the image can change depending on the characteristics of the person engaged in the act of looking. She is demolishing the notion that there is one Truth.

Finally, Halide Edib's third reason for writing her book on India links her to an eleventh-century traveler, Alberuni,[20] the author of an encyclopedia of Indian civilization. This at once lets her readers know that she is familiar with what has been written about India and again confirms her status as a visitor, an essential element of travel writing.[21] Alberuni was a medieval Muslim scholar, polymath, and founder of Indology, who was brought to India in 1017 by Mahmud of Ghazni, a Turkic conqueror and ruler. Halide Edib writes that she was "as strongly impressed by the Hind [India] of the twentieth century as Alberuni was of the tenth."[22] Her citation of Alberuni fulfills two functions. It establishes her as a well-educated person who can communicate effectively in English, but who is also familiar with the great scholars and philosophers of the East. She also tells her readers that "I wanted to leave as truthful and objective an account of my period as Alberuni has done of his ... the quality of Alberuni's work seems the highest among the strangers who have written about India."[23] While Halide Edib may have arrived in India ten centuries after Alberuni, they are both scholars and they are both Muslims. Both wrote accounts of India as they saw it.

18. Hulme and Youngs 2002, 3.
19. Adıvar 2002, 3.
20. As this is the spelling favored by Halide Edib Adıvar, I will use it in this text.
21. Youngs 2014, 7.
22. Adıvar 2002, 3-4.
23. Adıvar 2002, 3.

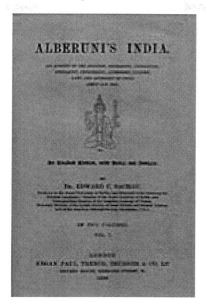

Alberuni's India. Google Images.

In the Turkish version, Halide Edib repeats her statement that reading Alberuni's "Tahkik-i Hind"[24] in English had enabled her to embark on this project.[25] The rather long paragraph includes all the information in the earlier English version and a great deal more. Edib describes Alberuni as an extraordinary man who was as much imbued with the soul of an artist, as he was a scientist.[26] Alberuni, she writes, was "originally Turkish but in terms of culture, he was a Muslim." While Islam is not emphasized in the English version, it became important for Edib to connect herself in the Turkish text to a non-Ottoman, Muslim intellectual. Thus, she is participating in the creation of a new Turkish imagined community with an expansive historical geography that precedes the Ottoman Empire.

24. Bīrūnī's completed *Kitāb taḥqīq mā li'l-Hend min maqūla maqbūla fī'l-ʿaql aw mardhūla* (The book confirming what pertains to India, whether rational or despicable) consists of a wide-ranging examination of Sanskrit scientific sources, supplemented by conversations with Hindu pandits whom Bīrūnī met while accompanying his patron, Sultan Maḥmūd of Ghazni, on military campaigns in northern India in 1030. Encyclopaedia Iranica online.

25. An English edition of Alberuni's text prepared with notes and indices by Edward Sachau, titled *Alberuni's India*, was published in 1910. This work is available online through many sources, including the Open Library website: https://archive.org/stream/Alberunisindiaac01biru#page/n5/mode/2up.

26. Ibid. Alberuni was born in Khorazm, which today is in Uzbekistan, and died in what is today Afghanistan. He was proficient in many languages but wrote in Arabic or Persian.

However, while Edib had excellent reasons for linking herself to Alberuni, the lack of an Ottoman tradition of travel literature referring to non-Ottoman Muslims may have also been part of her reticence about travel writing and her desire to connect her work to Alberuni's encyclopedia. Herzog and Motika, who published an extensive article on the Ottoman travelogue genre, argue that there were few Ottoman autobiographies and travelogues.[27] While there were many diaries of military campaigns, pilgrimages, and such that were written by travelers of necessity, such as government officials and military officers,[28] no overall picture or discourse that defined the non-Ottoman Muslim existed.[29]

This is Halide Edib's first attempt at telling a story about a place as opposed to a person or her nation. It is interesting that she chooses a model from the eleventh century, when there is an Ottoman travel narrative to India written in 1877. Ahmed Hulusi Efendi Şirvani was part of a British Ottoman delegation to India in 1877. He published a *seyahatname* (travelogue) (1883) that described his trip to India. For Ahmed Hulusi, however, travel reports also include "weird and wonderful events" in order to "provide useful information for his compatriots."[30] Halide Edib may not have had access to the narrative.

Adıvar's Turkish text has an additional section explaining how and why it differs from the original English version. Here, Halide Edib writes that the Turkish version includes everything that the English version includes, but that it is not a translation. The Turkish version, she tells her Turkish audience, was written separately and independently. Topics that may be of interest to Turkish readers are comparatively longer and those that may not be of interest are relatively shorter, she explains. Furthermore, she writes that the conclusions she has reached may not be those of other travelers to India or Indians.[31] Then she refers to herself in the third person – the reporter of *About India* is far from claiming that she has reached any definite or true conclusions about such a confusing and difficult topic.[32] I have argued elsewhere that when Halide Edib is called on to take actions that she finds intimidating she writes about herself in the third person singular.[33] Here again, by using this technique, she indicates how difficult she finds this task. Not only is India complicated and multi-layered, but she herself is not an

27. Herzog and Motika 2000, 162.
28. Herzog and Motika 2000, 155.
29. Herzog and Motika 2000, 195.
30. Herzog and Motika 2000, 155. It is not clear that Hulusi actually went on such a trip.
31. Adıvar 2002, 17.
32. Adıvar 2002, 17.
33. Micallef 2013, 151–71.

experienced "travel" writer, she explains to her readers. She is, neverthe-less, the first modern Turkish traveler to India to have produced a narrative detailing her impressions of India and Indians.

In the "Preface" and "First Words" Halide Edib establishes herself as a traveler who has a unique point of view. She is a Turkish, Muslim woman born in the Ottoman Empire, which she helps transform into the Republic of Turkey. Furthermore, through her education and travels she is proficient in both English language and culture. When we compare her to the male and female European travelers discussed in Bassnett's work we see that she has a unique voice in travel literature overall. However, Edib's insistence on writing about her identity and the existence of many "truths" make this text an excellent example of the new, twentieth-century self-reflexive travel narratives.

Introductory/On India's Threshold: The Credible Narrator

The "Introductory" in the English-language text becomes part of the section entitled "On India's Threshold" (*Hindistan'ın Kapı Eşiğinde*) in the Turkish version. In the English version, we are given three pre-glimpses to India, whereas in the Turkish version the readers are only provided with two. In addition, there are differences in details and explanations. An analysis of these two sections demonstrates the importance of prior information about places, objects or people in "how we see" them.

Three Pre-Travel Glimpses of India

Glimpse One: Fantastic Tales

The first line of the English "Introductory" is, "Tales had three ways of begin-ning in my country,"[34] which is followed by the first beginning. Whereas the Turkish version starts with "I heard the earliest mention of this country's name in the tales I heard during my childhood. Because two of the rhymes (*tekerleme*) in the beginning of the tales are particularly suitable to India I will repeat them here."[35] These opening sentences introduce the notion of tales and introduce the reader to the idea that the information they will receive here is not scientific and cannot be interpreted as objective or truth-ful. In the English version, her statement "my country" serves to emphasize the fact that while there is a country where she belongs, that is "hers", this country is neither India nor England. The utterance, "I heard about this

---

34. Adıvar 2002, 5.
35. Adıvar 2014, 21.

country in my childhood," assumes a communal Turkish space where children are told tales about places like India. There is no need to elaborate on "my country" because she is in a place and writing in a language where she is part of an "imagined community." However, her "country" has changed dramatically from her childhood to the time of her writing, 1935–37. The Republic of Turkey had replaced the Ottoman Empire of her childhood. Edib does not interrogate or elaborate this point. It would appear from her formulation that her "country" and her audience have remained the same through the seismic shifts in borders, boundaries, and populations that took place in the aftermath of World War I. Perhaps the explanation lies in the webs of belonging that she has created through her writing of people who share her Soul-Climate, Muslims, whether Persianate or Turkic, and those who speak her language (whether it be Turkish or English).

"'Once upon a time....' That is common to the whole world, but will not do for what I have to say about India. India is no longer 'was': it is very much 'is'."[36] This is the one of the three beginnings of tales "in her country" that is missing from Halide Edib's Turkish text. Halide Edib writes these lines in the English text where it serves to connect Turkey, India and the world in multiple ways. It indicates that humanity as a whole shares a story-telling tradition and that everyone in the world shares at least one way of articulating the entry to a fantasyland. An attempt to create a common human trait can be seen as an attempt to demystify those who have been seen as strange or exotic and upon whose otherness the English had defined their identity. One might ask why this beginning was excluded from the Turkish text. Had India, once the partition took place, reverted to a state of "was" rather than "is," or did the author deem this uninteresting for Turkish readers? Perhaps it was politically problematic at that point in time to discuss the partition of India, since the British and French involvement in the Middle East had led to the partition of the Ottoman Empire. Perhaps 1941, just about the middle of the Second World War, was not the time to remind the Turkish audience of British involvement in the demise of their own empire.

In India, Edib writes in the English version, there are ideas that will influence humanity for thousands of years and there are ideas in the present that belong to the distant past: "there are facts in its present condition which should belong to the jungle, to the early appearance of man upon earth."[37] The Turkish version is bereft of any allusions to evolution; it simply states, "belonging to the first days of humanity."[38] The English version ends with: "This is why the child of the twentieth century, who is wander-

36. Adıvar 2002, 5.
37. Adıvar 2002, 5.
38. Adıvar 2014, 21.

ing around there, is constantly face to face with the beginning of time and the end of time."[39] Edib's third beginning starts: "'once there was, and once there was not....' Thus the storytellers of our childhood began every Indian tale." This was her first glimpse of India. However, the same beginning in the Turkish text is introduced as "the *tekerleme* that is much suited to this strange country is '*bir varmış, bir yokmuş*,'" a literal translation of "once there was and once there was not." Again the English lines set her up as someone from a different culture than her intended audience, but also as someone familiar with India, since she grew up in a country where children were told tales about India that all began with a certain rhyme. The Turkish version does not at all indicate that anyone was being told tales about India, but rather marks India as a strange and exotic country. In both texts, Halide Edib describes her vision of India in terms of atoms and physics, setting herself up as a well-educated person who is capable of objectivity in scientific terms. According to Youngs, "women travel writers must become 'honorary men' in order to be recognized within a genre that is shaped so powerfully by a discourse of masculinity."[40] Are the references to science Edib's way of marking herself as an honorary man, not just someone well versed in the Western sciences? The remainder of the paragraph in the English version proceeds to link the India of these children's tales to the fantastic: "it was the invisible spirits who pulled the strings of power and shaped the destiny of its children."[41] Missing in the Turkish version, these lines are evidence of what Herzog and Motika call "Orientalism alla Turca." Edib tells us that she heard these lines as a child while the Ottoman Empire still existed and India was exoticized; it was the land of magic and spiritualism not the land of science and rational thought exhibited by the work of Western scholars such as Einstein.

These reflections by the author present us with an India and an author who is linked to East and West. The author is believable in both contexts because she belongs to the imaginary community of one and she knows India and England well enough to translate one for the other accurately. They also tell us that the author is a good storyteller.

Glimpse Two: The Governess/The Teacher

The differences in the way the second glimpse is described in the two publications show that the political and social environment and the chronological time when a story is narrated have an impact on how it is told. Halide Edib's

39. Adıvar 2014, 21.
40. Youngs 2014, 135.
41. Adıvar 2002, 5.

second glimpse of India is informed by what she is told by the wife of a tea merchant who had spent many years in India. The details about this character's nationality and role vis-à-vis Edib's life differ in the two versions of this narrative. Edib writes in the English-language text that her "English governess," Mrs. Percy, described the India of forty years ago, which according to my calculations would make it the India of the 1890s. The widow of an English tea-planter, her governess had spent thirty years in India.[42] In the Turkish version, the same character is introduced as a *hoca*, or a teacher, not a governess. We find foreign governesses in other Turkish narratives, both fictional and autobiographical, from this period.[43] A teacher, however, would be expected to have more professional training and qualifications than a governess. In the Turkish version, the readers are told that this teacher, who is not given a name, is of Irish extraction and the dates when she was in India are different. The Turkish reader is told that this woman had come to Turkey to teach forty years ago and she had spent more than twenty years in India as the wife of a tea merchant.[44] In both texts, this woman appears to be impossibly old, but perhaps this explains her views of India and its residents. That she is Irish, rather than English, softens the reactions the readers might have about the English upon reading her racist, fervently British imperialist comments. Her name in the English version, Mrs. Percy, is the kind of detail that strengthens the relationship between the author and reader, rendering the author more believable. In the Turkish version, the name is irrelevant. There were many nameless, older, foreign women tutoring or caring for children of elite Turkish households at that time.

The glimpse of India provided by the governess in the English version sounds more fantastic than a fairy tale. Through the voice of the nanny, Edib criticizes the colonial rulers and their view of themselves. From the governess's vantage point, the English are the main actors and the Indians are in the background. The Indians who are allowed to emerge in this tale of India are the serving classes and the untouchables. "Caste frontiers were eternal," the governess states in Edib's account. Edib states that the imperialist race created new lines, rather than erasing the old boundaries. However, the new lines were equally rigid. In the governess's view, white men had remarkable backbone and colored men were wild beasts and the unseen "succumbed before them."[45] The "unseen" in the Turkish version has been transformed into "snakes,"[46] but otherwise the texts are the same. In an interesting jux-

42. Adıvar 2002, 5.
43. For example: *Aşk-ı Memnu*, Halit Ziya Uşaklıgil and *An Ottoman Woman's Search for Freedom*, Zeyneb Hanoum.
44. Adıvar 2014, 22.
45. Adıvar 2002, 6.
46. Adıvar 2014, 22.

taposition of empire, gender and class, Edib, by providing the character of governess/teacher, positions herself as a privileged, modernizing, upper-class woman who sympathizes with people colonized by Western imperial powers. She grew up in an upper-class household where modernization im-plied giving girls access to education and foreign languages and adults were educated enough to know tales about India that they could share with the children of the household. Her critical comments about the British Empire reflect that there was a difference between what the English claimed that they were doing and what they actually accomplished. The fact that a mem-ber of the British imperialist mission, the wife of a soldier, had been reduced to serving an Ottoman household also tells the reader that the British Em-pire was perhaps overstretching when it shifted its gaze from South Asia to the Middle East.

An event that is represented significantly differently in the two texts is "The Mutiny," the widespread but unsuccessful rebellion against British rule in India in 1857–58 and a moment of great imperial crisis, referred to variously as a "rebellion" or "war of independence" by British and Indian historians.[47] In the course of this episode, over two thirds of the Bengal army, comprised of Hindus, Muslims, and Pathans, rose up against the British. The "mutiny" spread to become the largest rebellion against the British Empire in the nineteenth century.[48] The governess of the English version and the teacher of the Turkish text describe the Mutiny as the only instance in which the white man was taken "unawares." In the Turkish version, we are told that this was the 1857 rebellion. Edib elaborates, "When she narrated this I sensed a fear in my teacher's eyes that will follow the English who lived in India for eternity."[49] In the English version, she writes: "All this awesome up-heaval was due to the objection of some Indians to pig's flesh and fat.[50] The people had risen, not because of tyranny or oppression, but because they were made to touch the accursed swine-flesh by their masters."[51] For an English-speaking audience, this may have seemed absurd. The notion that the English would have forced the Indians to touch the pig or its flesh, but also the notion that a community would be upset enough about such a thing to overthrow a ruling class, might have seemed fantastical. To a Turkish au-

---

47. Anderson 2007, 1.

48. Anderson 2007, 2.

49. Adıvar 2014, 23.

50. The mutiny broke out in the Bengal army because it was only in the military sphere that Indians were organized. The pretext for revolt was the introduction of the new Enfield rifle. To load it, the sepoys had to bite off the ends of lubricated cartridges. A rumour spread among the sepoys that the grease used to lubricate the cartridges was a mixture of pigs' and cows' lard; thus, to have oral contact with it was an insult to both Muslims and Hindus.

51. Adıvar 2002, 6.

dience, however, which had recently fought a war of independence against a group of Christian nations, being forced to eat pork products would have symbolized a new version of the Crusades, a war with religious overtones. They would have been very sympathetic to the citizens of India.

Perhaps because this would have been rather inflammatory in a text published in 1941 in Turkish as the British were fighting the Nazis, in the Turkish version Halide Edib writes:

> What was the reason for this rebellion? ... According to my teacher this was far from a national independence cause, not against tyranny or oppression but a reactionary movement lacking in goals, born out of ignorance and extremism.[52] ... While the cause may have been represented differently, in both cases the punishment for the uprising was so severe that even the ghosts of the mutineers could not walk on the earth where they had been born.[53]

In the Turkish version, the teacher is describing a powerful British Empire facing an unreasonable and irrational mob. According to Halide Edib the British response was excessively harsh.

Glimpse Three: Literary Sources

Literary texts provide Halide Edib with her third glimpse of India. Once again, despite using the same material, the differing representations in the English and Turkish-language texts demonstrate her understanding of her audiences. In both narratives, the first author mentioned is Rudyard Kipling. Under the subtitle "The India of Fiction", or simply "Literature" in the Turkish version, Edib writes about her admiration for Kipling's *Jungle Book*, published in 1894. The time period described in Kipling's book would have coincided with the India described by Edib's governess/teacher. Edib writes about Kipling: "Never had genius captured animal life with such truth, though the form was fanciful; and no other land, ancient or modern, was such a home for animals. They lived their lives as animals should; yet they made one realize the oneness of all life on earth."[54] In the Turkish version, Halide Edib writes a longer evaluation:

> For some reason I was not that interested in these works that were about people. Maybe because I was of the age to sense that there was always a story genre in the way the Western world saw the East. But

---

52. Adıvar 2014, 23.
53. Adıvar 2002, 6; Adıvar 2014, 23.
54. Adıvar 2014, 23.

when I read the work called *Jungle Book*, the work that talks about animals, it was as if I had seen a brand new world. It is not possible to think of a country that is as real a home to animals as India. This great genius was describing how the animals live in such a way that, what appeared to one as products of the imagination at first began to appear realistic by the end.[55]

After decades of post-colonial studies one might criticize Edib for failing to see that even a book describing a country as an ideal setting for animals, could be orientalist in its own right and that perhaps a book advocating that "animals live as animals should," was referring to the various inhabitants and castes of a nation. However, given when she wrote this text, and what she told us previously about her uneasiness about the reader assuming that Halide Edib is writing the objective truth, we might just as well read this paragraph to mean that it is easier to be objective about animals than people.

The second literary glimpse in both books, subtitled "The Human Side,"[56] is provided by a much-loved Turkish playwright, Abdülhak Hamid,[57] whom she describes as "the greatest dramatic poet of late nineteenth-century Turkey."[58] Halide Edib writes simply that the play, "Lady Finten," was put on stage in 1908, although in the Turkish version she names the time period as the immediate aftermath of the Constitutional Revolution (1908–9), which would have been of more interest to the Turkish reader. The play is about an aristocratic English woman and her Hindu servant-lover, Davalagiro. In both of Edib's texts, the actress representing Lady Finten is described as unsuitable, "anything but English." In the English-language text, we also learn that she is a "puny Armenian actress." We are not given this information in the Turkish text since all actresses in that time period would have been members of the non-Muslim minorities. The Turkish audience would likely have assumed as much. In both versions, the Hindu lover is represented as strong and powerful. In the English version, his character is described as "un-Indian" because he raved about "tearing the darkness" and "facing the dawn" because of a desire, because of an aim.

Halide Edib describes a scene where Davalagiro, the Indian "coolie" proclaims:

I have taken the road with such determination that I will not turn my

55. Adıvar 2014, 24.
56. Adıvar 2002, 6.
57. In *Inside India*, Halide Edib refers to him as Abdul-Hak-Hamid, whereas in *Hindistan'a Dair* she refers to him as Abdülhak Hamid. For the remainder of the essay I will refer to him as Abdülhak Hamid.
58. Adıvar 2002, 6.

face from the goal, though my tombstone barricades my path. Neither
the white-capped waves, nor fire-spitting clouds – no, not even
volcanoes shall stop me on my way.[59]

Abdülhak Hamid's "coolie," an unskilled laborer, is a dramatically different source than Edib's governess/teacher and the "unseen" forces of Kipling.
In the play, the Indian servant is "not suited to the India we imagined."[60]
But who is "we"? Those educated in the British system? In the Turkish version, Edib cites the same lines and tells the reader that she interpreted them
as the imaginary lines of a romantic poet that were not true to life.[61] She
concludes, "Was it possible to imagine an Indian who could rip the dark cur-
tain of the night and face the morning?"[62] Is Halide Edib suggesting that the
British should be aware, especially after a traumatic moment like the Mutiny that they have already experienced, that perhaps they needed to adjust
"how they saw, what they saw." Perhaps the weak coolie of their gaze from a
different angle would turn into an Indian who could take charge of his own
destiny. Again with a twenty-first-century gaze it is easy to fault her for not
questioning the use of the British upper-class lady as the object of desire or
the stated need to protect her from such a coolie as an impetus for harshly
imposed colonial rule. Abdülhak Hamid is tapping into a deep-seated imperial fear that is replicated in many such situations of power and domination,
including a seminal narrative about the American south in the waning years
of slavery, *Gone with the Wind* (1936).

The Indians Halide Edib Met Before Traveling to India

In this section, which describes her encounters with people from India before her trip there, we have the most convergence in the presentation of
characters to her two audiences. In both texts, she warns her readers that
one must not judge a country by its citizens that one meets abroad. In the
English text, "A person without his background is like a floating plant, difficult to identify. Further, what is personal may appear national; and what
is national, personal."[63] In the Turkish text, "A man living abroad resembles
leaves that have been torn from their roots, floating on currents. His personal characteristics may appear national to you. A national virtue or fault may
appear personal."[64] Curiously, Halide Edib seems pre-occupied with making
a case for Indian masculinity.

59. Adıvar 2002, 7.
60. Adıvar 2002, 7; Adıvar 2014, 25.
61. Adıvar 2014, 25.
62. Adıvar 2014, 25.
63. Adıvar 2002, 7.
64. Adıvar 2014, 26.

First, she describes the Indians traveling on the ship she took to London in 1909, telling her readers in the Turkish version that she did not pay attention to her fellow first-class Indian travelers and, in the English version, that she simply did not pay attention to the other travelers. Rather, she writes, she is more interested in the working-class Indians, the stewards, and the sailors. Apparently, the first-class travelers are a community on the vessel. They may be of different ethnic, national, religious or language backgrounds but they are all united in their class designation. In both texts, she tells her readers that, in contrast to the English who were ordinary waiters, the Indians looked refined and sensitive. In both texts, she says that their faces could not have been a reflection of who they were, but rather "ancestral masks." In the Turkish version, she adds some complimentary lines describing the Indian waiters as having calm and brave eyes, as men who went about their duties with the look of men who worked with their minds and imaginations, rather than their muscles. They are serving, but they are dignified.

It is the Indian sailors who get the more peculiar descriptions. They are described almost like monkeys in the English text, where she tells us that she would not be surprised if they could embroider with their toes. In the Turkish version, they are described as being examples of the ugliest possible Indians, as strange creatures who appeared beside you at the most unexpected moments.[65] Furthermore, she writes, they carried the mark of those who had been stepped on for an eternity.[66] It is this that she seems to find most objectionable. Masculinity and servility cannot coexist for Halide Edib. Just as the lead man in Abdülhak Hamid's play is "un-Indian" because he is goal-oriented, a fighter and powerful, these men are ugly because they are servile. The "other" for her on the boat is the working class, the servile laborer who works with his muscles rather than intelligence. The "other" is not the British, the Indians, or the other first-class travelers.

In 1912 in Istanbul Halide Edib meets Dr. Ansari, who led the Indian Red Crescent delegation to aid in the aftermath of the Balkan disasters. In both texts, Halide Edib describes Dr. Ansari as "the most representative Indian Muslim."[67] In both texts, she focuses on his eyes: "They were purposeful eyes, very kind in spite of the unwavering determination of their depth."[68] However, while in the Turkish version she writes about their friendship and describes him as being similar to Turkish doctors, in the English text she makes an effort to describe him as masculine. She appears to be compensating for the English descriptions she has come across of Indian men.

---

65. Adıvar 2014, 27.
66. Adıvar 2002, 8; Adıvar 2014, 26–27.
67. Adıvar 2002, 8. This is how she spells Muslim.
68. Adıvar 2002, 8; Adıvar 2014, 27.

She writes that his clothes "had that masculine elegance associated with London," and that the younger members of the mission were like "our own young people."[69] It is not clear who the "our" refers to in this text, but it is missing in the Turkish version.

We have another interesting historical silence next. In the Turkish version, she skips to 1925, but in the English version she discusses the Indians she met in 1918, the Indian regiments of the occupying forces – the colonial representatives. Then, in 1919, she met the Indians, who were trying to help Turkey and the Khilafat movement (1919–24), a pan-Islamic political movement launched in India to influence the British and to support the Ottoman-held title of Caliph.[70] This movement, which for her Turkish audience evoked the past, had a different significance for India and her English-speaking audience.[71]

In both texts, 1925 is described as the period when India takes on a confusing picture and when Indian Muslims face difficulties living in India amid scenes of disorder and misery. Halide Edib writes,

> "India is a prison, and we all are prisoners and slaves," said a
> Muslim. A Hindu painted a terrible picture of dire poverty against a
> background of shameless luxury. "There are a few hundred languages,
> and a few thousand castes at loggerheads—can there ever be an
> Indian nation under such conditions," wrote a journalist.
>
> Above these blurred scenes of disorder and misery gradually rose
> the figure of Mahatma Gandhi.[72]

The same passage as rendered in the Turkish version:

> In 1925 India appeared as very confusing place to me. In London an
> Indian Muslim I had known since the Balkan War said to me, "India is
> a big dungeon, all the Indians are prisoners." Every Hindu intellectual
> that I met told me about his country's misery, the people's poverty,
> and hunger. A journalist who had inspected India in those days
> explained to me that India would not be able to be an independent,
> single nation. "How can it be?" He was saying, "There are a few
> hundred languages, a few thousand castes!"[73]

After a few lines, Gandhi is mentioned:

69. Adıvar 2002, 8.
70. See Minault 1982 for further information.
71. Adıvar 2002, 8.
72. Adıvar 2002, 8–9.
73. Adıvar 2014, 27.

Mahatma Gandhi slowly emerged after 1919 from what appeared to us to be India's dark and confusing condition.[74]

India's multiplicity is described as a liability in the modern world that emphasized homogenized nation-states. This comes through clearly in both texts. Halide Edib knows what happened in Turkey, what had already happened to the Armenians before the collapse of the Empire, to the Greeks with the population exchanges after the establishment of the Republic, and to the Kurds who rebelled against the Turkish Republic. In all cases, poverty and misery are present. In both cases Gandhi represents a potential beacon of light.

Both texts proceed to a paragraph that is almost identical, about how, at the point of arrival in India, she had listened to many Indians of different persuasions, but that together they lacked "coherence," or *ahenk* as she writes in Turkish. After this, she arrives in India, ready to discover and present a more coherent version, or a version that she presents as a coherent subject.

A comparison and analysis of two texts, one in English and one self-translated into Turkish about a trip Halide Edib Adıvar took to a third country, India, reveal much about the multi-faceted nature of identity, the acts of seeing and representing oneself or others. Adıvar's complex positionality, her linguistic background, class affiliations, education, and religion all surface in different ways in different times and situations, as she seeks to get the same point across depending on whom she is addressing. She is unlike the male or female travelers described by Bassnett. As someone whose culture was an object of curiosity and study, she is an author who has first-hand knowledge of how faulty or limited one's vision can be if one has only one point of access to a culture or its people. She is one of the few men or women who has not only read what has been written about the Ottoman Empire and Turkey but also has the power and authority to participate in the conversation. In writing about India, whether in English or Turkish, with the frame she provides in the Preface and Introductory, Edib is self-reflexive and honest about what is shaping how she sees, and at the same time successful in her effort to convince her readers that she is a trustworthy, first-person narrator who has the authority to take us with her on her voyage.

74. Adıvar 2014, 27.

Bibliography

Adıvar, Halide Edib. 1928. *The Turkish Ordeal*. New York: The Century.

———. 2002. *Inside India*. First edition 1937. Delhi: Oxford University Press.

———. 2014. *Hindistan'a Dair*. Istanbul: Can Sanat Yayınları.

Anderson, Clare. 2007. *The Indian Uprising of 1857-1858 Prisons, Prisoners and Rebellion*. New York, London, Delhi: Anthem Press.

Bassnett, Susan. 2002. "Travel Writing and Gender." In *The Cambridge Companion to Travel Writing*, edited by Peter Hulme and Tim Youngs, 225–42. Cambridge, New York: Cambridge University Press.

Buzard, James. 2005. "What Isn't Travel?" In *Unravelling Civilization: European Travel and Travel Writing*, edited by Hagen Schultz-Forbert, 43–69. Berlin, New York: Peter Lang.

Hasan, Mushirul. 2002. "Introduction" In *Inside India* ix–lxi. Delhi: Oxford University Press.

Herzog, Christoph, and Raoul Motika. 2000. "Orientalism 'alla turca': Late 19th / Early 20th Century Ottoman Voyages into the Muslim 'Outback'." *Die Welt des Islams*, New Series, Vol. 40, Issue 2. *Ottoman Travels and Travel Accounts from an Earlier Age of Globalization*: 139–95.

Hulme, Peter, and Tim Youngs, eds. 2002. *The Cambridge Companion to Travel Writing*. Cambridge, New York: Cambridge University Press.

Micallef, Roberta. 2013. "From the House with Wisteria to Inside India: Halide Edib's Journey to the Symbolic." In *On the Wonders of Land and Sea: Persianate Travel Writing*, edited by Roberta Micallef and Sunil Sharma, 151–70. Boston: Ilex Foundation.

Minault, Gail. 1982. *The Khilafat Movement: Religious Symbolism and Political Mobilization in India*. New York: Columbia University Press.

Smith, Sidonie, and Julia Watson. 2010. *Reading Autobiography: Interpreting Life Narratives*. 2nd edition. Minneapolis, MN: University of Minnesota Press.

Youngs, Tim. 2014. *The Cambridge Introduction to Travel Writing*. New York: Cambridge University Press.

A Glimpse of the American West:
A French Schoolteacher's 1893 Pioneering Adventure

Mary Beth Raycraft

FRENCH SCHOOLTEACHER Marie Dugard (1865–1931) set off for an American adventure on June 24, 1893. Boarding the transatlantic ship *The Westernland* in Antwerp, Belgium, Dugard embarked on a four-month journey that would take her across the ocean and then from coast to coast across the United States. Unlike most of the other travelers discussed in this volume, Dugard's opportunity to travel to the United States came about for professional reasons, as she was invited to join the French delegation to the International Congress of Education. Held in July of 1893 at the World's Columbian Exposition in Chicago, the Congress brought together educators from around the world for several days of lectures, panel discussions, and exhibits.[1] By selecting Dugard as the sole female member of the French delegation, the Ministry of Education signaled her growing reputation as an outstanding teacher, writer, and advocate for girls' schooling. Although she was still in the early years of a promising teaching career, Dugard had already distinguished herself as a pioneer. Most notably, she was among the first group of women to earn the advanced diploma of the *agrégation* and to enter the newly professionalized teaching corps in the French public school system. Upon completing this rigorous degree in 1886, largely through self-study, Dugard was hired to teach in one of the girls' public lycées that had been established following the passage of the *loi Camille Sée* in 1880.[2] This law, which put into place a state system of secular public instruction for both boys and girls, prompted new efforts to train and recruit female teachers. At the time of her selection as a delegate, Dugard was employed as literature and philosophy teacher at the Lycée Molière. One of three girls' public schools in Paris, the Lycée Molière was often the setting for discussions regarding the curriculum and goals of girls' education in Third Republic France.[3] Dugard was among the first teachers recruited to teach at the Lycée Molière upon

1. National Education Association 1894.
2. See Offen 1983, 252–54 and Rogers 2005, 205–8 for discussions of the Camille Sée Law and its implications for girls' education.
3. See Jean de Paris 1888, 2 for a description of the opening ceremony of the Lycée Molière, which featured speeches by numerous dignitaries on the importance of girls' education.

its opening in 1888 and she taught there until her retirement in 1930. In addition to her strong teaching credentials, Dugard had also demonstrated a talent for writing. Just a year before her trip to America, Dugard's article on the need for reform in girls' education was published in the newly established journal, *La Revue universitaire*.[4] That same year, Dugard communicated her eagerness to shape curriculum through the publication of an anthology, *La Culture morale*, which was designed for use as a textbook in high school philosophy classes.[5] Throughout her career at the Lycée Molière, Dugard also demonstrated strong interest in religion. In fact, Dugard had converted from Catholicism to Protestantism just a few years before her trip to the United States. Inspired by a Protestant minister, Dugard had embraced a more personal, humanitarian approach to faith that she would continue to explore throughout her life.[6] As Dugard boarded the ship bound for New York, this thirty-year old unmarried woman of modest means brought with her a professional interest in discovering American educational institutions and a more personal curiosity about the status of women in the social, political, and religious life of the United States.[7]

Dugard's American itinerary speaks to the double vantage point that she brings to her travel adventure: that of a schoolteacher undertaking a professional obligation as a delegate and that of a young French woman eager to meet Americans and to explore the New World. Dugard arrived in New York Harbor on July 3, 1893 and spent a few days in the city before heading west to Chicago, following an overnight stop at Niagara Falls. At the International Congress of Education, she gave a well-received presentation, in which she explained the structure and goals of girls' education in France.[8] Rather than return directly to the east coast as she had originally intended, Dugard veered off her planned itinerary and headed west. Traveling on the transcontinental railroad, she undertook an ambitious six-week tour that included stops in Salt Lake City, Portland, and San Francisco as well as the Grand Canyon and Pike's Peak. The unexpected addition of the western excursion gave Marie Dugard an exceptional opportunity to refine her ideas about American and French approaches to education, gender roles, religious life, and social conventions, and to organize her notes in preparation for a

---

4. Dugard 1892a.

5. Dugard 1892b.

6. Mestral-Combremont 1932, 109–15. Marie Dugard's obituary describes her religious conversion in the late 1880's from Catholicism to a more personal, free-thinking faith. *Revue universitaire*, 41:1 (1932), 114.

7. See Raycraft 2015 for more information about Marie Dugard's life and the influence of her trip to America on her later works.

8. National Education Association 1894, 213.

publication based on her observations. Two years after Dugard's return to France, she published *La Société américaine; moeurs et caractère, la famille, rôle de la femme, écoles et universités* (1896), which was honored with a prize from the *Académie française*.[9] While many accounts of American life by French travelers appeared between 1875 and 1900, the enthusiastic reception of Dugard's book shows that she brought a fresh perspective and approach to the subject and to the genre.[10] Critics on both sides of the Atlantic offered favorable reviews of *La Sociéte américaine*. André Balz, in his weekly *chronique* in the daily paper *Le XXe siècle*, suggested that Dugard had revived a genre introduced by Tocqueville in his *Democracy in America*, combining a travel narrative with personal observations on American society.[11] In *La Revue universitaire*, another French reviewer pointed to the originality of Dugard's hybrid text, in which her own reactions are interspersed with evidence gathered from interviews, official documentation, and literary sources in an effort to depict and explain the customs of the New World to her readers.[12] An American reviewer praised Dugard's measured tone: "Many Europeans during recent years have discussed American institutions but few with so much insight and fairness as Mlle. Dugard."[13] This lively chronicle of late nineteenth-century American life through the gaze of a French schoolteacher offered a new look at the people, cities, and customs of the New World. At the same time, Dugard's account of her travel experience gave her an opportunity to explore and expand on her ideas in the more loosely structured format of the travel narrative.

The freshness of Dugard's account is evident from the opening pages as she interweaves a scholar's eye for facts and figures with a colorful first person narrative. In contrast to her earlier publications that were addressed primarily to education professionals, the format of *La Société américaine* allowed Dugard to experiment with a more informal, digressive style. Drawing on her status as an educator, Dugard presents herself as an inquisitive traveler eager to share her knowledge with readers. Her narration thus functions as a natural extension of her teaching mission. Unlike most other late nineteenth-century French travelers to the United States, Dugard had an excellent command of English, which allowed her to engage directly with the people she met. In fact, she incorporates dialogue directly into her text, allowing readers to hear the voices of the American men and women she

9. Dugard 1896.

10. See Portes 2000 for a comprehensive overview of late nineteenth- and early twentieth-century French travelers' accounts of America.

11. Balz 1897, 1.

12. Anon. La Revue universitaire. 6:1 (1897), 76.

13. Monroe 1898, 283.

meets. Dugard also establishes an ongoing conversation with her readers, frequently addressing them with *vous* and anticipating their reactions and questions. Although she includes lengthy descriptions of the people she meets and the places she visits, her travel narrative goes far beyond these prosaic details as she investigates striking differences between what is happening in American and French homes, schools, universities, and churches. Dugard's text is also remarkable in that she includes many lengthy footnotes. By interweaving her observations with references to scholarly sources and statistics, Dugard creates a personal and persuasive travel narrative. Shifting fluidly from description, to discussion, and finally to social commentary, Dugard shapes her chapters with an eye toward exposing the narrow-mindedness of French attitudes toward education, religion, and women's status in the home and in the world.

In order to explore the different layers of this unusual text, this essay takes the form of a textual commentary that follows the chronology of Dugard's travel narrative. Drawing on Mary Louise Pratt's notion of the traveler's gaze, I examine Dugard's gradual transition from outsider to insider as she develops a more comprehensive perspective of the complex ethnic, religious, economic, and social world of the American West and seeks to explain it to her readers.[14] I also address the link between travel writing and initiation as Dugard used this writing project to give new textual life to her ideas on education, marriage, and religion.[15] In the first section, I discuss the French fascination with the American West during the nineteenth century and Dugard's growing interest in this region. The second section focuses on Dugard's reactions to the people and places she encounters in the West, including Mormons, Native Americans, Chinese Americans, and men and women of different social and professional backgrounds. The final section explores how touring and subsequently recording her reactions to the West led Dugard to reconsider some of her preconceived ideas regarding American and French society and marked her initiation into an increasingly engaged and polemical stance that would influence her writing upon returning to France.

The Lure of the West

Growing up in late nineteenth-century France, Marie Dugard and others of her generation would have encountered colorful stories and images centered on the American West. During the 1820's and 30's, for example, French

14. Pratt 2008.
15. Uden 2018, 24. This aspect of my analysis has been inspired by Uden's comments on the travel narrative as a place to give "new textual life" to ideas previously explored in other literary forms.

readers enthusiastically read translations of James Fenimore Cooper's popular tales of Native American life, including *The Last of the Mohicans* (1826).[16] Dugard was clearly acquainted with Cooper's work, as she makes direct reference to his tales in her depiction of Native Americans in her travel narrative.[17] French curiosity regarding the American West reached a peak in the mid-nineteenth century, paralleling the excitement surrounding the 1849 Gold Rush. As French gold seekers headed west, numerous books and articles focused on life in California began to appear on the market.[18] Later in the century, several French travelers ventured west and published impressions of the exotic landscape and rustic manners. Louis Simonin's *À travers les États-Unis* (1875) includes descriptions of Salt Lake City and San Francisco, Jules LeClercq's *Un été en Amérique* (1877) focuses his exploration on the Grand Canyon and Pike's Peak, while the Rocky Mountains are the subject of Edmond de Mandat-Grancey, *Dans les montagnes rocheuses* (1885).[19] Two French women preceded Marie Dugard on the western trail and published their impressions. Françoise de Saint-Amant traveled to San Francisco in 1851 with the goal of establishing a business there. In a series of letters to her husband published in book form as *Voyage en Californie, 1850, 1851*, she described the difficult trip as well as the eccentric cast of characters she met in San Francisco during the early years of the gold rush.[20] Louise Bourbonnaud, a wealthy French widow, world traveler, and member of the *Société géographique* visited the western United States in 1889.[21] In her account of a whirlwind cross-country train trip, Bourbonnaud shares descriptions of a number of western cities, mostly viewed from the safety of the train car or the comfort of a French-owned hotel. A traveler who drew on her experiences to proclaim the superiority of French culture, Bourbonnaud's descriptions focus primarily on negative depictions of inefficient servants and African Americans and Chinese immigrants.

Beyond these fictional tales and travel accounts, nineteenth-century Parisians also had a chance to "see" some lively representations of the American West. For example, in the 1840's, American painter George Catlin (1796–1872) exhibited his dramatic portraits of Native Americans in Paris.[22]

16. James Fenimore Cooper (1789–1851) resided in Paris between 1826 and 1833. Translations of his popular tales of Native American life, including The Last of the Mohicans (1826) appeared in France soon after their publication in America.

17. Dugard 1896, 80.

18. See Rohrbough 2013, 162–74 for a comprehensive discussion of non-fiction accounts, short stories, novels, and articles in the French press regarding the California Gold Rush.

19. Simonin 1875, Leclercq 1877, Mandat-Grancey, 1884.

20. Saint-Amant 1851.

21. Bourbonnaud 1889, 51–89.

22. Catlin, Dippie, and Gurney 2002.

These life-sized depictions of Native Americans in full dress captivated Parisians, including the poet Charles Baudelaire, who attended Catlin's show and subsequently published an enthusiastic review in his *Salon de 1846*.[23] In addition to the paintings that comprised his "Indian Gallery," Catlin created a live show in which Native Americans reenacted traditional dances. Later in the century, Buffalo Bill Cody (1846–1917) presented his circus-like show "The Wild West" at the 1889 Paris Exposition Universelle and attracted thousands of enthusiastic spectators.[24] Both the characters and codes of the Wild West appealed to French readers and spectators, who were intrigued by the individualistic spirit and pioneering energy associated with this region.

While Marie Dugard was familiar with the cultural referents of the American West, she was increasingly drawn to this region for its reputation as an open-minded and forward-thinking haven. In fact, during the late nineteenth century women from across America and overseas, including British traveler Isabella Bird (1831–1904) and Indian explorer Pandita Ramabai (1858–1922) headed west to see this frontier, where it was rumored that women were challenging gender restrictions and helping to rewrite traditional rules governing politics, education, and work.[25] Nina Baym points out that throughout the nineteenth century, "the West was seen to allow women to become capable, physically active, independent, honest, and forthright. Ideas of bigness and spaciousness, of freedom from convention, of physical development, contribute to a sense of the western heroine as a new kind of person."[26] As Dugard learned more about the West through her conversations with Americans during the early weeks of her trip, she developed a fervent curiosity about its reputed progressive ideology.

Seeing the West

Dugard's choice of the transatlantic ship *The Westernland* for the ocean crossing was fitting for a trip that would eventually draw her to the western edge of the United States. The first mention of the West occurs early in Dugard's travel narrative, while she was still aboard the ship. In contrast to the lighthearted shipboard adventures of another French traveler discussed in this volume, Marc-Antoine Caillot, Dugard did not waste a minute and immediately set to work observing Americans during the crossing.[27] Most notably,

23. Baudelaire 1846, 240–41.
24. See Kasson 2000, 84–89 for a discussion of the enthusiastic reaction of French audiences to Buffalo Bill's show in Paris during the 1889 Exposition Universelle.
25. Bird 1879, Kosambi and Ramabai 2003.
26. Baym, 2011, 9–11.
27. Goldsmith 2018, 174–75.

she listened attentively to American passengers describe the West with its dramatic landscapes, immigrant populations, and independent women: "They describe for me ... in the still wild Far West ... independent morals, a free and strong existence, a gigantic battle against nature."[28] While in New York City, Dugard heard more about the distinctive character of the West and explained to her readers that she had been advised to explore this region in order to gain a more complete picture of American life: "They tell me that New York, a cosmopolitan city that looks toward Europe, cannot give one a fair idea of the United States and, in order to have a glimpse of both the young and the old America, it is necessary to visit both the West and the East."[29] Dugard's attraction to the West is clearly evident during these early days of her trip and becomes even more apparent as she heads to Chicago.

Once Dugard arrived in Chicago, her experiences in the city and at the Fair played a crucial role in her decision to add the western trip to her itinerary. In descriptions of the people she observed in the street, on the streetcars and at the Fair, Dugard repeatedly points out the social, ethnic, and regional diversity of the United States, including the intriguing dress and manners of westerners. Beyond her encounters in the city, Dugard's experience as a delegate at the Congress of Education was critical in terms of exposing her to ideas about American education and giving her an opportunity to meet teachers from around the United States and abroad. At the Congress, Dugard gave a well-received presentation in English on girls' schooling in France. After describing the curriculum and goals of French girls' education, Dugard concluded her presentation by candidly expressing admiration for the progressive nature of girls' schooling in America: "We know that you have done more for the education of women than any other nation in the world; we think that we have much to learn from you."[30] From these remarks, it is clear that Dugard planned to visit a number of schools and universities in the hope of seeing how certain aspects of the American approach to girls' education might be adopted in France. In fact, she made numerous professional contacts at the Congress of Education who would later welcome her to their schools and university campuses.[31] In this way, she had an opportunity to tour campuses, meet students and teachers, and ask questions about curriculum, teacher training, and working conditions. By early August Dugard had made the decision to modify her planned itinerary.

28. Dugard 1896, 10–11. All translations are my own except where indicated otherwise.
29. Dugard 1896, 24.
30. Dugard 1894, 213.
31. Compayré 1893, 409. Gabriel Compayré, one of Dugard's fellow French delegates, described the enthusiastic reaction of American teachers to her Congress presentation.

On August 9, 1893 Dugard sent a letter to the *Ministère de l'Instruction publique* asking for an extension of her leave from her teaching position at the Lycée Molière until January 1, 1894. In the letter, Dugard explained that although she had learned much from the exhibits and the presentations at the Fair, she had not yet had a chance to visit schools in different cities.[32] So determined was Dugard to stay that she even offered to cover her travel expenses with personal funds. Moreover, she actually set out on a six-week tour of western cities before even mailing the request, which was postmarked several weeks later in Portland, Oregon. Dugard's resolve to see the West foregrounds the dynamic turn her writing would take in her depictions of the dramatic landscape and diverse group of westerners she would encounter. Having finished with her professional obligations at the Fair, Dugard was free to take on a new role as the narrator of her own unplanned western adventure.

In contrast to Dugard's brief descriptions of New York and Chicago, where she struggled to take in the fast urban pace of each city and situate its inhabitants, her depiction of the West is more complex. Indeed as Dugard moved westward, her travel account concurrently expanded with a 107-page travelogue that follows her route across this region. Since the western excursion was not directly connected with her official role as a French delegate, Dugard was free to follow her own itinerary. Although it appears that she was traveling with a small group of people, as she repeatedly uses the pronoun *nous*, Dugard chooses not to name her fellow travelers. Using a diary-like format with dated entries, Dugard presents her impressions in three geographically organized chapters: "The Prairie and the Salt Lake," "From Salt Lake City to San Francisco," and "California." Each chapter opens with lengthy descriptions of the light, terrain, and colors that she observes from the protective window of the train compartment. Intent on capturing the distinctive characteristics of each region, Dugard emphasizes the varied landscapes of the west, including the prairie, the arid plains of Colorado and Wyoming, the California coast, the Grand Canyon and the Rocky Mountains. At times, Dugard seems visually overwhelmed by the contrasts she finds in the West, explaining: "the country is too vast, its oppositions too extreme."[33] As Bruce Greenfield points out, describing the dramatic western terrain posed a challenge for late nineteenth-century visitors: "Western mountain ranges, deserts, and canyons, on a scale and assuming forms that beggared most travellers' experiences, elicited new kinds of descriptive writing."[34] Nonetheless, Dugard systematically strives to present an overview of the geographic and historic features of each city and tourist site on her route.

32. Dugard 1893.
33. Dugard 1896, 82.
34. Greenfield 2002, 213.

While Dugard struggled to depict the geographic variation of the West, she found it even more difficult to understand and convey the spectrum of ethnic and social diversity. During her first weeks in the West, Dugard was taken aback by the mix of westerners that she observed in the spaces or contact zones frequented by tourists – train cars, restaurants, hotels, schools and universities.[35] Following the well-trodden western loop of the transcontinental railroad, she made an effort to get off the beaten path to explore cities and meet a range of westerners from different religious, ethnic and economic backgrounds including Mormons, Native Americans, Chinese immigrants, teachers, and workers in hotels and restaurants. Armed with many of the stereotypes surrounding the West and its inhabitants, words often fail her when she first encounters new ethnic and religious groups, and she repeatedly tells readers that it is necessary to see the people of the West – *"il faut les voir"* – in order to make sense of this region. [36]

Dugard's first stop on the train route west was Salt Lake City, which provided an ideal opportunity to discuss the history and practice of Mormonism and to initiate a broader discussion on the state of religion in America.[37] Her narration takes a distinct turn here, as she interweaves descriptions of Salt Lake City with historical context. She begins by describing for readers the unusual geographic features of Salt Lake City. Recognizing, however, the French fascination with the Mormon religion, Dugard quickly shifts the focus to this sect and its curious history: "I reread their story, curious about the energy that it unleashes as well as what it reveals about the trend toward mysticism ..."[38] As Dugard explains the origin and tenets of Mormonism, she downplays the sect's eccentric practices and instead emphasizes its exemplary sense of American individualism, describing the Mormons as "extraordinary people, whom it is necessary to see firsthand, in order to understand certain extremes of American individualism."[39] Dugard subsequently invites readers to follow her inside the impressive Mormon Tabernacle, where she finally addresses the practice of polygamy and debunks its prevalence: "Mormon society is no longer what it used to be. What we imagine still in Europe with polygamy and the strange practices brought on by these morals, no longer exists as of a number of years ago."[40] Additional evidence of progressive at-

35. See Pratt 2008, 8, for a discussion of the term "contact zone" as "the space in which peoples geographically and historically separated come into contact with one another."
36. Dugard 1896, 57, 85.
37. See Portes 2000, 78 for a discussion of the European fascination with the Mormons.
38. Dugard 1896, 58.
39. Dugard 1896, 57.
40. Dugard, 1896, 69. Although Dugard is accurate in that plural marriage had been outlawed in Utah in 1890, some Mormons continued to practice polygamy. See Radke-Moss, 2008, 127–28 and Hafen 1997, 342–77.

titudes is presented following a visit to a Mormon home and university. A Mormon leader referred to as "Docteur X" invites Dugard to his home for dinner, where she meets his articulate wife and young children. [41] Through a description of her lively conversations with this engaging couple , Dugard offers an example of a modern Mormon marriage.

Dugard finished her tour of Salt Lake City with a visit to the University of Utah, which had been established by the Mormons in 1850. Not only was this Dugard's first visit to an American university but it also was her first experience seeing coeducational classrooms, as in late nineteenth-century France, girls and boys attended single sex schools. Although French public universities were open to women, few applied and even fewer were admitted, as the curriculum of the girls' *lycée* did not provide sufficient preparation for university courses. Before touring coeducational American high schools and universities, Dugard had expressed skepticism about the potential moral consequences of coeducation. However, after spending time in a classroom at University of Utah, she was impressed by the academic caliber of the curriculum and admired the respectful rapport between young Mormon men and women. She was particularly intrigued by the Mormons' attempt to create a university setting where the teaching of moral values was directly integrated into the curriculum and social life.[42] Dugard's encounters with Mormons in the Tabernacle and in domestic and university settings allowed her to present numerous examples of the modern-day Mormon life and to debunk stereotypes associated with this religious sect. In fact, Dugard's depiction of the Mormons and of the acceptance of this sect in American society provided her with a strategic opportunity to highlight religious diversity and tolerance in the United States.

Energized by the individualist spirit and determination that she believed characterized indigenous American Mormonism, Dugard continued west toward Portland, Oregon. En route to Portland, Dugard caught her first glimpse of Native Americans as the train passed through the Umatilla Indian reservation in Idaho's Snake River Valley. Dugard's descriptions of Native Americans suggest her attempt to reconcile her long-held images with the people she observes and to communicate the complexity of their political and social situation with readers. Karen Morin points out that the train played an important role in bringing late nineteenth-century travelers and Native Americans into contact: "Train transportation itself was key to how travellers represented western Native peoples, because it was on the trains or at depots along the railroad routes that travellers and Native

41. Dugard 1896, 71.
42. Dugard 1896, 72.

Americans most often encountered one another."[43] Dugard's first description of Native Americans on the prairie is in fact grounded in her perspective from the window of the train car: "groups of women enveloped in colorful shawls gathered in the grass and gazed toward the horizon while the men, dressed in animal skins and red coats allowed their horses to drink at the waterfall."[44] She enhances the scene by drawing on well-worn images from works of James Fenimore Cooper (1789–1851) and Henry Wadsworth Longfellow (1807–82): "a thousand tales of Cooper and Longfellow, a thousand legends of primitive life – warriors returning from combat crowned with eagle's feathers, hunters chasing buffalo in the mountains, young people dancing around a fire ... flood the imagination.[45] Although the scene on the reservation brings to mind fictional depictions of an earlier time, Dugard is quick to point out that the situation of Native Americans has dramatically changed. No longer foraging on the prairie or hunting in their native territory, Native Americans had been relocated to federally run reservations and consequently were removed from both traditional food sources and practices. Instead, they wandered from one government station to another, in search of allotted rations of flour, lard, and sugar.

A few weeks later in the trip, an unexpected encounter with Native American women in a train car allows Dugard to accentuate further the gap between literary images and the situation of this displaced people.[46] During an overnight train ride from Flagstaff, Arizona to Pike's Peak, Dugard describes being awakened by a group of Native American women:

> I opened my eyes: five or six Indian women were leaning over me,
> their flat hair framing prominent cheekbones painted with ochre
> and tattooed with mysterious lines; they gently placed in our hands
> grapes from California, brightly colored pieces of pottery, and rudely
> fashioned toys, with such inviting gestures and sad faces.[47]

Here Dugard has a chance to see Native American women up close and to carefully examine their distinctive physical characteristics, noting their cheekbones, facial paint, and hair. Dugard skillfully juxtaposes the traditional appearance of the women with the tawdry wares they are attempting to sell to tourists in the train car. These brief glimpses of Native Americans

43. Morin 1998, 312.

44. Dugard 1896, 79.

45. Dugard 1896, 80.

46. See Morin 1998, 316 for an insightful discussion of the gap between the literary images of Native Americans and nineteenth-century travelers' encounters with displaced, impoverished Native Americans at train stations.

47. Dugard 1896, 110.

from the contact zone of the train car or station serve to confirm Dugard's disillusionment regarding the poverty and rootlessness of the displaced tribes.

While Dugard had fully anticipated encounters with Native Americans in the West, she was clearly surprised and disoriented by the large number of Chinese workers she met in hotels and restaurants in Oregon and California. In contrast to her depictions of other ethnic and religious groups, Dugard's comments on Chinese immigrants are openly racist. She repeatedly criticizes their appearance, customs, living conditions, and food as a way of emphasizing how different they are from other immigrant groups who have successfully integrated into American life.[48] Upon arriving in San Francisco, she openly complains that "one spectacle spoils this likable city and abruptly gives you a sense of the unfinished nature of the Far West: the Chinese, more numerous there than in Portland, and more ruthless."[49] In these descriptions, Dugard abandons her measured tone and conveys with stark candor her impressions of Chinese immigrants. Determined to get a better understanding of the living conditions and customs of the Chinese, Dugard took a guided tour of San Francisco's Chinatown. Her exposure to this ethnic neighborhood, which included a visit to an opium den, simply reinforces her disgust: "they are forty thousand strong, teeming like rodents, which they resemble with their rapacious aspect, their sharp teeth, their thin tails, and even their subterranean habits."[50] Despite her scathing criticism of the Chinese, Dugard makes an effort to understand better their presence in America. In discussions with American acquaintances, for example, Dugard learns of the importance of Chinese labor in the western economy, particularly in the construction of the railroad and the development of mines.[51] Although Dugard never reconsiders her negative opinion of Chinese immigrants, the strong presence of this ethnic group in the wildly diverse American West further demonstrates to her and her readers that hardworking individuals of all backgrounds are welcome on the western frontier.

Marie Dugard's confusion and prejudice concerning ethnic diversity is paralleled by the slippery social boundaries she discovers in the West, especially in the case of the young women working as waitresses, chambermaids, and domestic helpers in restaurants, hotels, and homes. Having already encountered inattentive servants in New York and Chicago, Dugard explains

48. Berglund (2005) points out that European visitors' tours of Chinatown usually served to confirm negative impressions of the Chinese.

49. Dugard 1896, 93.

50. Dugard 1896, 94. The translation of this passage is taken from Roger 2005, 206.

51. Dugard 1896, 103.

to readers that female workers in the West are even more impertinent: "As one moves away from the east, the appearance and pretentions of domestic servants become even less tolerable." [52] Despite her frustration with what she perceived as impertinence, Dugard was intrigued to learn from an acquaintance that "these young girls are not domestic servants in the sense that we understand it in Europe."[53] In fact, as Dugard's friend points out, many of the young women working as waitresses and domestic servants in the West were actually university students earning money for their studies. The idea that a young woman employed as a waitress or a domestic worker could also be a university student was unimaginable within the strict social and economic boundaries of late nineteenth-century France. By sharing this conversation with readers, Dugard manages at once to express frustration about American workers while ironically showcasing the economic and educational opportunities available to determined young women of modest means.

Some of the young women working in western hotels and restaurants might well have been students enrolled at coeducational Leland Stanford University, known as Stanford University today. During her stay in San Francisco, Dugard was invited to tour the campus at the invitation of an American professor. Established in 1891, the university was committed to coeducation and already counted 227 women among its 800 students. Dugard was especially drawn to the idea articulated by Stanford's founders that women were equal to men and therefore should enjoy the same educational and professional opportunities. As she toured the campus, Dugard was surprised to discover impressive laboratories and libraries that were open to both men and women students. Even more striking were the articulate, energetic professors who spoke so positively of their jobs and students. In contrast to the centralized, bureaucratic administration of public high schools and universities in France, Dugard admired the freedom of this private institution to create its own curriculum and hire its own teachers. Measuring the energy and enthusiasm of the faculty as well as the dynamic university founded upon progressive ideas against the French context, Dugard can only lament, "one feels very far away from Europe." [54]

Venturing to the Southwest, Dugard concluded her western excursion with an adventurous mule trek in the Grand Canyon and a scenic outing to Pike's Peak. These final touristic visits offer Dugard a chance to present herself as a fearless pioneer, exploring the depths of the canyon and the

52. Dugard 1896, 85.
53. Dugard 1896, 85.
54. Dugard 1896, 100.

peaks of the mountains as her energetic trip to the West winds down. The stunning canyon and mountain perspectives seem to mirror the vast opportunities offered by the West to both women and men, regardless of ethnic or religious background or economic standing.

Making Sense of the West and Looking Toward the Future

Following her six-week western adventure, Dugard began the three-day return trip to Chicago and used the long hours on the train to reread her notes and summarize her findings. In this final chapter dedicated to the West, entitled "Across the West," the travel narrative recedes as Dugard's focus shifts to a discussion of what she had seen thus far of American life in a digression that spans forty-nine pages. She explains her project: "In the relative tranquility of the return trip, impressions which had confusingly piled up, begin to sort themselves out and following this contact with the west ... it seems that we can begin to tease out a few of traits of the American character."[55] Undertaking a careful analysis of what she had witnessed up to that point, Dugard enumerates both positive and negative aspects of American life. In this section, Dugard's vantage point shifts from that of a foreign observer to an informed and scholarly expert as she adds an abundance of footnotes to support her commentary. After navigating the often confusing yet exhilarating educational, religious, and social settings of the West, Dugard candidly admits that the firm educational, religious, and social hierarchies of late nineteenth-century France seem stifling in contrast. Echoing Tocqueville, Dugard uses the metaphor of youth to stress the vigor, vitality, and candor of America: "a younger world where a new civilization is emerging, stronger and healthier than ours, based on action and independence."[56] In fact, Dugard strategically uses the final chapter of the western section of her book as an opportunity to contrast the sprawling freedom and open-mindedness of the West with the narrow-mindedness of French attitudes toward education, religion, and gender relations. In terms of education, Dugard praises the independent administration of American institutions, where even public schools and universities had the power to hire teachers, set curriculum, and introduce new programs. Dugard also expresses envy at the job opportunities and flexibility enjoyed by American teachers. By describing the advantages of a teaching career in America, including possibilities for promotion, the ability to move from one city to another, and fewer bureaucratic rules, Dugard openly articulates her growing disillusionment with the constraints of her job as a public schoolteacher in late nineteenth-century

55. Dugard 1896, 113.
56. Dugard 1896, 111.

Paris. She goes so far as to describe teaching in America as "an adventure with opportunity on the horizon" in contrast to the French teacher's destiny to follow "a bleak path toward a measly retirement."[57] Dugard's authentic voice comes through here as she measures what she has seen against the more rigid professional context that awaits her back home in Paris.

In addition to exposing important differences between the situation of teachers in France and the United States, Dugard was intrigued by the larger question of how American women were negotiating inclusion in educational, social, and professional spheres. In coeducational classrooms at both the University of Utah and Stanford, Dugard took note of the access that female students had to a university education as well as the respectful rapport between the sexes that seemed to extend beyond the classroom. Although she had misgivings about the value of coeducation at all levels, she admitted that interaction between young men and women in classrooms created a solid foundation for the loving relationships she had observed between husbands and wives in American homes. Especially impressed by the respectful behavior of men toward women, Dugard shared with her readers how easy it was for women to travel and move about freely in the United States compared to Europe: "American women can go everywhere alone, even crossing the United States from east to west, without being bothered by an offensive word or glance."[58] In this supportive environment, she points out that women develop a strong sense of independence and self-reliance that prepares them to participate more fully in domestic, professional, and political life. Later in her conclusion, Dugard goes so far as to contrast the American woman with her French counterpart: "here woman is not the illogical and impulsive being that we know in Europe, she is a creature of another species and she is already being called la 'New Woman,' la Femme Nouvelle."[59] This striking juxtaposition of the fin de siècle woman in Europe and in America effectively highlights the contrast between traditional European attitudes that continued to shape French women's education and experience and the forward thinking ways of modern American women that Dugard admired during her visit.

Dugard's admiration for individual freedoms in America is echoed by her appreciation for the independent status of educational and religious institutions. In contrast to the small-minded attitudes toward religion back home, she discovers a place where spiritual exploration and religious tolerance are flourishing in America. The atmosphere of mutual respect among

57. Dugard 1896, 114.
58. Dugard 1896, 138.
59. Dugard 1896, 280.

religious groups, with a shared commitment to charity and goodwill, stood in opposition to the simmering tensions between Catholics and Protestants back in Paris as Dugard explains: "Our bitter and petty religious quarrels are unknown here."[60] Dugard grounds this discussion of religious freedom and tolerance in the American intellectual tradition, citing Ralph Waldo Emerson as a model.[61] For Dugard, Emerson's break from traditional religion and his role in the transcendentalist movement mirrors her yearning for a new kind of religious practice, open to exploration of different traditions and rooted in social activism.[62]

After leaving the dusty trails of the West, Dugard returned to Chicago and quickly boarded a train for Washington D.C. In this final section of her book, Dugard's increasingly confident narrative voice shows that her perspective and outlook has changed. Back on the East Coast, Dugard expresses sadness at leaving behind the wide horizons and independent spirit of the west. She experiences a sense of dislocation and claustrophobia and laments that in contrast to the West, the east coast "almost felt like Europe."[63] Traveling the western loop had both energized her and allowed her to see and share evidence of progressive ideology at work in education, religion, and social life. The western adventure also gave her an opportunity to explore the boundaries of the travel narrative, interweaving description of sights and settings, reflections on her disenchantment with life in Paris as a professional woman, and polemical commentary calling for change in France. Although she regretted leaving the West, the lively independence and youthful freshness she had seen there influenced her reactions as she undertook visits to schools and universities on the east coast. Watching and listening to American women and men in the East, she immediately focused on the progressive tendencies that she had been exposed to in the West including coeducation, women's roles in domestic and professional life, and religious tolerance.

Marie Dugard's travel narrative offers an intriguing example of a professional woman documenting her reactions to the people, ideas, and places she encountered during her American trip. Both Dugard's decision to see the western United States and her narrative of the adventure in *La Société*

60. Dugard 1896, 147.
61. Dugard 1896, 149.
62. Dugard was clearly drawn to Emerson's ideas and visited his gravesite in Concord, Massachusetts. Upon her return to France, she published four books, including a biography Emerson, sa vie, son oeuvre (1907), an anthology, Pages choisies d'Emerson (1908) and two translations of his works: Société et Solitude (1911) and La Conduite de la vie: essais politiques et sociaux (1912).
63. Dugard 1896, 158.

américaine were pioneering. Covering the vast territory of the western rail-road loop, Dugard was able to develop a more independent voice as she shared with readers her impressions of the west. In addition, the positive reception of *La Société américaine* in both France and the United States le-gitimized Dugard's authority as an outspoken advocate for girls' education and helped launch her career as a public intellectual.[64] What Dugard had witnessed in the West, including coeducation, religious tolerance, and social mobility, galvanized her to advocate for better educational and economic opportunities for French women and a more open-minded consideration of religious faith. For example, shortly after returning to Paris, Dugard pub-lished a widely discussed article about the inferior working conditions of women teachers in French public schools.[65] A few years later, in her 1900 book *De l'éducation moderne des jeunes filles*, she stressed the importance of en-couraging self-reliance in young girls, a trait she had noticed in the women of the west.[66] Dugard further expanded on the importance of education and access to professions for women of all social backgrounds in her 1910 book, *Amour et Mariage*.[67] In many ways, *La Société américaine* thus marks Dugard's initiation into a more forceful, socially engaged approach to writing. Indeed, Dugard's exploration of a broad range of topics in *La Société américaine* al-lowed her to experiment freely with narrative techniques and polemical strategies that she would draw upon in her prolific writing career, which included twelve books and many articles.[68] Both the eye-opening trip to the American West and her hybrid and multi-layered approach to the narrative of the experience allowed Marie Dugard to redefine herself and prepared her to engage in a range of new forward-thinking roles including feminist, alternative religionist and social critic.

64. For example, Dugard was named a member of the organizing committee in 1900 for the Congrès international de l'enseignement secondaire and also the Congrès international des oeuvres et des institutions féminines.

65. Dugard 1895, 129–38.

66. Dugard 1900.

67. Dugard 1912.

68. In addition to her works on Ralph Waldo Emerson, Dugard's books published after 1893 include those with a focus on education, De l'éducation moderne des jeunes filles (1900), De la formation des maîtres de l'enseignement secondaire en France et à l'étranger (1902), L'Évolution contre l'éducation (1910) ; on religion, De La Culture et la vie (1917), Les Étapes (1931) ; and a novel centered on religious exploration, Les Deux Françoises (1920).

Bibliography

Anon. 1897. *La Revue universitaire.* 6.1:76.

Balz, André. 1897. "Chronique," *Le XIXe siècle: journal quotidien politique et littéraire,* 10 janvier, 9802:1.

Bassnett, Susan. 2002. "Travel Writing and Gender." In *The Cambridge Companion to Travel Writing,* edited by Peter Hulme and Tim Youngs, 225–41. Cambridge: Cambridge University Press.

Baudelaire, Charles. 1846. "Salon de 1846." In *Oeuvres complètes.* Paris: Éditions du Seuil, 240–41.

Baym, Nina. 2011. *Women Writers of the American West, 1833-1927.* Urbana: University of Illinois Press.

Berglund, Barbara. 2005. "Chinatown's Tourist Terrain: Representation and Racialization in Nineteenth-Century San Francisco." *American Studies* 46:2.

Bird, Isabella. 1879. *A Lady's Life in the Colorado Mountains.* New York: G. P. Putnam's Sons.

Bourbonnaud, Louise. 1889. *Les Amériques: Amérique du nord, Les Antilles, Amérique du sud.* Paris: Librairie Léon Vannier.

Catlin, George, Brian W. Dippie, and George Gurney. 2002. *George Catlin and His Indian Gallery.* New York: W.W. Norton and Company.

Compayré, Gabriel. 1893. "Les Congrès scolaires à Chicago." *Revue pédagogique,* 22:409.

Dugard, Marie. 1892a. "L'Enseignement des jeunes filles: quelques mots sur la réforme de l'enseignement secondaire." *Revue universitaire, Supplément,* 1/1:8–16.

———. 1892b. *La Culture morale.* Paris: Armand Colin.

———. 1893. Dugard's letter to Ministère de l'éducation is included in her personnel dossier. F/17/23835. Dugard correspondence, 9 August 1893. The dossier is located in the Archives Nationales, Pierrefitte, France.

———. 1894. "The Secondary Education of Girls in France." In *Addresses and Proceedings of the International Congress of Education of the World's Columbian Exposition,* 213. New York: National Education Association.

———. 1895. "Le Surmenage des femmes professeurs dans l'enseignement des jeunes filles." *Revue universitaire,* 4/1:129–38.

———. 1896. *La Société américaine, moeurs et caractère, la famille, rôle de la femme, écoles et universités.* Paris: Hachette.

———. 1900. *De l'éducation moderne des jeunes filles.* Paris: A. Colin.

———. 1902. *De la formation des maîtres de l'enseignement secondaire en France et à l'étranger.* Paris: A. Colin.

———. 1907. *Emerson, sa vie, son oeuvre.* Paris: A. Colin.

———. 1908. *Pages choisies d'Emerson*. Paris: A. Colin.

———. 1910. *L'Évolution contre l'éducation*. Paris: A. Colin.

———. 1911. *Société et Solitude*. Paris: A. Colin.

———. 1912. *La Conduite de la vie: essais politiques et sociaux* . Paris: A. Colin.

———. 1912. *Amour et mariage*. Paris: Librairie Fischbacher.

———. 1917. *De la Culture et la vie*. Paris: Librairie Fischbacher.

———. 1920. *Les Deux Françoises*. Paris: Librairie Fischbacher.

———. 1931. *Les Étapes*. Paris: Je sers.

Goldsmith, Beth C. 2018. "Travel, Adventure and Self-Fashioning: A Frenchman's Journey to New Orleans in 1729." In *Illusions and Disillusionment: Travel Writing in the Modern Age*, edited by Roberta Micallef. Boston: Ilex Foundation

Greenfield, Bruce. 2002. "The West/California: Site of the Future." In *The Cambridge Companion to Travel Writing*, edited by Peter Hulme and Tim Youngs, 207–22. Cambridge: Cambridge University Press.

Hafen, Thomas K. 1997. "City of Saints, City of Sinners: The Development of Salt Lake City as a Tourist Attraction 1869-1900." *Western Historical Quarterly*, Autumn: 342–77.

Kasson, Joy S. 2000. *Buffalo Bill's Wild West: Celebrity, Memory and Popular History*. New York: Farrar, Straus, Giroux.

Kosambi, Meera. 2003. *Pandita Ramabai's American Encounter: The Peoples of the United States (1889)*. Edited and translated by Meera Kosambi. Bloomington: Indiana University Press.

Leclercq, Jules. 1877. *Un été en Amérique: De l'Atlantique aux Montagnes Rocheuses*. Paris: Plon.

Mandat-Grancey, Edmond de. 1884. *Dans les Montagnes Rocheuses*. Paris: Plon.

Mestral-Combremont, J. de. 1932. "Marie Dugard." *La Revue universitaire* 41.1:109–15.

Monroe, Will S. 1898. *Educational Review*, 16/10:283.

Morin, Karen M. 1998. "British Women Travellers and Constructions of Racial Difference across the Nineteenth-Century American West." *Transactions of the Institute of British Geographers*, 23/3:312.

National Education Association. 1894. *Addresses and Proceedings of the International Congress of Education of the World's Columbian Exposition, July 25-28, 1893*. New York: National Education Association.

Offen, Karen. 1983. "The Second Sex and the Baccalauréat in Republican France, 1880-1924." *French Historical Studies*, 13/2:252–54.

Paris, Jean de. 1888. "Nouvelles diverses." *Le Figaro*, 8 octobre. 2.

Portes, Jacques. 2000. *Fascinations and Misgivings: The United States in French Opinion, 1870-1914*. Translated by Elborg Foster. Cambridge: Cambridge University Press.

Pratt, Mary Louise. 2008. *Imperial Eyes: Travel Writing and Transculturation.* Second Edition, New York and London: Routledge.

Radke-Moss, Andrea G. 2008. *Bright Epoch: Women and Coeducation in the American West.* Lincoln: University of Nebraska Press.

Raycraft, Mary Beth. 2015. "Marie Dugard Takes Notes: The Spirited Reaction to 1890s America in *La Société américaine* (1896) By A Parisian Secondary School Teacher of Girls" *Forum for Modern Language Studies,* 51.3, 316–34.

Roger, Philippe. 2005. *The American Enemy: The History of French Anti-Americanism.* Translated by Sharon Bowman. Chicago: University of Chicago Press.

Rogers, Rebecca. 2005. *From the Salon to the Schoolroom: Educating Bourgeois Girls in Nineteenth-Century France.* University Park: Pennsylvania State University Press.

Rohrbough, Malcolm J. 2013. *Rush to Gold: The French and the California Gold Rush, 1848–1854.* New Haven: Yale University Press.

Saint-Amant, Madame de. 1851. *Voyage en Californie, 1850 et 1851.* Paris.

Simonin, Louis. 1875. *À travers les États-Unis.* Paris: Charpentier.

Uden, James. 2018. "Gothic Fiction, the Grand Tour, and the Seductions of Antiquity: Polidori's *The Vampyre* (1819)." In *Illusions and Disillusionment: Travel Writing in the Modern Age,* edited by Roberta Micallef. Boston: Ilex.

The Travels of a Japanese "Girl":
Yoshiya Nobuko's 1928–29 World Tour

Sarah Frederick

HIS CHAPTER looks at a Japanese woman writer who travels west to east, south to north, perhaps against the grain of European and North American images of women's travel literature – the white woman traveling and finding herself in exotic spaces. But perhaps equally remarkable and different is this traveler's insistence on viewing her movement in terms of her own childishness rather than her development. The travelogue emphasizes stopping, retelling, and returning. This return is not so much to Japan per se as to her "girlhood" and the cosmopolitan world of Japanese girls, which is her usual readership and object of representation. I argue that the travelogue of this queer traveler from Japan is constructed to highlight a non-developmental and non-linear narrative, instead creating the opportunity to travel along multiple pathways that open up spaces for difference in both form and identity.

The popular author Yoshiya Nobuko (1896–1973) embarks on her world tour in 1928 with the woman whom she will later adopt as a partner, Monma Chiyo.[1] She travels until 1929, funded by proceeds from her own serialized fiction. Her 1930 travelogue based on this trip, *Details from Other Countries* (*Ikoku tenkei*), jokes about the similarity between her send-off party and "a wedding reception," ironically highlighting her own refusal to "grow up" and marry a man. Momna having recently moved into her home, she gestures at the honeymoon genre of travel literature. The narrative goes on to emphasize multiple and alternative routes, often ones facilitated by forms of media that allow for shortcuts in making a connection. Her writing focuses on new forms of affiliation and mobility that might not have been possible before.

Here the stance of the "girl" (or *shōjo*) who is still absorbing fresh information from multiple sources is key to the non-honeymoon nature of her trip. Eve Kosovsky Sedgwick writes of a reading mode similar to that of the *shōjo*:

---

1. The chapter follows Japanese name order with the family name preceding the given name.

[A]bsorption of the child or adolescent whose sense of personal
queerness may or may not (yet?) have resolved into a sexual
specificity of proscribed object choice, aim, site, or identification.
Such a child – if she reads at all – is reading for important news about
herself, without knowing what form that news will take; with only the
patchiest familiarity with its codes; without, even, more than hungrily
hypothesizing to what questions this news may proffer an answer....
[This state is a] speculative, superstitious, and methodologically
adventurous state where recognitions, pleasures, and discoveries
seep in only from the most stretched and ragged edges of one's
competence.[2]

I argue that Yoshiya embraces such a reading mode when approaching her
travels. She always distances herself from the traditional Japanese travelogue
that often seeks to display competence over the landscape through allusion
and, in some of the oldest Japanese sources like the *Tale of Ise*, over the local
women, as part of coming of age and poetic inspiration. Yoshiya's travelogue
highlights instead the range of possibilities that she and her readers might
imagine by opening up situations they may never have experienced directly.
In her own childhood in the 1910s, and in that of her readers, girls have been
able to access new identities, Japanese and other, through emerging print
culture, new fiction aimed at adolescent girls, translated fiction and thought,
cinema culture, and travel itself. *Details from Other Countries* does not narrate
any particular national or sexual identity, but instead highlights an inchoate
queer view on the world, made legible through episodic storytelling.

   Yoshiya Nobuko wrote fiction from her debut in the late 1910s until her
death, and was arguably the most widely read Japanese writer for much of
the twentieth century.[3] Beginning as a contributor to the girls' magazines
that she read in the 1910s, submitting short poems or vignettes, she went
on to win a newspaper fiction contest for *To the Ends of the Earth* (*Chi no hate
made*) in 1919, and in the late 1910s began receiving pay for her manuscripts,
including the extremely successful series *Flower Tales* (*Hana monogatari*).[4] Her

---

   2. Sedgwick 1997.
   3. There is not a great deal of scholarly writing on Yoshiya Nobuko in Japan, although
the past decade has seen increased interest. An important mass-market book is Tanabe 1999.
There is minimal translation into other languages. Recent translations are "Foxfire" (Yoshiya
2000); "Yellow Rose" (Yoshiya 2016). Her novel *The Ataka Family* (*Ataka-ke no hitobito*) is available in a Japanese-produced 1950s translation in *Info* magazine; it was also translated into
French and Danish in book form in the 1950s (Yoshiya 1957 and 1961), a fact that she recounts
poignantly in her memories of Hayashi Fumiko, who had, soon before her death, told Yoshiya
of her ambitions of writing a novel that would be translated into French (Yoshiya 2008). All
translations here are my own unless otherwise noted.
   4. This began publication in a magazine in 1918, but she began receiving significant roy-

works came to be serialized in newspapers, girls' magazines, and women's magazines, and drew huge audiences with their characteristic flowery writing style and masterful use of romance and domestic fiction plots. She was incredibly prolific throughout her life and is even said to have sat by her father's deathbed with pen in hand, and her diary entries from July and early August 1945 still have her writing and delivering manuscripts as air raid sirens go off daily. Although not considered part of the Japanese canon, her work has invited some scholarly attention among those interested in issues of sexuality.[5] An important aspect of Yoshiya's public persona was her lifelong relationship with another woman, Monma Chiyo (later adopted as Yoshiya Chiyo); as a result of this relationship and some of her fictional works, she has come to be seen as something of an icon of lesbian fiction, or, as it is more often expressed in Japan, an icon of other related categories with such names as "S" (romantic sisterly relations), *dōseiai* (same-sex love), or the sub-genres of *anime* and *manga* referred to as GL (Girls' Love) or *Yuri* (lily).[6] Although this relationship was known, Monma did not like being photographed, and when she appeared in Yoshiya's writing she was referred to as "M" for Monma or "T" for (T)chiyo. Yoshiya's fan base was never limited to women who identified themselves with a particular sexual orientation, or to women at all. But her depictions of erotic relationships and other deep emotional bonds between girls and women are also seen as a major influence for the creation of the entire category of *shōjo shōsetsu* (girls' fiction), and especially for the forms of erotic relationships among adolescent girls, particularly in the subsequent works of girls' animation and comic books. More generally, her stories have remained highly influential throughout Japan's rich graphic novel culture (*manga*), particularly *shōjo manga* (girls' manga), where her stories are often retold.

Depiction of exotic and foreign spaces was used prevalently in twentieth-century girls' fiction to create spaces for different ways of experiencing sexuality and gender that often ran against the motivations of a patriarchal state or the school system. These tendencies persist in contemporary Japa-

---

alties only later in the series and particularly from its book editions. This remained one of her most popular series of works, and remains in print today. One story is translated as "Yellow Rose" (Yoshiya 2016).

5. Komashaku 1994; Robertson 2001.

6. I am being somewhat quick with the distinctions between Japanese and non-Japanese named categories. "Rezubian" is used in Japan, and clearly many of the "Japanese" terms are English words. In addition, the American group Yuricon has been influential in using the term "Yuri" for this purpose; it was a 1970s counterpart to the term "Barazoku" (Rose Tribe) used for gay men, which was then used primarily in soft-pornography depicting girls together. Yuricon members began to reclaim the category for labeling products depicting romantic and sexual relations among women, and this has had some influence in Japan as well. This is explored in a new special issue of the intellectual magazine *Eureka* (December 2014).

nese girls' comics and television dramas, where there is often the conceit that a school in Japan has fantastic, castle-like architecture, and has a Catholic or British boarding-school feel. It may never even be suggested that the characters are not Japanese or that the spaces are outside Japan, but the difference from the normally rather utilitarian high school and university architecture to which readers likely commute each day sets the scene for subversion of other aspects of normality, such as same-sex erotics, gender bending, or incursion of the other-worldly.[7]

Indeed the status of the "girl" in Japanese culture at the time of Yoshiya Nobuko's trip in 1928–29 is central to considering her travelogue. The concept of the "girl" (*shōjo*) in the early twentieth century emerged to describe this nascent identity for young women who through the education system increasingly had some independence from their parents, sometimes living in school dormitories or simply spending time at school away from home. Due to extended school life and sometimes working as schoolteachers or in white-collar jobs, middle class "girls" also had an extended period of adolescence before marriage. Many of the cultural texts depicting and aimed at these young women highlighted the mobility associated with this group. In some cases this was a real form of mobility, but just as often it was explored via reading material about adventures, and, in the 1920s, increasingly film and radio media. Girls' magazines depicted the lifestyles of girls the same age in other cities of the world, and films brought images, often anxiety-filled or inducing, of young women in urban areas around the world. For other young women, these same stories were the object of aspiration or fantasy. There was massive migration from the countryside to urban centers, but many fewer who left Japan entirely. Those who did leave more usually did so as part of a family emigration to Brazil, California, Korea, or (somewhat later) Manchuria. Nearly all of the upper-class women in a mobile situation to travel on their own funds eventually married under financial and/ or familial pressure, usually "staying put." Many of the most well-traveled female figures were married to men who were travelers themselves, with some quite important exceptions such as author Tamura Toshiko and librarian and translator Sakanishi Shiho.[8]

In this emerging culture, Yoshiya Nobuko becomes a particularly salient figure. She was able to achieve physical mobility through travel and also to

---

7. Examples are too numerous to list, but many of these elements are seen in *Revolutionary Girl UTENA* (*Shōjo Kakumei UTENA*), which is also influenced by Yoshiya's *Two Virgins in the Attic*. The 2009 television drama "Mei's Butler" also contained these elements and was based on a comic book, though its storyline was a more conventional teenage romance plot, albeit one with the fantasy of exorbitant wealth and being waited on by handsome young men.

8. See for example, Horiguchi 2011; Frederick 2013.

have the financial resources from her writing to remain unmarried. This is one aspect of her maintaining connections to a "girl" identity through-out her life. To her contemporaries and even until today, there has been something inspiring about her success as a writer and the mobility that it allowed. Her success granted the wherewithal to live without financial sup-port from a husband, to live alone with a woman partner, and to travel – this last the focus of this chapter.

The travelogue contains voluminous front matter to whet our appetite. Its prologue is written by Tokutomi Sohō (1863–1957), head of Minyūsha (the publisher), an important historian and a major figure in journalism and publishing, particularly known in connection with *Kokumin Shinbun*. He was also a colonialist who came to be an important proponent of imperial-ism and Japanese colonization of Manchuria. Tokutomi has not yet read the book, so his comments afford a good place to embark on the journey:

> I should preface my remarks honestly by noting that I have not
> yet read this book. But since I am ordinarily an admiring reader of
> Yoshiya, I believe that when this woman's eyes and hands touch
> this new subject and this new visual realm, her work will capture an
> even more extraordinary palette than we have seen before. Yoshiya's
> sentences are not naïve or unsophisticated; I would characterize
> them, on the contrary, as frank and uninhibited (*muenryo*). It is that
> frankness and lack of inhibition that has the power to charm a certain
> type of reader. It is beguiling. I am not yet certain what Miss Yoshiya
> will have acquired from her tour of the various civilized nations of the
> world. But if, by some small chance, her writing bears the traces of
> aestheticizing, it will be a great loss. I look forward to writing later to
> express the feelings I have after reading this book.[9]

Even if the book to come is a dish he has not yet tasted, he looks forward to it with palpable anticipation. Referring constantly to sensation, he says the colors and visual world that her hands and eyes will touch will represent the "civilized world" in a fresh way. He subtly argues *against* the image of the "girls' fiction" writer as naive, or as aestheticizing, to argue that instead she is uninhibited, a quality that grants her the potential to experience the world with intensity and passion, suggesting interest and emotional attach-ment. It is a thick and vivid representation.

In my readings of the travelogue, and of Yoshiya in general, there is *both* a realistic boldness, and something that might be seen as more dramatic, if not aestheticizing. She shapes the experiences, creatively invoking story-

---

9. Yoshiya 1930, 1–2.

telling clichés. But it is unlike the poetic travelogues of Yosano Akiko (who also appears in the front matter) and more closely tied to the tradition of the classical poetic travelogue (*kikō*). Hers is instead very much a travelogue of the modern era, explicitly the age of cinema and photography. As Rey Chow writes: "The compelling sense of photographic realism in film is ... punctuated with an equally compelling sense of melodrama – of technologically magnified movements that highlight the presences unfolding on the screen as artificial and constructed experiments."[10] Similarly, Yoshiya's representations here can be utterly realistic, directly conveying the thing that she saw via photograph and direct language, while *also* dramatizing their presence via their re-representation in story. She accomplishes this combination of realism and drama through representation of moments of personal encounter, ones that result in a moment of identification, empathy, or understanding. An audience of and producer of what Miriam Hansen has called "vernacular modernism," Yoshiya is always interested in the ways story segments and conventions can pick up audiences as they move, and the ways they can be manipulated and modulated, and with melodramatic storylines can bounce off the realities, encounters, and political situations. Hansen notes that cinema is "a discursive form in which individual experience could be articulated and find recognition by both subjects and others, including strangers" (and Yoshiya often uses the term *étrangère* for herself in France), and (as Yoshiya often does) "engaged the contradictions of modernity at the level of the senses."[11] For Yoshiya, the sensory might come via the effects of her own flowery writing and accompanying illustrations, or the direct experience allowed by the mobility produced in modern times (trains, ships, automobiles), or viewing or adapting cinema or literary translation. And I would note that it was *not* family prestige, but modern mass-market publishing and the education of larger numbers of potential readers, not only but especially girls and women, that gave her access to such mobility. These experiences and representations were a source of affective connection with other human beings, even as she reflected critically on the gaps in such identifications, and the dangers of their excesses.[12] The complex interaction of the sensory and its transport is true of both her fictional and her "documentary" work.

    We see here also the aspect of cosmopolitanism in her situation. Through schooling, print culture, and media representation, Yoshiya is tied as a

10. Chow 2000, 167.

11. Hansen 1999, 70.

12. This was especially true in her early postwar writings, which pull far back on the "excess" and make statements that wartime Japan was a time when people had gone mad (Yoshiya 1975).

younger girl to an international culture that becomes important to her later direct experience of the world through travel. Important to the discourse on cosmopolitanism is its potential for forming affective relationships with other individuals or groups of people who might be foundations of ethical action; the discourse's failure is also of course one criticism of the concept. We can see that Yoshiya attempts to maintain an ideal of personal connections, even as their possibility begins to break down in the face of military expansion in Asia. Throughout her writings in Asia, she attempts to connect to individuals, and particularly young women, in the places she visits.

While her sexuality is not explicitly in play in the travel writings, it is worth linking her meditations on cosmopolitanism and connection with the other to her thinking about same-sex relations. In January 1921, she wrote a piece in *Shin shōsetsu* (New Fiction), strongly affected by the British socialist and proponent of same-sex and platonic love Edward Carpenter (1844–1929), in which she argued that thick relations of "longing" among girls in their school years could be the foundation for social ethics and for love among humankind:[13]

> In Carpenter's *Love's Coming of Age* [1896], he points to friendship-love. When it occurs between older and younger *shōjo*, or else between an instructor and student, it can be extremely advantageous from an educational perspective, and almost immeasurably so. When this happens, the younger *shōjo*'s feelings towards the older do not stop at taking her as a love object; she worships her as a sort of hero for her own spirit and imitates her. Meanwhile, the older girl is touched by the dearness of that younger *shōjo* ... and she develops a beautiful ethical, social, and unselfish character.... Their sensibility grows like a beautiful flowering grass, nurtured in those soft embraces while showered with spring rains. It grows day by day in the heart of a young *shōjo*, and, just like the ocean tide receding from the shoreline, the longer all of that sentiment overflows and is cherished, the more sublimely powerful the generosity that forms in its wake.[14]

While same-sex love is not an explicit subject in the travelogues and the

13. Yoshiya 1921. Carpenter's writings were likely brought to her via the translations of feminist Yamakawa Kikue, particularly his *Love's Coming of Age* (Carpenter 1921; see also Frederick 2017). Carpenter is not well known today, but he was a major influence in the early part of the twentieth century, particularly for his ideas about homosexuality and ethics, and about gender and poverty. He used the term "structure of feeling," now commonly associated with Raymond Williams. While Carpenter did travel to India and was influenced by Hindu thought in later life, these factors do not seem to be an influence on Yoshiya at this time. See Tsuzuki 1980; Leib 1997; Maiwald 2002.

14. Yoshiya 1921.

presence of her own partner on these trips is subdued, we can see echoes of this argument in her travels to both France and in Asia.

Setting Out

Details from Other Countries depicts Yoshiya's first trip abroad. Leaving in the autumn of 1928, she traveled for a year to France, with side trips to Germany, England, and Italy, and then returned to Japan via America. She had received large royalties from the newspaper serialization and book form of a novel named, appropriately enough, *At the Furthest Reaches of the Sea* (*Umi no ki-wami made*, 1922) and used the proceeds to make this trip. There were many Japanese artists and poets in France at this time, with a peak presence in 1928–29 of over 800 in Paris and 900 in France in 1928.[15] Yoshiya and Monma rented a long-stay apartment in Paris in a building that still stands at 14 Rue Quatrefages[16] and, like many of her contemporaries, she studied French at the Tokyo Athénée Français, which opened in 1913 and still operates today.[17] Although she set down roots in these semi-long-term lodgings, her writings and their framing focus on what she might bring back to Japan via her writing, whether fictional or journalistic. Her travel writings are well observed about her locales, but tied powerfully to major social forces in Japan at the time: in particular, class tensions and issues surrounding the proletarian literature movement with which Yoshiya was never associated, as well as between gender and class and changes in gender roles.

The opening pages of *Details from Other Countries* feature two photographs of Yoshiya Nobuko. The first is called "Beneath the Paris Eiffel Tower on a Morning with Dusting of Snow." At first glance, this is a cliché photograph with the Eiffel Tower, but it is in fact a skillfully composed photograph, with Yoshiya's placement paralleling and framed by the formal stands of trees. We can see footprints in the snow and Yoshiya bundled up in a fur coat. The second, labeled "One Year Later, Back from Abroad in the Her Beloved Study," has Yoshiya lying comfortably in a sweater and skirt, head resting on a soft pillow surrounded by a few books. This scene invokes the word *natsukashiki* (nostalgic) to modify her study, setting up the book with the

15. Hirofumi 2004, 11.

16. Though unremarked in her travelogue, this street is the site of the oldest urban mosque in France, built in 1926 before Yoshiya's trip.

17. The school does not have detailed records of her time there, but she appears to have been a student in 1923, and at that time the languages taught there were French, Latin, and classical Greek. There are no accounts of her learning any classical languages. (Correspondence with Athénée Français, November 5, 2011.) In the travelogue, there are several indications that she spoke English to people in other places in Europe, and sometimes used an interpreter, as she did in Italy.

familiar discourse on nostalgia that permeates the girlhood literary genres and Yoshiya's fiction oeuvre. But what is the nostalgia for? It is not precisely a nostalgia for "Japan," and I think we can see via contrast with late 1930s and early 1940s writings that Japaneseness is not the category at the forefront of her mind at this time. Nostalgia for "home" includes very much the western things (and clothing as we see) that are part of the cosmopolitan girlhood seen in her fiction and the magazines she published in from the beginning of her career, and it is important that "nostalgia" is not about cultural difference at this point. In fact, within the travel essays, she often writes with humorous criticism about nostalgia. Her first entry on Paris, for example, notes that the many Japanese in France become members of the "Patriotic Party" in the Paris winter, because "it is so dark compared to our country, which was, after all, named for being the place from which the sun shines." She observes them as they "turn the other cheek and become Francophiles come May when all of the flowers are in bloom."[18] At the same time, she shows sympathy for those living abroad becoming lonely and oddly attached to Japan because of their situation and their own position as immigrants in those places.

Returning to the front matter, her choice of epigraph to express the mood of the book is a piece by Théodore Aubanel (1829–86), a Provençal poet, as translated by Ueda Bin in the collection *Kaichōon* ("Sound of the Tide"), an important 1905 collection of translated European poems, which introduced symbolist poetry to Japan and initiated the Japanese symbolist movement, despite its inclusion of works by Dante and Shakespeare and a wide range of nineteenth-century poets.[19] Published in Yoshiya's childhood, this volume took on greater popular prominence with the translator and anthologizer's death in 1916, just as Yoshiya was beginning to submit her own poems and essays to magazines. As with many of her generation, her own writing style was heavily influenced by the Japanese used in translations of European literature, particularly collections like this that brought

18. Yoshiya 1930, 123.

19. The other poets translated in this collection include Gabriele D'Annunzio, Charles-Marie-René Leconte de Lisle, José-Maria de Heredia, Sully Prudhomme, Charles Pierre Baudelaire, Paul Marie Verlaine, Victor-Marie Hugo, François Edouard Joachim Coppée, Wilhelm Arent, Carl Hermann Busse, Paul Barsch, Theodor Storm, Heinrich Heine, Robert Browning, Christina Rossetti, Emile Verhaeren, Georges Raymond Constantin Rodenbach, Henri de Régnier, Francis Vielé-Griffin, Albert Victor Samain, Jean Moréas, Stéphane Mallarmé, and Arturo Graf. Although most of the translations were completed from English- or French-language versions only (even in the case of Italian poems, for example), the results (generally excellent in their own right) have remained the dominant translations of a number of these works. See Jackson, Jr., 1991.

European poetry to a general educated audience. As she embarks on a trip to France, it is clear that she has in her mind a space that is to her exotic, but also connected to her own via translations of this sort. This is one English translation of the original:

> To the other side of the sea
> In the hours I spend in dream
> Often I'm off on a voyage
> Oft times my trip is bitter
> To the other side of the sea.[20]

Ueda's translation deploys the lovely phrase *umi no anata* ("you, of the sea") which has an affinity with *kanata*, "the distant reaches of the sea," while placing greater emphasis on a "you" that might be at that distant place. Throughout the collection, he includes this turn of phrase "you, of the sea" in multiple poems invoking "the sea." These references to the sea echo the title of the collection, a reference to the Buddha's sermons having the power of the sound of the waves (*jaladharagarjita* in Sanskrit), and is used by Ueda to evoke the power he sees in these poems from overseas. Yoshiya borrows these sentiments and Aubanel's to launch her book.

Yoshiya writes her own prologue for the travelogue, which again focuses on transnational transportation of experience. The book is a reproducible stand-in for authentic pressed flowers from her travels:

> I had gathered up the fallen *marronier* blossoms of Paris, daisies from farms in the suburbs of London, and placed them in between the pages of my travel diary with thoughts of giving them to my younger friends when I returned to my home country – this book is like a collection of little pressed flowers from my travels. As there could never be enough for all to whom I would like to give these gifts, I wish that there were more. Thus, as though carrying seeds from travels to a foreign country and by my brush, I write so as to make more flowers bloom from that source and to hold on to those times even a little bit longer.[21]

Nostalgia and a desire to create affinities and memorable images of another

20. Translation in Streight 1996, 62; Streight also provides the standard French thus: "Au pays d'outre-mer / dans mes heures de reverie, / bien des fois je fais un voyage, / je fais souvent un amer voyage au pays d'outre-mer." The original Provençal, from section 11 of Aubanel's The Split Pomegranate, reads: "De-la-man-d'eila de la mar / Dins mis ouro de pan-taiage / Souvènti-fes iéu fau un viage / Iéu fau souvènt un viage amar / De-la-man-d'eila de la mar."

21. Yoshiya 1930, 3.

place that are then transferred to those girls who are "younger" and probably still in Japan is a guiding force of her writing.

The first ten pages of her travelogue tell the story of her send-off party, which seems to have marked in a firm way her place in the literary community. The list of figures associated with Yoshiya's send-off is impressive, and includes the great poet Yosano Akiko, major fiction writers such as Mushakōji Saneatsu and Kataoka Teppei, Hani Motoko, a prominent woman publisher of *Fujin no tomo* and educator, and powerful editor and writer Kikuchi Kan, who sent flowers for her departure from the train station.[22] With much fanfare, the young writer and her "bride" Monma set off to Europe. Meanwhile, Yosano includes a line in her poem requesting of Paris that Yoshiya not be disdained as an "oriental traveler" (*tōhō no anazurawashiki tabibito to kimo wo omowanu Pari tanomaru*). This awareness of French orientalism among her compatriots, and Yoshiya's reflections on and criticism of it will be an important aspect of her travel writings.

Across Asia

It is important to remember that travels to almost all places in "the West" involved traversing some portion of Asia. Those going to Europe sometimes traveled by boat via Southeast Asia, but increasingly used the trans-Siberian railway. Yoshiya's first stop is northern China, and she writes entries on Manchuria, Harbin, Siberia, and Moscow.

In Manchuria, she has understood in a direct way "how frightful the Russo-Japanese War was for the first time.... For this alone, it was worth visiting the battle sites in Manchuria before traveling to foreign countries."[23] She visits the site of the Battle of Mukden of 1905, site of a decisive and brutal battle of the Russo-Japanese War that cost 10,000 dead and 90,000 casualties. She feels with a new intensity the difficulties of war via a set of sensory stimuli: she "can hear the sound of countless battle comrades crying out as they climbed the embankment" before going silent, and is told by the tour guide that Russian soldiers "had toasted bread on the surface of concrete graves."

> I felt deeply then the horrors of war. Amongst the scars of the
> artillery battle and the scattered rocks and clay they had left there,
> wild chrysanthemums grew, and here and there were purple blooms:
> a sorrowful apposition. This was not the elegant world of Bashō's
> "Summer grasses / in the soldiers' footprints/ the traces of dreams" –

22. Yoshiya 1930, front matter.
23. Yoshiya 1930, 34.

it was so much more painful than that. For four to five years after the war, we are told, the soil in this area still glistened eerily, saturated as it is with blood, and blood-stained military hats and accessories still rise to the surface from time to time.[24]

She distinguishes between Bashō's poignant, but aestheticized and elegant phrasing, and the physical pain she experiences in her chest at the thought of the strange brightness of the blood gleaming as though still wet in the soil. Her affinity with the space is articulated largely through the Japanese deaths there, though the focus of her rhetoric is the very general categories of "war" and "peace," and the ways they manifest in concrete items (artillery, rubble, blood) that represent sensory experiences (pain, death, hunger) and a failure of sympathy. This is also the first cinematic scene: toasting bread on a grave. These visual descriptions contrast with the Manchurian travel writings of Yosano Akiko, the poet mentioned earlier as launching Yoshiya's visit. Yosano's travelogues rely heavily on poetic associations that display her mastery of Chinese and Japanese poetry, and were published earlier in the year of Yoshiya's trip. Yoshiya rejects that mode in favor of one that has qualities of cinema and photography, and that highlights her cosmopolitan identification with people she meets and sees rather than with the landscape.[25]

In Yoshiya and Monma's brief stop in Moscow, we see her highlight a network of same-sex couples, while also trying to think in a direct way about the Russian Revolution. Nakamoto Yuriko (later Miyamoto) and her companion Yuasa Yuriko were staying in Moscow at that time and were excited to tell Yoshiya and Monma what to see there, saying that they really must stay longer. While this proletarian writer is often known in the postwar era as the wife of poet Miyamoto Kenji, she traveled extensively with her female friend Yuasa in the 1920s.[26] Unable to change their tickets, however, Yoshiya and Monma were obliged to make a whirlwind tour. While not mentioned in the travelogue itself, a later, post-World War II publication says that their tour guide was a Korean man, of whom the ladies said, "Oh, that there is a real pro, you're all set."[27] But in the late 1920s, interaction with a Korean guide was perhaps less remarkable, with Korea a colony of Japan at the time; instead, Yoshiya will focus on Europeans who know Japanese or about Japan,

24. Yoshiya 1930, 33. In reference to one of Bashō's more famous poems from Okunohosomichi (Narrow Road to the Far North): Natsukusaya, Tsuwamono dono, Yume no ato, which is contextualized as Basho's reflection on a battlefield.

25. Yosano 2001.

26. "The Breast" has been recently translated by Heather Bowen-Struyk in Bowen-Struyk and Field 2016, 364–93.

27. Yoshiya 1973, 11.368–70.

especially a German woman who travels alone with two children and speaks good Japanese. She chooses to sit near the "two older modern girls" rather than the one American man in a different car. As the women travel across Asia, their sisterly relationships with other women travelers are a focus. Even when Yoshiya focuses in on the topic of the revolution, her place of attachment is a young teacher, one not unlike those depicted in her fiction: "But what left the strongest impression by far was the Revolution Museum (*Kakumei hakubutsukan*). What I will never forget were the elementary students who seem to have come from somewhere near Moscow to see it on a field trip, and their woman teacher charismatically describing to the sad looking children before her the brutal tragedy of the revolutionaries captured, bound at the feet and lined up to be shot."[28] The force of the dramatic is highlighted above the politics of these events.

Paris 1928–29

Yoshiya and Monma reach Paris in October, and after a short hotel visit and a stay in the home of one Madame Bruhn, move to the apartment. Rather than a month-by-month look at her time in Paris or any sort of broader reflections on Paris and France, we see short episodes or reflections on particular categories of people or things ("French Children," "Girl Students," "Flower Shops," "The Shoestore"). A closer look at these essays reveals content sometimes less anodyne than these titles might suggest, and also a resistance to speak of anything universal or "French" about these spaces.

In "Shoestore," Yoshiya tells of buying comfortable shoes in advance of an excursion to Nice scheduled for the next day. While shopping in the store, a woman comes in with somewhat disheveled hair and no hat, despite the cold weather, and Yoshiya notes, "no Parisienne would go out without a hat!" The woman stares longingly at the cheapest and simplest shoes in the store. Yoshiya's view pans to her feet to see what is left of her footwear, writing that these "could hardly be called 'shoes' – the worn items that had no heel remaining were more like straw sandals." The woman soon goes away, with the eighty-franc shoes still far out of reach. Yoshiya leaves the store with her sports shoes under her arm only to see the same woman approaching a beggar she had passed by earlier. As Yoshiya had passed him, she had paused awkwardly for some seconds, fumbling in her purse to find change. Realizing she had only larger bills prepared for her trip, in the end she gave nothing. She now sees the woman, who does not have enough money for decent shoes, drop a coin in the cup:

28. Yoshiya 1973:,11.369.

My entire body was as though colliding with *Shame,* and then
swallowed up by it. As when disembodied in the midst of a dream, I
just felt like throwing whatever bill I had – five or ten – and just run
away. Ah Paris! Under that label of "Woman of Paris," was not that
woman from the shoestore one of them, if anyone was? And yet, the
woman who was the woman able to buy a pair of shoes was not her,
but me.

On one level this vignette resembles a story of insight through travel: a
young woman understands poverty through seeing it in another space. But
emphasized here are two other aspects. One is the storytelling element,
the way this situation can be taken with her fresh eyes and turned into a
singular, emotionally laden moment, resonant with a whole tradition of
Christian stories about charity that have filtered to her through her reading and schooling in Japan. The other is the problem of identifications that
Yoshiya explores here. Recalling Yosano's remark about being an "oriental
lady," Yoshiya shows the way that expectations of the Parisian, expectations
that have informed both her own self-image and that of her readers, are
complicated by reality. Such images, rather than simply disappearing after
being revealed, leave her unable to act, fumbling for money. Just as her re-
writings of these stories in multiple formats creates multiple identities, her
replaying of what she wished she had done (given a lot of money and run
away) explores the many possible ways of being an "oriental lady" in Paris,
including ones informed by melodramatic storytelling and the social and
multiple realities of Parisian women themselves.

A similar method is employed in a section called "Lipstick," which depicts
an evening that Yoshiya and Monma experienced spending time with some
French prostitutes at the introduction of some male Japanese friends.[29]

The dance hall was called PARADISE, the sort of name that you might
see on a Japanese café, and was a fairly high-class place. And that is
where I was introduced to her by a Japanese person, whom I'll call A.
Mademoiselle Rosette was her name, and she was a petite, beautiful
woman wearing a black silk spring coat and black clothing. A's friend
B told me, "For someone in this line of work, she is Petit Bourgeois
and lives in a normal way, but does this to earn spending money.... Try
talking to her about novels. She really reads quite a bit."

After dancing a while, she goes to the ladies' room, and Rosette comes as

---

29. It is likely that among these men is popular writer and critic Kume Masao, with whom
Yoshiya was known to spend time during this trip. They also became fellow travelers in Shang-
hai in the late 1930s when writing war correspondence.

well. After taking out her compact and fixing her make-up she offers Yoshi-ya her lipstick:

> "Here, try it. The color will suit you well." A sudden bout of *nerves* suddenly flared up in me and made it difficult for me to accept the lipstick that was on offer. I said, "Thanks, but that's too much," and refused, only to regret it later. If only I had accepted, it would have been a once-in-a-lifetime experience, me painting my own lips with the lipstick of a Parisienne flower of the night.[30]

Later they part, Yoshiya giving her ten francs, and she and Monma receiving a hug goodnight. Monma says, "When a woman is poor and has no one to support her, sometimes there is no other path for you in life than to go into that profession." Several days later, in the second scene of this essay, Monma points out someone in the Metro, a young woman who cleans the station: "If that girl dressed herself up, she would be just as pretty as Rosette, but rather than do that kind of job, she is working here instead." Yoshiya thinks of how hard this woman works, and that she, Yoshiya, would never be likely to pay her ten francs or be pleased to borrow her lipstick. In fact this woman wears no lipstick, and the description is of her bedraggled but "pure" beauty: "In the very same Paris, two women have these different trajectories," Yoshiya remarks. She imagines what the woman would say if you asked her why she did not become a prostitute instead: "'I myself would just not like to do that.' Is probably what she would say."[31] Particularly interesting given Yoshiya's own sexuality is her reflection on the fact that she should have wished for simulated bodily contact with the prostitute via the lipstick, while she did not do so with the cleaning woman. The class aspects of her own sexuality and representations of romance become suddenly clear to her, and even more so to Monma, who is criticizing French society, Rosette, and Yoshiya all at once. The romantic, exoticized image of the glamorous and sexually alluring Parisienne that has come via literature and film is disrupted by the doubling of these "two women in the very same Paris."

Movies

By contrast, we can see throughout Yoshiya's travelogue an interest in juxtaposing direct visual and physical experience with literary, journalistic, and cinematic representations, in an only partly chronological format. Her travel observations in Paris, which take a form like the scenes I have just described, are followed by essays about movies she saw while she was traveling. While

30. Yoshiya 1930, 146.
31. Yoshiya 1930, 151.

she discusses plots and formal qualities of some films, the focus is rather on the physical spaces of the theaters, the audiences, her own visceral experience of seeing a movie in these places far from home. The most interesting is her recounting of seeing an independent, small-release film in France.[32] Yoshiya goes to the Studio des Ursulines near where she is staying, to see a film which she calls "The Lives of Ragpickers" (*Kuzuya no seikatsu*), which I suspect may be the documentary *La Zone*, 1928, directed by Georges Lacombe.[33] The framing for her discussion is a letter of reply to a friend back in Japan, Miss T, who has written to her of her own experience of empathy through movie-going. While Yoshiya was not at all a part of the proletarian literature movement in this period, she understands at this moment in Paris the possibility of identifying across class and across nation, writing of this in her letter. Her friend has written in a letter of going to see a leftist play and finding herself shouting along with her fellow audience, "Fools!" "Enemies!" and when the capitalists and petty bureaucrats come on stage, feeling for the first time in her life that "her whole body was struck with a singular happiness." Then her friend goes home as if in a dream, only to feel ashamed later. Yoshiya chastises her young friend, reminding her that Japan is in many ways an enviable country, given that Miss T had a family among whom she could study the piano and French cooking. She says that it has felt difficult to seek such a singular happiness in Paris itself. But she was reminded of Miss T's letter when she sees *La Zone*, "a film which allowed her, an *étrangère*, a glimpse of the lower stratum of Paris." She describes this movie scene by scene:

> The first scene shows a cart that collects trash from all of Paris. Dumped into it are piles of rubbish found in the basements of apartment buildings. Driving around the city, it is filled with refuse before returning.... A young girl sorts the items, collected by her father and brother ... an old newspaper, the cover of a magazine, a fallen button, a small broken dish, a single glove, a sock with a hole, a torn corset.... She tidies them all beautifully, and amongst them the girl's eyes fall on the cover of a used book. *AMOUR.*

Rather than leading into a romantic love story, however, the film depicts the girl and her mother selling items at a flea market, and then the family sitting together in the evening, as she looks longingly at the found book. Between the flea market and home, the girl experiences an intense fantasy moment:

32. The extended discussion appears at Yoshiya 1930:206–10.

33. As of this writing, I am unable to identify the French film's name with any certainty, but Lacombe's *La Zone*, about ragpickers, was shown in Studio des Ursulines in 1928; Yoshiya's Japanese title is *Kuzuya no seikatsu*, and her entry is dated Spring, 1929.

outside a shop she hears music flowing from a music box and dances, "her whole body as though gently taken over by a dream, and moving like the heroine of an old romance, and then twilight comes to Paris. The audience smiles." At the end of recounting the film, Yoshiya returns to this observation of the audience, placing herself firmly within it. As the film fades gently out from the poignant home scene, the audience applauds over and over:

> [T]his is a direct greeting to the characters of this film. That is because this was a documentary. This was their real life. This was the beauty and beauty born out of the reality of their lives. In the hearts of the audience, who thus saw the life of this group of workers, could be felt a warm friendship. And they must feel a kind of love towards those characters' lives. They must feel the same level of satisfaction as when they see a beautiful fictional story in a movie. I certainly felt this way. In place of the "one happiness" you had told me about in the letter, T, I felt a "one human love" (*hitotsu no ningen ai*).

She feels the power of the movie might come from the audience's legacy of their ancestors' fighting a revolution, but she is impressed that she too could experience, through the same film, the sort of emotional transformation in faraway Paris that her friend described in her letter from Japan. Interestingly, a contemporary review of *La Zone* in *Cinémonde* focuses on the fact that these trash sorters are strangers to other Parisians: "For us, the zone was as unknown as Papua. And like Papua, we know it today because of a documentary."[34] Yoshiya seems to have sensed the same extraordinary quality of that distance and connection in the theater.

But there may be something amiss with Yoshiya's movie review. Although early scenes are nearly identical to what Yoshiya described, something is quite different. The "Amour" in the book and the young woman dancing – these are not scenes that appear in the film. Perhaps some portion of the film has been lost? More likely, Yoshiya frames it with an eye to her work as a storyteller. Yoshiya seems unable to resist a romantic twist, and seeks to explore the untapped melodramatic potential of this social realism. It is not a cheapening of this serious bit of realism, but rather a way of capturing the effect of the moment of viewing, when she sensed a form of pleasure, of drama, of attachment to the characters among the audience members. This "love" goes back to her 1921 essay, "Loving One Another," where love for a woman could also lead to love for humankind.

---

34. Daniel Abric, "La Zone: Petit film trés amusant," Cinémonde 17:314, as quoted in Flinn 2009; my thanks to T. Jefferson Kline and Richard Abel for assistance in identifying this film.

Miss America

While Yoshiya's romantic dream trip was to Paris, she ultimately enjoys America, which suits her girl aesthetic. She playfully titles the first section on America, "The Girl I Looked up To – Meeting Miss America." In fact, there were no Miss Americas in 1928 and 1929 due to a variety of scandals that had dogged the pageant, including a nudity scandal and resentment that one Norma Smallwood, the first Native American winner in 1926, had earned over $100,000 (more than Babe Ruth) for her public appearances. To Yoshiya, Miss America is just a symbol of America, but she runs the joke deep enough into the section to fool her readers. She says that many in Japan are very critical of this "Miss" for her materialism, but "how could such a lovely face be all bad?" She "feels like Columbus going off to discover Miss America" for herself. She is struck instantly by the way the tastes in America are new and less solidified than in Europe. Where the "Miss Europe" would certainly be of high birth, in the end, she likes America better due to this quality of newness.

In America, she arrives in Boston, travels to New York City, Niagara Falls, and Chicago. She loves the hotels in Chicago and particularly large public bathrooms. At the back of her book she includes a story, "A Landscape without Men: A Story from Mademoiselle X" (*Otoko no inai fūkei: Mademoiselle X no hanashi*), which is largely an ode to the ladies' room. As a schoolgirl, she despised the toilet and might even be willing to get married if she did not have to use one again. But all of this changes when she sees this grand ladies' room in Chicago, where legs more lovely than The Rockettes with gorgeous silk stockings line up below the doors. She says that in Japan she will build a western toilet: if she only has the space, she will make room for fifty, have a party and invite only women. Yet this humorous essay also reflects a larger theme of the chapters on America. While she enjoys a few aspects of New York, she is drawn more to the frontier, from Chicago to California, as closer to her girlishness, as well as the West Coast's more hybrid affiliation with Asia via proximity. We see this when she visits Los Angeles, the "Movie Capital," her tour of Hollywood given by Kamiyama Sōjin (1884–1954) and his wife.[35] Kamiyama, often credited as simply "Sojin" or "So Jin," who appeared as the Mongol prince in *The Thief of Baghdad* (1924) and as Prince of Persia in the 1927 *The King of Kings* (he never played a Japanese man), but returned to Japan in the talkie era.[36] Sōjin takes her into the sets. Typically, rather than

---

35. Yoshiya 1930 196–97.

36. Kamiyama Sōjin was also a friend of author Tanizaki Jun'ichirō, who wrote the preface for his autobiography.

being starstruck by Hollywood, she dares say she is tired out by walking through whole cities and villages set up for the films (just as she fell asleep watching a Wagner opera in Germany). Moving north from Los Angeles she reaches San Francisco, where she turns out to have many former classmates and is put up in their various guest rooms and treated to meals: "I had little need to draw on my spending money." She is toured around in their personal cars, including that of one Dr. Ishikawa, who, "perhaps being a doctor drove with some caution even as he broke the speed limits," but is most struck by the fact that even a landscaper (*uekiya san*) commutes by car: "In America ... one in four people owns a car. A car is nothing more to them than another pair of *geta*!" In Japantown she notes names of hotels and restaurants that use the names of their various hometowns in Japan, such as "Aichi Hotel," and expects that no doubt people from those areas "coming with their youthful energy to make their way working in America will find those names appealing." Meanwhile San Francisco art museums contain Japanese art objects in large collections such as one could never see in Japan itself, for example a collection of hundreds of *netsuke* tobacco cases. It is here that she says that, back on the East Coast, the "Miss America" with all the economic power she had did not seek out these sorts of things, but was in more of a Europhile mode, drawn to the neo-Renaissance architecture such as that seen in the large movie theaters. Perhaps, she suggests, "the second generation of nouveau riche families there cannot help, from a psychological standpoint, beginning to try to mimic the styles of older money." She admires the west coast, because she seems to identify best with the more hybrid, new-money frontier, where Japanese émigrés and American new money seem to seek different forms of cultural interaction. But she is also aware of the ways that there is imbalance between Miss America and Japanese workers in California: a Japanese navy training ship comes into port, and she realizes that for this community this is a major event, "like a festival," because they see their compatriots there looking impressive. She talks with many young Japanese women living in California and feels that their "loneliness" leads to a sort of patriotism. The mobile girl is placed in an unstable position even as it creates opportunities and various futures, from Sōjin's stardom as an "oriental" actor to a worker in Japantown to a bestselling woman writer. This variety is highlighted in the final portions of the travelogue.

At the end of the journey by sea to Japan, Mt. Fuji comes into view. Oddly, this is a story told twice. One is her own travelogue; the other is a novella, one of three works of related fiction included in the travelogue volume.[37] In

37. One additional story is that about the public ladies' room in Chicago. A third, "Saumon no fume" (Smoked Salmon in Paris), is about an expat couple living in France: beginning with

the story, she projects her experience onto a young woman art student who meets a man on the boat. The student experiences a clear nostalgia at seeing Mt. Fuji, though her love for the man will also compromise the results of her education abroad. Yoshiya herself sees Mt. Fuji but just feels it reminds her how much *work* she has to do when she gets back to that study answering fan letters, making deadlines, and paying for her trip! We see now a bit of playfulness in her relaxed pose on the sofa. Returning to Sedgwick's reader looking for information about herself, a paranoid reading might read the fictional version of reaching Mt. Fuji as a heterosexual escapist plot with a nationalist ending, the other side of the liberated working woman writer. But we could also read them as multiple futures, maybe those of girl readers imagining how they might be in parts as yet unknown.

---

a discussion of expats becoming attached to miso or matsutake mushrooms in Paris, the story delves into their marital tensions and domestic violence, and how these play out in special ways in a different cultural setting (232–52).

Bibliography

Bowen-Struyk, Heather and Norma Field, eds. 2016. *For Dignity, Justice, and Revolution: An Anthology of Japanese Proletarian Literature.* Chicago: University of Chicago Press.

Carpenter, Edward. 1921. *Kaapentaa ren'ai ron.* Translated by K. Yamakawa Kikue. Tokyo: Daitōkaku.

Chow, Rey. 2000. "Film and Cultural Identity" In *Film Studies: Critical Approaches,* edited by J. Hill and P. C. Gibson, 167–73. Oxford: Oxford University Press.

Delavenay, Emile. 1971. *D. H. Lawrence and Edward Carpenter: A Study in Edwardian Transition.* New York: Taplinger.

Flinn, Margaret C. 2009. "Documenting Limits and the Limits of Documentary: Georges Lacombe's La Zone and the 'Documentaire Romancé.'" *Contemporary French and Francophone Studies* 13:405–13.

Frederick, Sarah. 2013. "Beyond *Nyonin Geijutsu,* Beyond Japan: Writings by Women Travellers in *Kagayaku* (1933–1941)," *Japan Forum* 25:395–413.

Frederick, Sarah. 2017. "Yamakawa Kikue and Edward Carpenter: Translation, Affiliation, and Queer Internationalism," in *Rethinking Japanese Feminisims,* edited by Julia Bullock, Kano Ayako, and James Welker. Honolulu: University of Hawaii Press: 187-204.

Hansen, Miriam. 1999. "The Mass Production of the Senses: Classical Cinema as Vernacular Modernism." *Modernism/Modernity* 6:59–77.

Hirofumi Wada. 2004. *Pari Nihonjin no shinshō chizu 1867–1945, Shohan.* Tōkyō: Fujiwara Shoten.

Horiguchi, Noriko. 2011. *Women Adrift: The Literature of Japan's Imperial Body.* Minneapolis: University of Minnesota Press.

Jackson, Earl, Jr. 1991. "The Heresy of Meaning: Japanese Symbolist Poetry." *Harvard Journal of Asiatic Studies* 51:561–98.

Kamichika Ichiko. 1921. "Dōsei ren'ai no tokushitsu," with the heading "Futari no josei no mitaru dōseiai." *Shinshōsetsu.* Reprinted in *Senzenki dōseiai kanren bunken shūsei* (Tokyo: Fuji Shuppan, 2006), 3:150–51.

Komashaku Kimi. 1994. *Yoshiya Nobuko: Kakure feminisuto.* Tokyo: Riburo-poto.

Leib, Frank B. 1997. *Friendly Competitors, Fierce Companions: Men's Ways of Relating.* Cleveland: Pilgrim.

Maiwald, Michael. 2002. "Race, Capitalism, and the Third-Sex Ideal: Claude Mckay's Home to Harlem and the Legacy of Edward Carpenter." *MFS Modern Fiction Studies* 48:825–57.

Robertson, Jennifer. 2001. "Yoshiya Nobuko: Out and Outspoken in Practice and Prose." In *The Human Tradition in Modern Japan*, edited by Anne Walthall. Wilmington, DE: Scholarly Resources.

Sedgwick, Eve Kosofsky. 1997. "Paranoid Reading and Reparative Reading, or You're so Paranoid, You Probably Think This Introduction Is about You." In *Novel Gazing*, 1–37. Durham, NC: Duke University Press.

Streight, David. 1996. *Théodore Aubanel: Sensual Poetry and the Provençal Church*. Saintes-Maries-de-la-Mer, France: Édicioun dóu Gregau.

Tanabe Seiko. 1999. *Yume Haruka Yoshiya Nobuko: akitomoshi tsukue no ue no ikusanga*. 2 vols. Tokyo: Asashi Shinbunsha.

Tsuzuki, Chushichi. 1980. *Edward Carpenter 1844–1929: Prophet of Human Fellowship*. New York: Cambridge University Press.

Yosano Akiko. 2001. *Travels in Manchuria and Mongolia* (Kinshū ihoku no ki). Translated by Joshua A. Fogel. New York: Columbia University Press.

Yoshiya Nobuko. 1921. "Aishiau kotodomo." *Shinshōsetsu*: 78–80. Reprinted in *Senzenki dōseiai kanren bunken shūsei* (Tokyo: Fuji Shuppan, 2006), 3:150–51.

——.1930. *Ikoku tenkei*. Tokyo: Minyūsha.

——.1964–65. *The Ataka Family* (*Ataka-ke no hitobito*). Translated by Takehide Kikuchi. Monthly. April 1964–May 1965. *Info*, n.p.

——.1957. *Coeur des Ataka* (*Ataka-ke no hitobito*). Translated by J.-G. Mills and M.-L. Bataille. Paris: Stock.

——.1961. *Familien Ataka* (*Ataka-ke no hitobito*). Translated by Ingebor Stemann. Copenhagen: Aschehoug.

——.1973. *Yoshiya Nobuko zenshū*. 11 vols. Tokyo: Asahi Shinbunsha.

——. 1975. "Haiku nikki." In *Haiku*, 24(8): 68–78.

——. 2000. "Foxfire" (*Onibi*). Translated by Lawrence Rogers. *The East* 36:41–43.

——. 2008. "Juntokuin fuyo kiyomi daishi." Reprinted in *Kuroshōbi no otometachi no tame ni tsumuida yume*, by Yoshiya Nobuko, 93. Tokyo.

——. 2016. "Yellow Rose" (*Kibara*). Translated by Sarah Frederick. Expanded Editions. Electronic book. Online. http://www.expandeditions.com/second-edition-yellow-rose-may-2016/